CHOOSING

Ellie Klipp

People are talking about

CHOOSING

Most parents are unaware of what goes on at school. An edge-of-your-seat read.
> Jorge Tovar, Senior Pastor – Jordan River Church, Laredo, Texas

Guides Tracy and her high school friends through the deceptive transgender maze. I didn't want the book to end—a real page turner.
> Dr. Laura Haynes, Retired Psychologist, Chair of Research and Legislative Policy, National Task Force for Therapy Equality

Masterfully weaves science and logic in an engaging tale for tweens and teens, showing how young people are swept under transgenderism's spell.
> Dr. Michelle Cretella, Executive Director of the American College of Pediatricians

Entertainingly equips teens, tweens, and parents against transgender ideologies. A fun read and a potent tool.
> Andre Van Mol, MD, Co-Chair of Adolescent Sexuality Committee, American College of Pediatricians

Tackles a controversial topic in a unique and positive way.
> Dr. Tim Clarey, Geologist and Author of Dinosaurs: Marvels of God's Design

See full endorsements at end of book.

1

Tracy bit the inside of her cheek just hard enough to keep herself from yawning. She twisted her toes inside her shoes, then straightened them.

It didn't help.

If something didn't happen soon, she was doomed.

The last time she yawned in Mr. Holmes' face, he sent her to detention, and then her parents said she couldn't go out to pizza with the other kids after school, and then her best friend Charlie—*her best friend!*—got to go out for pizza with all the popular kids, including Deke.

Yeah, Deke—the school's football star.

It wasn't Charlie's fault. Charlie was cute. Everyone liked Charlie. She was smart and actually really nice. Her long dark hair and flashing black eyes didn't hurt either.

Tracy sometimes resented her friend's casual relaxed manner and ease in making friends. Especially boyfriends. Or friends who were boys—not exactly *boyfriends* because Charlie never seemed to stick with one guy.

Which just wasn't done. You know, if you were dating a guy, you weren't supposed to be flirting with other guys. And you couldn't go with two guys at the same time. Or at least those were the unspoken rules at Tracy's school. Which didn't really affect Tracy as no one ever asked her on a date anyway.

But Charlie was the exception. She made her own rules. She was friendly with all the boys and went out with anyone she wanted, but no one called her a—well, you know.

3

Tracy's mom wouldn't let her use that word. She wasn't even supposed to *think* that word. But how can you not *think* something if you overhear it all the time in the bathroom at school when other girls were talking? You know, it just pops into your mind even if you try not to think it.

Anyway, Charlie got away with being friendly with all the guys—and even the girls, who didn't seem to get mad when she talked with their boyfriends. It was bizarre. But that was Charlie.

Hey, if Tracy had hung around Alex at Starbucks, for example, where he worked after school, instead of just picking up her latte and casually throwing a "thanks" over her shoulder, Wendy would be furious. That's just the way it was.

Tracy's mom said it was different when she was young. You could date several guys at once. Weird, right? But that was way back before kids had their own cell phones.

In Tracy's world, girls couldn't talk to other girls' boyfriends.

Except for Charlie. She could. She talked to all the boys. She could talk and laugh and bat her eyes at the guys and no one got mad at her.

But Tracy had never seen Charlie talk to Josh. That was weird because who would even care if you talked to *Josh?* He was a nerd.

Not nerdy really—Josh wasn't weird or dressed like a geek or anything. In fact, Tracy thought he was sort of cute, with reddish brown hair and a few freckles.

And he wasn't actually clumsy even though Josh did tend to bump into things a lot. But that was because he walked around with a book or a phone in front of his face all the time. Always looking something up. Too focused on whatever he was checking to notice girls. Or if he noticed them, he never asked any of them out anyway.

Come to think of it, Tracy realized she had never seen Josh talking to any girl. And she couldn't imagine a girl having a crush on Josh. He was sort of *unnoticeable*. Like the old set of reference books in the library that no one looked at anymore because it was so much easier to use the internet to look something up.

Josh just didn't seem—*approachable*. He usually looked like he was absorbed in his own bubble of thought and didn't even acknowledge you were there. So none of the kids in the popular cliques talked to him.

But everyone talked to Charlie, and Charlie could talk to any of the guys.

It was a mystery to Tracy how that worked. What kind of magic did Charlie have that all the guys seemed to like her? And the girls, too. No one resented her popularity either. Except maybe Tracy herself, ironically—her best friend. Yet at the same time it seemed to Tracy that someone was always mad at *her*, even when she hadn't meant to offend anyone.

She frowned, mulling over Charlie's mysterious appeal. And that was when Mr. Holmes struck.

"Does this displease you, Tracy?" he asked sarcastically.

"Wha-what? Uh, I'm sorry, would--would you repeat that?" Tracy stuttered.

"If your highness would deign to join the rest of the class," Mr. Holmes hissed, "we were discussing the assignment of committees for your history project. You seemed displeased with your teammates."

"Oh, no—no, it's fine. It's good. I'm fine." Shut up, Tracy told herself, before you get in more trouble.

But it wasn't fine. If she had been listening, she would indeed have been displeased. She was stuck with Megan and Marline.

2

Megan and Marline. The Dixie Duo. Except that they were not from Dixie. They were from Ohio. But they put on the thickest southern accent you could imagine and drawled their "howdies" and blinked their fake eyelashes at the boys while the other girls groaned and rolled their eyes behind their backs.

But not the boys. The girls saw right through it all but the boys—especially the jocks—treated them like something special.

That wasn't the worst of it. Both Megan and Marline seemed to have left their brains—if they ever had any—in Ohio when they moved here. They were—well, there was no other way to say it—they were dumb.

Not un-smart. More like turn-off-your-brain dumb. They could learn if they wanted to, but they didn't want to. All their energy was directed to one thing only—attracting male attention. So they parked whatever brains they had at the curb and used their other—uh, *assets*—to get by, even with the teachers.

Most of the teachers put up with their act, the fake innocence and false remorse when their assignments were late.

Even Mr. Holmes.

That was another thing Tracy didn't understand. It was easy to tell Megan and Marline were lying with their fake southern lip-quivering excuses. "Oh, Mr. Holmes, I'm so sorry. I didn't realize that was due today..." At least it was easy for Tracy to see.

So many things were clear to her that adults just didn't seem to get.

And one of the clearest was that Mr. Holmes should never have decided to become a teacher. Not only did he turn what could have been a fairly interesting class into an hour of terminal boredom every school day, but his addiction to *projects* extended the torture beyond reading the text to creating what she thought were boring dioramas and posters that took hours of extra time. Tracy thought she had left that kind of make-work assignment behind in middle school.

But maybe being paired with Megan and Marline wasn't so bad after all. They wouldn't do a lick of work—she was sure of that—which meant Tracy could whip out the project without their interference. That would cut the time the assignment would take. And she could make a credible job of it. Get Mr. Holmes off her back for a while.

The bell rang. Tracy shuffled her papers into her notebook and picked up her backpack. She edged forward between the rows of desks and joined the queue shoving out the door. Charlie waited for her in the hall.

They walked toward English together.

"What's the matter?" Charlie asked. "You look upset."

"Oh, it's just that class," Tracy responded. "You know Mr. Holmes. He put me on a project with the M's."

Charlie giggled. "Not the M's. Oh, darlin'. Well, y'all make it a right-special project now, okay honey-girl?" Charlie put the southern accent on thick.

Tracy rolled her eyes and scooted to the right as a big guy on the football team barreled down the hall. He acted as though Tracy was invisible. At the last moment he swiveled his head and called over his shoulder, "Hi there, Charlie. Hey, are you coming to practice today?"

"Sorry," Charlie answered, half turning around. "Gotta go to the dentist."

"Bummer," the boy grunted as he swept on down the crowded hallway.

"Check-up or toothache?" Tracy asked her friend, concern showing in her eyes.

"Neither," Charlie laughed. "But I don't feel like going to sit on cold bleachers and make goo-goo eyes at macho guys working off their testosterone this afternoon."

7

Tracy shook her head. That was another thing Charlie could do. Not that it was a good thing. But either way, Tracy just couldn't do it. If she tried to lie—even a harmless little white lie—her cheeks burned and her eyes watered and everyone knew she was fibbing.

Anyway, was there such a thing as a harmless little white lie? She remembered when her cousin Jackson had told his mom—her aunt—on the phone that he was watching his little brother Joe in the backyard when actually he was playing video games on the computer in the den.

It wasn't a big lie. He could look out the window and see his little brother toddling around out there. But Joe was only two and a half at the time, so of course he didn't know he shouldn't eat those pellets of fertilizer that had fallen out of a tear in the bag his dad had carried to the garden shed the day before.

Later that day when Joe got really sick and her aunt rushed him to the hospital, Jackson insisted he'd been watching Joe the whole time. The truth was he hadn't seen Joe eat the pellets so he had no idea why his little brother was sick. The docs suspected some kind of poisoning and got the toddler straightened out, but Jackson's lie delayed the docs figuring out the right treatment because no one thought to scour the backyard for the source of the problem. It could have turned out really bad.

Jackson never did tell his parents the whole truth—that he let Joe go in the backyard alone. But he told Tracy all about it once when his family was visiting her house. (Her cousins lived way out in California but they came to visit every summer.) He was feeling guilty, she guessed. Then he made her swear to keep it a secret on pain of—well, he never did say on pain of what. But he made it clear she would be very sorry if she ever said anything. And ever since then he'd acted like he was mad at her, even though she'd never said a word. Go figure.

Anyway, that *little white lie* wasn't so harmless. Depending on how many fertilizer pellets he had eaten, her little cousin could have died.

3

But it didn't matter if there *was* such a thing as a little white lie anyway as far as Tracy was concerned. Because she just couldn't do it. Or rather, she could never get away with it. She could tell the *truth* and look guilty. But Charlie made it look easy. Charlie made everything look easy.

Tracy sighed. "Are you ready for the math test?"

Charlie smiled as another group of boys hailed her in passing. "Of course, aren't you?"

"I never feel ready," Tracy moaned.

She pulled the door to their classroom open and waited as Charlie swept in first.

"Oh, you worry too much," Charlie grinned. "You always do well."

They found their seats and pulled notebooks from their backpacks. Tracy felt eyes on her and glanced up to see Mrs. Peters studying her. She beckoned for Tracy to come up to her desk.

"Yes, Mrs. Peters?" Tracy asked anxiously.

"Tracy, how would you like to change to AP math?" the teacher responded quietly.

"AP? I—I don't know," Tracy stuttered. "That's awfully hard, isn't it?"

"Not if you do your homework," Mrs. Peters rejoined. "And you do. Plus your test scores are always among the highest. I think you would do very well in AP."

"Oh. Well, thank you, Mrs. Peters," Tracy swallowed. "Can I ask my Mom and Dad about it tonight?"

"Of course. We wouldn't switch you until the semester break anyway, so that gives you two weeks to do a little study at home to catch up on some things they've already covered."

Oh great, Tracy thought, she could spend Christmas vacation studying math. That did not sound like a good idea after all.

"If you need a little help, I could suggest an excellent tutor," Mrs. Peters continued. "Your parents would have to pay him, though. He's looking for a way to earn a little money after break, so it could help you both."

"A tutor?" Tracy mumbled doubtfully.

"Yes, you probably know him—Josh Bullard."

Tracy froze, not sure whether she was intrigued or terrified. "Uh, Josh? Yeah, I know who he is, but I don't really *know* him." She paused. "You think he'd be willing to—uh, to tutor me?"

"Of course. He has done it before with other students. He's actually very good at it. Just talk it over with your parents and let me know in a day or so."

"Okay. Thanks, Mrs. P."

Tracy stumbled back to her seat in confusion. Josh was so intimidating. Well, not personally. Personally he was like a walking encyclopedia that you could reference if you needed a quick fact. The rest of the time most of the kids ignored him.

She'd never really thought about Josh much. He just didn't seem like the regular guys, even though he was kind of cute. But not somebody you'd wish you could have pizza with.

Academically he was tops in everything. It was all so easy for him. Like Charlie. Except that he was a lot smarter than Charlie.

Josh would probably think she was really dumb. Which she was. Well, not actually. She did pretty well in all her classes, but she really had to work at it. For him, it seemed like when he heard something once, he remembered it. And understood it. While she had to wrestle with math concepts and sweat over remembering formulas and dates and names and all the things you had to regurgitate on tests.

Tracy couldn't quite picture Josh Bullard sitting next to her at the kitchen table showing her how to do a math problem. Should she offer him pizza? Did he even like pizza? Of course he liked pizza—everybody liked pizza, even *ner*—no, not a nerd. Just somebody different.

He did seem nice enough. He was tall and slim. Sort of reddish-brown hair. A little wave in his hair, longish bangs. Brown eyes? And those freckles were kind of cute. Although that would not have anything to do with their tutoring sessions. She knew that. She knew Josh of all people would be strictly business.

She wondered what he would really think of her. As a person, she meant—not as a student. He seemed older than the rest of the kids, although of course he was only a year older than she was, a grade ahead. It was just that he didn't get—uh, silly. That was it. She'd never seen him act silly like the other boys, or rowdy or crazy or the way her brother acted some times when she just wished he would disappear. Well, not really. But at least stop embarrassing her in front of her friends.

But, as she'd said, academically Josh was tops in everything. So he would probably be a good tutor. A great tutor. And she'd need a really good tutor if she was going to catch up to AP level after Christmas vacation.

How did she, Tracy Elizabeth McKenzie, who struggled with everything from homework to social stuff end up with Charlotte (a.k.a. Charlie) Louise Smeldan and Joshua—hmm, she didn't know his middle name—(why would she know his middle name?)—Joshua *Unknown-Middle-Name* Bullard?

Charlie wasn't brilliant but her regular classes seemed easy enough for her, and socially—well, Tracy knew about that for sure. As for Josh—there was no social aspect to Josh, at least not anything that she knew of, but academically he was a star.

It was the story of her life. As far as most of the kids were concerned, she was a nobody in either category, socially or academically. Oh well, Tracy sighed, at least neither Charlie nor Josh were boring. Not like the unbearable M's. And hanging out with Josh might give her a certain *cachet* or status in an odd way. Not that hanging out with Charlie had. But at least it should be—*interesting.*

"What was that all about?" Charlie whispered as Tracy slipped into her seat.

"Tell you later," Tracy answered.

Charlie looked curious. Almost jealous in a way. She knew something was going on, and Charlie was usually the one who knew everything first.

11

Tracy felt a certain satisfaction. She knew something Charlie didn't, and she'd be having Josh at her house—just about the only boy in school as far as Tracy could see who wouldn't fall all over himself to get a chance to have a coke with Charlie. And she herself could offer Josh a coke or juice—or pizza. Definitely pizza.

Pizza always helped her study.

4

The doorbell rang at precisely 6:45 p.m. Tracy wasn't surprised. That was what she would expect of Josh. Punctuality. Not her forte. But for Josh—yeah, just another way that he was excellent.

Tracy wiped her hands on her jeans and sighed. Okay, here goes nothing, she thought.

The cold air hit her as she opened the door and she shivered.

"Hey, you okay?" Josh asked, cocking his head. His winter coat was zipped up. It looked like it was sheep-skin lined.

"Yeah, fine. I'm—I'm fine," Tracy sputtered. "It's just cold out there. Brrr."

"Yeah, it is." He paused. "Should I come in so you can shut the door?"

"Oh, right—of course. Come on in."

Great beginning, Tracy thought, making him just stand there until he had to *ask* if he could come in.

He set his backpack on the floor of the entry hall and shrugged out of his coat. Then he looked expectantly at Tracy.

"Uh—oh, come on back to the kitchen," she stammered. "We'll study at the kitchen table. We've got some snacks, too."

"Super," Josh grinned. "I'm always hungry. I mean, we just finished dinner at my house. But I always appreciate snacks."

Tracy paused as they passed the door to the living room where her parents sat. Her mom was reading a book, her legs tucked under her on the sofa and wrapped with a throw blanket. Her dad, ensconced in a leather recliner, was working on his laptop.

"Mom, Dad," Tracy said, "this is Josh. Josh Bullard. He came to tutor me in math, like we agreed."

13

Tracy's dad stood and stepped forward. Josh closed the distance as they both extended their hands and shook.

"Glad to meet you, Mr. McKenzie," Josh said politely. He nodded toward Tracy's mom, who remained seated but smiled. "And you, Mrs. McKenzie."

"Thank you for coming to tutor our daughter," Tracy's dad said. "AP math is a great opportunity. But she'll need to catch up."

"I'm sure she'll do fine, Mr. McKenzie," Josh responded.

"We'll let you get to it then," the man replied.

Tracy led the way on down the hall past the bedrooms. The kitchen and den were at the back of the house. All the houses on her block—in fact, she suspected all the houses in her subdivision—were laid out that way.

Tracy's dad said the developers did not create that floorplan because they were thinking of parents being able to watch their kids play safely in the back yard. The developers did it that way, he said, because they could save development costs by making the houses long and narrow with super skinny side yards—just five feet on each side of the house. So they could squeeze more house fronts on a street. More houses for less infrastructure cost.

In her neighborhood the garage and utility room and a small multi-purpose room—like a study or small living room—were at the front. Then came the bedrooms off a long central hall, and the den across the hall from the kitchen. The more expensive houses had multiple stories, of course, with media rooms like movie theaters and extra bedrooms and bathrooms upstairs.

Her grandparents' house was different. It was in a small town in the Midwest. Probably built way back in the 1960s. A large open living room was up front—it was what you saw when you opened the front door. So people in the living room could watch neighbors out their front windows, or sit on their front porches and hail their neighbors as they walked by.

No one in Tracy's neighborhood ever sat on the front porch. The porches in her neighborhood were small decorative affairs, just big enough for an over-sized ceramic pot. Or a set of pots in graduated sizes, some as big as four feet tall. They were massive and expensive. Show pieces. Usually people didn't even put a potted plant in them.

Tracy liked the way her grandparents' house faced the street, so you got to know your neighbors. On her street, people opened their automatic garage doors, drove their cars in, and entered the house from the garage. They hardly ever saw their neighbors. She only knew the ones right next door. So she was surprised by Josh's next statement.

"I live seven blocks down. About mid-way down on the block," he said.

"You do?" Tracy was astonished. "I had no idea."

"Yeah, so I walked down."

"I—I didn't know," Tracy said again. "Uh—I mean, I've never seen you walking by."

"It's easier to walk down the other way and turn the corner to go up to the street that leads to the school," Josh answered. "Lots of times my Dad drops me off at school on his way to work anyway."

"Yeah, my Mom drives me most of the time. I'm usually a little bit late," she admitted, "and it *is* kind of far."

"Hardly any of the kids walk to school," Josh said. "My parents say they always walked—and a lot farther than we do."

"I know," Tracy rejoined, grinning. "My Dad says he walked two miles each way..."

"...uphill in the snow," Josh finished, his eyes twinkling.

Tracy thought he was even more attractive with that half smile on his face.

Josh gestured to the table with his chin.

"Oh, sorry. Yes, please have a seat," Tracy said apologetically.

Josh draped his heavy jacket over the back of a chair. He took some books out of his backpack and dumped them on the table. As he sat down, Tracy slid a cookie plate across the table. Then she sat in the seat to his left.

"Umm, these are good," Josh said as he picked up a cookie. "Did you bake these?"

"My Mom and I did together. We both like to bake."

"If you make these chocolate chip cookies every time, I'll tutor you every night of the week!" Josh joked as he picked up a second cookie. "May I?"

"Of course. Take as many as you like," Tracy said.

She began to relax. Maybe this wasn't going to be as bad as she thought. Josh seemed pretty much like a regular guy after all. Maybe cookies would be the key to making these sessions less nerve wracking. After all, wouldn't any girl be a bit nervous sitting next to a super-smart, kind of cute boy that she didn't really know?

She wasn't used to talking to guys—that is, guys other than her brother and his goofy friends. But they all treated her like a pest, not a girl. Just because they were two years older. As for her younger brother—his friends were little runts always messing with her stuff or playing tricks on her.

And the boys in her classes either ignored her or were goofballs anyway. Some of them were good students but they did the stupidest things. Like the time a bunch of them thought it would be fun to spray cake frosting on all the hall locker combos. The frosting dried hard, and then nobody could get their lockers open.

But Josh seemed okay. Maybe even though he was smart, he was going to turn out to be a regular guy.

"Okay," Josh said, wiping some crumbs off his notebook. "Open your book to page 89. Let's start by finding out just how much you know about..."

Tracy forced herself to pay attention. She had let her mind wander. She was thinking that maybe next time she'd offer Josh pizza.

5

"So how did it go?" Charlie hissed, leaning over across the aisle.

"Fine," Tracy mouthed, motioning with her hand to push Charlie away. Her English teacher, Miss Fellows, was turned the other way writing on the blackboard, but she didn't want to get in trouble for whispering during a pop quiz.

After class Charlie pursued her question as the girls swam through the surging crowd of students in the halls on the way to their next class.

"I told you, it was fine," Tracy shrugged nonchalantly.

"So what do you mean—fine?" Charlie pushed. "Was he a good tutor? He never seems to talk. Is he as quiet as at school?"

"No, of course not," Tracy replied shortly.

"Hey, give it up, girl. A little dish here, you know?" Charlie continued. "Do you think he's cute? Was it awkward?"

"No," Tracy snapped irritably. "I mean, no it wasn't awkward. He's a good teacher. And he's a real gentleman. My parents were impressed."

"Hmm," Charlie hummed. Her eyes narrowed. "You *like* him, don't you? Tracy's got a crush—"

"Stop it, Charlie." Tracy was more than irritated now. She was flat out mad. "Stop being stupid, Charlie. Of course I like him, but not like that. He's—hey, he's okay, that's all. He's a good tutor."

"Yeah right," Charlie said wryly, a smirk on her face.

Tracy wondered—not for the first time—why she called Charlie her best friend.

"Oh well," Charlie shrugged, "whatever. Hey, I'm going with Sharon for a latte after school. You wanna come?"

17

"Naw, I have to go home and babysit my little brother."

"Why?"

"You know why. The same reason I always have to go home right after school on Tuesdays and Thursdays."

"Is your mom still taking those classes at city college? Isn't she a little old to be going to school?"

"My parents say a person is never too old to keep learning," Tracy retorted.

Charlie looked apologetic. "Oh yeah, she's studying to be a nurse, isn't she? That's hard work—a lot of studying."

Tracy nodded, mollified by her friend's response. "Anyway, I have to get home right away because Toby's school lets out twenty minutes after ours."

"How long does it take you to walk home?"

"Only about fifteen minutes, but Toby's school is just two blocks from our house," Tracy explained for the umpteenth time to her friend. "So I have to hoof it after school. No time for lattes."

"I'm glad I don't have any bratty siblings," Charlie sighed.

"Toby isn't a brat," Tracy flared. "Honestly, Charlie. You can be such a pain."

"Yeah, but you love me anyway, eh, girlfriend?"

Charlie batted her eyes. Tracy didn't know whether to be madder or to burst out laughing.

That was the trouble with Charlie—she drove Tracy crazy but she had been her friend since third grade. She stuck through all the shifting cliques and klatches of girl friendships that morphed throughout the school year. She could count on Charlie to hang out with her at lunch, gossip with her at the locker, and walk with her between classes. Her best and oldest friend.

Except that after school, Charlie usually ran off with the popular kids and Tracy walked home alone.

Which was okay actually, because sometimes Tracy got awfully tired of the talk about movies and boyfriends and clothes. She wasn't really into fan clubs or fashion, and since she'd never had a real boyfriend herself, the bragging the other girls did about their own boyfriends got a little old. Especially when she didn't think most of the boys were that special anyway.

Her walk home gave her a chance to chill. Really chill, in this weather. It was a time when she didn't have to do anything but put one foot in front of the other. That was automatic, so she could think about things. Sort of think without thinking. It somehow helped to clear the cobwebs out of her brain. And it helped to make little upsets seem just that—little. Nothing to worry about.

Besides, she actually liked to look at the different houses on the way home. They all had brick or stone fronts but the developer had varied where he put the front door—one at the left corner but at the next house, the right corner or toward the middle.

The windows were different, too. Some were square with dividers—muntins, she thought they were called. They divided one big window up into little squares, which she thought was a rather elegant old-fashioned look. It was probably expensive to have muntins. Her house just had regular windows with a bottom sash that pushed up.

Some of the more expensive houses had windows with a curve at the top that met at a point, kind of like an old church window. Tracy thought that was a romantic look, like an ancient castle.

Toby came running down the street as she reached the front door. He looked upset.

"Hi, Trace," he called, pushing past her and dropping his backpack on the floor inside the door. "Do we have any more of those cookies Mom baked?"

"I think there are some left," she said, shoving his backpack with her foot so she could close the door. "Look on the counter next to the fridge."

Tracy took her backpack and coat to her room and put her things away. When she went down to the kitchen, she found Toby already sitting at the kitchen table eating cookies. He had poured himself a glass of milk and was doodling on a piece of paper.

"Hey, Trace," he muttered as she took a glass out of the cupboard. "How do you know you're a girl?"

"Huh?" she blanched. "Where did that come from?"

"Just—you know—what makes you think you're a girl?"

"Tobe, what a silly question," Tracy scoffed. "When you're born, the doctor looks—you know—at your bottom and tells your parents whether you're a boy or a girl."

"Yeah, but what if you've got the wrong body? Like you're a girl in a boy's body? A girl with a boy's bottom?" Toby continued.

Tracy turned to look at him, glowering. She expected to see a smart-aleck grin as if he thought this sort of smutty talk was cool. But he looked small and confused and frightened.

"You can't be a girl with a boy's bottom, Toby," she said. "That's crazy."

"Well, this boy—or girl—at my school says you can," her little brother insisted. "And the principal said we have to call Jason—that's his name—or her name—or whatever—Jessica from now on."

Toby looked like he was going to cry. Tracy stared at him in consternation.

"And he gets to go in the girls' bathroom now," the boy added.

"What?" Tracy exclaimed. "That's just crazy. You must have it all mixed up."

"No, honest. That's what the principal said," Toby said. He swallowed and sniffled. "It's kind of scary. I mean, I've known Jason ever since kindergarten. And now he says he's been in the wrong body all this time."

"That's absurd." Tracy shook her head. "Hey, I'm sure it's just some sort of mix-up. You misunderstood. Don't worry about it."

"No but—see, that's why I asked you how you know you are a girl. Because what if I'm really a girl. I mean, I don't want to be a girl. I want to be a boy. I *am* a boy. I mean, I've always been a boy, right? But what if I was wrong? My teacher says I might be wrong."

Tracy could see that Toby was really upset. Tears were starting to roll down his cheeks. Well, he wasn't the only one upset. Tracy was getting mad. What kind of nonsense was Toby's teacher saying that she would get a seven-year-old boy so confused?

Hey, most kids knew the difference between a boy and a girl by age two—and knew which one they were. Four-year-olds had it figured out that boys grew up to be men and girls grew up to be women. Between age five or seven, kids knew that even if a man put on a dress (like for a silly skit at camp), he was still a man. Even though he looked like a woman in the skit, he was really a man.

So obviously Toby's teacher couldn't really be saying Toby might be a girl!

If Toby hadn't been so upset, Tracy would have burst out laughing. The very idea of her little brother being a girl! It was ridiculous. Ludicrous. It would be like saying black was white and up was down and sweet was sour. It just didn't make sense.

"Okay Toby, look," Tracy soothed. "Just don't worry about it right now. We'll talk to Mom and Dad when they get home, okay? Let's watch some cartoons."

Toby brightened. Toby usually didn't get to watch cartoons until he'd finished whatever homework his second-grade teacher had sent home. But Tracy figured today she could make an exception.

She thought it was cruel to give little kids homework anyway, but that was the system. Sit in class all day and then come home and do work sheets. If *she* was a teacher...

The phone interrupted her daydream. "Hello?" she answered. It was Charlie.

"Trace, did you hear what the principal at your brother's school told the kids today?"

Tracy could hear the shock in Charlie's voice. She glanced at the clock. Her mom would not be home for another hour, and her dad for half an hour after that. She didn't want to sort this one out on her own. If only they would come home early today!

"Uh, yeah. Toby just told me."

"They had a party for a kid who changed his gender in the second grade, Sharon says. So what do you think? Is Toby upset?"

"Which Sharon?" There were three Sharon's in her English class.

"Pepper's older sister."

"Pepper—wait, who's Pepper?" Tracy was getting exasperated. Charlie had a tendency to talk in circles and throw in lots of names, as if Tracy *knew everyone* like she did.

"Pepper is a girl in Toby's class," Charlie explained. "I told you I was going for a latte after school. With Sharon and Wendy? You know, where Wendy's boyfriend works after school? He always gives me extra whipped cream and chocolate drizzle when I go with Wendy."

Tracy realized Charlie was talking about Popular Sharon. Tracy never hung out with her. She always felt like wallpaper around that Sharon.

21

"And Sharon said?" Tracy prompted. "What does Sharon have to do with anything?"

"I told you. Sharon is Pepper's older sister," Charlie hissed.

"Yeah, and Sharon went with you and Wendy to get a latte, and—?"

"Right, that's what I said. And just as we ordered, Sharon's little sister Pepper called her on her cell phone. She had just gotten out of class."

Tracy waited impatiently while it sounded like Charlie took a bite of something, probably an energy bar—Charlie loved to eat energy bars. "Come on, Charlie. Tell me what Pepper told Sharon."

"Pepper said her teacher and the principal had a transgender celebration party for a little boy in her second grade class," Charlie mumbled with her mouth full.

"Transgender celebration? What does that mean?" Tracy sputtered.

"It means this kid—a little boy—*came out* as a girl. He told everyone he was really a girl and he was just in the wrong body but inside he was really a girl. He'd known it for a long time, he said."

"And the teacher didn't correct him or straighten him out or something?" Tracy gasped. "I mean, that's absurd."

"Well, it's kind of a thing these days you know," Charlie sighed.

"No, I don't know," Tracy exploded. "That's nonsense. What do you mean, it's a thing."

"Oh Trace, sometimes you are such a dork. I know your mom is real strict about what you get to watch on television and she has all kinds of parental controls on your computer, but still—you *do* know the show about Jazz, don't you?"

"Of course," Tracy huffed. "I know what jazz is."

"No, not jazz like the music—Jazz like the boy, or girl."

"Well, which is it," Tracy snapped. "You don't even know if this kid is a boy or a girl?"

"Hey, don't get mad at me," Charlie countered. "I'm just the messenger. Jazz is—or was—a boy and now he says he's a girl. He says he knew he was a girl when he was only two years old and now he's a teenager so he's been a girl for quite a while," Charlie elaborated. "So I guess I should say *she* is a girl now. I guess. Maybe. What do you think?"

"I think you're nuts. I think Jazz is nuts. This is just plain crazy. You can't be born in the wrong body," Tracy scoffed.

"Yeah well, a lot of people say you can," Charlie countered. "So how do you know *you* are right?"

"Because I'm not *nuts*." Tracy practically spit the words.

"Or at least you're not *trans*," Charlie said in her *I-will-explain-this-to-you-patiently-child* voice.

It drove Tracy to distraction when Charlie adopted that woman-of-the-world tone. "Trans?"

"Transgender. You're not transgender, Trace. So you just don't get it."

"I don't get it because it's totally illogical and fantastic and insane," Tracy muttered. "Look, I gotta go talk to Toby. I'll talk to you later, Charlie."

"Okay, no prob," Charlie chirped. "See you tomorrow."

Tracy dropped her cell phone on the table as if she'd just been told it was poison ivy. She needed to get into the den and check up on Toby. And she *really* needed to talk to her mom.

6

Tracy really didn't want to talk to anyone at school the next day. She especially didn't want to talk to Charlie—or rather to have Charlie keep yammering at her.

She hated it when Charlie tried to keep explaining the whole transgender thing to her. Charlie had quickly adopted the popular line about how it was possible for someone to be born in the wrong body and it was mean and intolerant and bigoted—or just plain ignorant—not to support a person, especially a kid, who said they were really the *other* gender.

The whole idea made her uncomfortable. Suddenly everybody was talking about gender. Kids were looking at their friends as if trying to assess how male or female they were, what sex or gender they really were. And it focused a lot of attention on bodies and who was obviously having the changes that puberty caused and who was *behind*. Like Tracy.

Tracy hadn't *developed* that much, which her mom said was normal for her age. (Her mom said *she'd* been a late developer.) But a lot of the girls—like Charlie and the M's Megan and Marline—sure had.

She thought about her mom, who was slender and athletic at forty. She was afraid she was going to have a "boyish" figure like her mom. Which meant that right now the guys sometimes called her a stick. That hurt but it was silly. She'd always been able to laugh it off. It actually hadn't been that big a deal.

But now with all this transgender talk at school, she felt like kids were looking sideways at her wondering if the reason she didn't have a developing figure was because she was really a boy. Which didn't make any logical sense, because the whole transgender idea was that it didn't *matter* what your body was like—it was what you *felt* like inside.

But logic seemed to have been totally swept aside. Tracy found that frustrating. First, it just didn't seem logical that anyone would think they were in the wrong body. Gee, she'd always felt like she had the wrong nose. That is, she'd always hated her nose. It was kind of round on the end, like a blob. Charlie, of course, had a straight nose, narrow and straight on the end. Like a movie star.

So Tracy had always thought she had the wrong nose in the sense that she didn't *like* her nose because she thought it didn't look right on her face. But she didn't think she had the wrong nose as if it was somebody else's nose—a boy's nose or the nose Charlie should have had instead of her. It was *her* nose. She knew that. She didn't like it but she was stuck with it.

It was the same with your biological sex or gender, Tracy thought. You might not like what sex you were, but that's what you were born and that's what you were. You just couldn't change it. You couldn't pretend you were the other sex just because you wanted to be the other sex.

Except that's exactly what the kids were saying. Charlie insisted it was possible.

"You can have surgery to correct your body," Charlie told her.

"Like what? How do you make a little boy into a little girl? You can't exactly cut off his thing, you know," Tracy objected.

"Yeah, you can," Charlie flung back. "Just look it up. There's all kinds of information on the internet about it."

"That's just bizarre," Tracy shot back. "It's crazy. It's just wrong—and gruesome. Gee, how does a boy go to the bathroom if you cut off his—you know?"

"Penis. It's not a bad word, Trace," Charlie snapped with a superior scowl.

"Well, I don't like to say it," Tracy said gruffly.

"Oh, don't be such a prude," Charlie hissed.

The way Charlie was acting, Tracy really didn't want to hang out with her, even though she didn't have to hurry home on Wednesdays to babysit Toby.

25

Charlie and Wendy and Sharon (the popular one) and a few more girls from her class were all going together for pizza after school. The pizza place was easy walking distance from the school and it was a great place to hang out in the winter. There was a center fire pit with artificial logs that looked just like a real wood fire.

Tracy loved to stare into the fire and soak up its warmth with the wind howling outside. So she would have gone with Charlie, but now the kids were all gossiping and laughing about this transgender thing. She didn't want to go and talk about that all afternoon. Especially since she didn't agree with what most of the girls were saying now.

It seemed as if Sharon had convinced the whole gang that you actually could change your gender if you wanted to. She was kind of the ringleader in a clique of hip kids (including some of the boys) who were almost a cheering club for that little boy in Toby's class, that Jason kid who now said he was a girl and should be called Jessica.

The whole transgender cheering gang seemed to have sprung up overnight. Tracy hadn't ever heard the kids gossip about this *trans* idea before the transgender celebration party at the elementary school. It just seemed to erupt like a volcano. Because now the kids—the popular kids—were really pushing it.

Well, Tracy didn't like it so she wasn't going to go with them for pizza. Yeah, she'd love to go for pizza with Charlie but she wouldn't feel comfortable going with the others or pretending to agree with this whole gender thing. Yet if she objected, they would exclude her. So she just wouldn't go.

The only problem was that meant there was no one left to hang out with. Except Zoe.

Zoe was an odd duck. She usually hung around for a while after school, but off by herself. Charlie was always right in the middle of the popular gang of lower classmen after school when both boys and girls gathered in the front courtyard. But Zoe never had the courage to walk up and join them. She knew she wouldn't be welcome.

So Zoe would be off to the side of the courtyard and Tracy could go up to her and talk to her today now that she herself didn't want to join the girls. But she wouldn't do that. If she started talking to Zoe, the other girls would see and then she'd be excluded for that reason also.

So she didn't. She didn't go up to Zoe and say hi. She did sort of smile at her as she passed. Her mom was always telling Tracy that she should be nice to Zoe, should be friendly, because Tracy didn't know what her home situation was or why she always seemed unhappy. Well, I'd be unhappy too if my clothes looked as weird as hers did, Tracy always thought when her mom started that lecture. But she never said it, of course. Her mom wouldn't let her talk back like that.

The only thing left to do was to walk home alone. She waved gaily to the girls as if she had something important and fun to do after school and walked off briskly.

After all, she thought, the really interesting stuff might be what her mom told her in the five minutes before Toby got home from school. Her mom and dad and some of the other parents had met with the principal at the elementary school that morning for a meeting. She'd really like to know how that went and what her parents found out.

Ha, she thought, then she'd know something Charlie didn't, because none of the girls going to the pizza hut had parents who were upset by this transgender thing. So none of them had asked for a meeting. So Charlie wouldn't find out what the principal said in the meeting unless one of the kids whose parents had gone called her.

Like Tracy. She could dish the gossip to Charlie this time instead of the other way around.

Tracy grinned to herself as she walked. She was beginning to like this new feeling of knowing something sort of confidential before Charlie did.

7

"Mom?" Tracy called as she opened the front door. "You home, Mom?"

"In here," her mom called from the kitchen. "Come on back."

Tracy took her backpack and jacket to her room and put them away before heading to the kitchen.

"Umm, that smells good, Mom," she said as she entered.

"I baked cookies. I think Toby may need a little pick-me-up when he gets home today so I baked his favorite, oatmeal raisin. And I made extra because Josh is coming over to tutor you tonight."

Tracy's heart sank. Oh no, not Josh. She'd forgotten that tutoring had been changed to Wednesday night this week. She didn't want to deal with a boy right now. She meant a real boy, not one of her brothers. Nate and Toby didn't count.

She wouldn't feel comfortable with Josh tonight. Not with all this gender stuff that the kids were talking about. All the emphasis on bodies and who had which body and whether somebody was really a girl in a boy's body or a boy in a girl's body or—or what? She couldn't keep it straight.

Tracy rubbed her forehead. It used to be so simple. It was still that simple, wasn't it? It gave her a headache to think about it. She decided to forget it and enjoy a cookie.

Tracy had hardly settled on a kitchen chair with a glass of milk and a cookie when Toby burst through the front door.

"Mom?" he yelled.

Her little brother sounded a little frantic, Tracy thought. She looked up in consternation as her mom suddenly scooted around the table and hurried down the hall.

What had that kid gotten into now, Tracy sighed. He had a knack for getting into the wackiest scrapes. Like the time they went to the opening of a new McDonalds because the Ronald McDonald clown was going to be there and Toby—just three years old at the time—loved Ronald McDonald.

The fast-food restaurant had a stage set up behind their parking lot, back by the big green dumpster that the garbage truck lifted with the massive steel fork on its front. The kind of fork that swung up over the truck when it was driving down the road.

There were round steel posts about four feet tall and five inches in diameter at the four corners of the dumpster. They were painted the same forest green as the dumpster.

One of the posts had a little hole—one tiny little hole about a quarter inch in diameter. The hole was about three feet off the ground. If you looked in the hole, you could see that the steel was almost a quarter inch thick. Those posts were strong hunks of steel! Tracy guessed that was to keep cars from crashing into the trash bin.

Tracy's mom brought her and Toby to the opening party because her little brother wanted to see Ronald McDonald and there were going to be free treats. The three of them were standing next to the dumpster near the stage at the back of the parking lot. Toby wanted to be right up close to Ronald.

Ronald McDonald—that is, the guy who was hired to play Ronald McDonald—was up on the stage in his clown costume singing and dancing and joking with the crowd. There were a few band players providing music. All the kids and their parents seemed to be having a good time.

The show lasted more than an hour. Some families left and new groups of kids arrived. Finally Ronald McDonald signaled it was time to pack up the show and the crowd started to melt away.

That's when Tracy's mom found out that Toby couldn't move. He had stuck his little finger in that one tiny little hole in the post by the dumpster and he couldn't get it out.

First Tracy's mom tried to wiggle or twist it out. Several other parents also gave it a go and even Ronald, when he noticed what was happening, got down off the stage and tried to jiggle Toby's finger loose. All to no avail. Finally someone called the fire department.

29

The firemen were careful and gentle but Toby's finger was getting awfully sore from so many adults wiggling and jiggling his hand to try to unstick that little finger. It started to swell. All the firemen's tricks including soap and salve didn't budge his little finger.

In the end the firemen decided they needed to cut the post with a big saw to get Toby unstuck. Tracy's mom was upset and nervous, afraid they'd cut Toby's finger off by mistake. But Toby was real brave.

The firemen got a special tool like a mini chain saw out of their truck and started walking over to where Toby stood anchored to the post by his little finger.

Just at that point a skinny pony-tailed man wearing a smeared white apron came out the back of the McDonalds kitchen with a small bowl. He went up to Toby, kneeled down, pulled a gob of grease out of the bowl with his index finger and massaged it around the post hole. In two seconds flat, Toby pulled his finger out and everyone cheered.

The firemen looked relieved as they packed up their saw. The cook shrugged and went back into the kitchen. And Toby got to go up on the stage with Ronald McDonald for special treats.

Toby wasn't upset about the whole affair. After all, he got special attention from Ronald McDonald. But Tracy remembered that none of the seventy-five to a hundred other little kids in the parking lot that day got their fingers stuck in holes. Only Toby.

So Tracy wasn't alarmed by Toby's frantic calls. He was always getting into some dumb scrape or another. What had he gone and done this time?

She could hear her mom's soothing tones as she talked with Toby but they were far enough away that she didn't bother to try to distinguish their words. She was sure she would hear about Toby's misadventure in all its lurid detail soon enough. He liked to tell her every detail, usually two or three times.

So for now Tracy ignored whatever was happening in the front hall and pulled a magazine her mom had left on the table over toward her cookie plate. It was one of those flea market decorating magazines her mom liked. The front showed a picture of an old bicycle wheel frame made into a rustic chandelier complete with hanging crystals. Tracy thought it was a clever re-purposing idea and she was all for conservation and recycling, but she really wasn't into bling.

Just then Tracy's mom and her little brother walked quietly into the kitchen. Her mom had her arm around Toby's shoulders and Tracy could see that he'd been crying. Hard.

Without even asking, Tracy had a feeling she knew what the problem was—and that Toby wasn't the only one who was going to be upset before the end of the day.

8

Tracy started to open her mouth to ask what was going on but her mom narrowed her eyes and shook her head slightly from side to side. Tracy got the signal to keep quiet. She pretended to be absorbed in the flea market magazine.

Toby dropped into a chair and sighed heavily. "It's just not fair, Mom," he mumbled.

"I know, sweetheart," his mom answered. "It's completely crazy. But we can't always control situations. You know Dad and I are trying to work this out with the school."

"I don't want to go back," Toby said. He spoke so softly that it took Tracy a few seconds to be sure she had heard him correctly.

"I understand," his mom replied gently. "But you have to go to school, hon."

"But can't I go to another school, Mom?" he pleaded.

"Well, that's one thing your Dad and I are considering," Mrs. McKenzie answered. "It's a bit complicated, sweetheart. We're working on it."

"Good," Toby sighed. "Because I don't want to go back. Ever. Like tomorrow."

Tracy's mom paused in the middle of pouring a glass of milk. "Uh, Toby, that's not—"

She was interrupted by loud knocking on the front door. They had a perfectly good doorbell. Tracy could never understand why some people insisted on practically knocking the door down instead of just ringing the bell.

"I'll get it, Mom," she said, jumping up out of her chair and hurrying down the hallway. "I'm coming, I'm coming" she hissed under her breath as the knocking continued.

She had barely opened the door when Mrs. Blake from three doors down blurted out, "Is your mom home?"

"Yeah, she's in the kitchen."

"Excuse me, Tracy." Mrs. Blake abruptly pushed past her and swept on down the hall calling, "Lara—Lara, I've got to talk to you."

Both taken aback and intrigued, Tracy followed Mrs. Blake down the hall into the kitchen.

"Uh, Trace, you stay here with Toby, okay?" her mom said, moving her eyes in a way that said *do-what-I-say-no-questions-asked-and-be-nice-to-your-brother.* "Alison, let's you and I go into the living room to talk," she continued as she ushered Mrs. Blake back down the hall.

Tracy sighed with frustration and dropped back into her chair. She didn't like to be treated like a little kid who couldn't hear whatever gossip was going to be shared by the neighbor. She had finished her cookie and she wanted to go to her room and do her own thing. But when she looked at Toby's tear-stained face, she felt bad and relented.

"Hey, lil bro, what's going on?" she asked gently.

"I—I got in trouble," he sniffed. "At school."

"Yeah," she encouraged. "So what'd you do?"

"I didn't *do* anything," he said softly, tears welling at the corners of his eyes.

"Well, you must have done something," Tracy objected. "Who got you in trouble?"

"The principal."

Wow, Toby must have pulled a really good one, Tracy thought. Mr. Pullman always seemed so mellow with the kids.

"The principal? So what is it that you *didn't do wrong* that got you in trouble with Mr. Pullman?" Tracy pushed.

"I just said Susie was right when she cried."

"Who's Susie?"

"She's a girl in my class."

"Yeah, so...?"

"So she was crying and I said she was right, it was wrong."

Sometimes it was like trying to squeeze orange juice out of a corn stalk to get Toby to tell something straight. Her mom always said it was like trying to make a silk purse out of a sow's ear, but Tracy liked to make up her own similes.

Was that a simile? She wasn't sure. Mrs. Fellows had taught them similes and metaphors but Tracy always got them mixed up. Or maybe that was an analogy. Argghhh, she groaned to herself. Why couldn't they just read the books instead of having to analyze motivation and style and all that? None of that would ever help her figure out what Toby was saying anyway.

The point was that Toby never told a story straight. You had to pull it out of him in pieces. And when he was talking about other kids that you didn't even know, it got even more confusing.

"So Susie was right and *it* was wrong?" Tracy patiently repeated. "What was it?"

"What he did. Or she did. But he's not a she so it's wrong and Susie was right."

Tracy rubbed her forehead. "Toby, I know you're upset, but I can't figure out what you are talking about," she said slowly. "Please start from the beginning and tell me what happened."

Toby gave her a look like she was a real *dummkopf*. "I just told you," he said. "Jason shouldn't have gone in there because he isn't a girl and Susie *is* a girl so she got upset when he went in there and so she cried and then she got in trouble and I said she shouldn't be in trouble because she was right and then I got in worse trouble and then everyone was mad at me and said I was mean and dumb and I don't want to go back."

Tracy chewed on her lip and thought a minute. "Uh, is Jason that boy who says he's a girl?"

Toby nodded.

"So Jason went into—" Tracy asked.

"The girls bathroom."

"The *girls* bathroom?"

Toby nodded again.

"Ah, now I got it," Tracy muttered. "So Susie cried and you said Jason shouldn't go in there because he's a boy and your teacher said he's not a boy anymore?"

"Yeah. Which is stupid. He is a boy. He's been a boy for the whole time I've known him. Since kindergarten."

"You're sure?" Tracy wasn't expecting an answer to that one. She was just filling a space with words while she tried to figure out what to say to her brother. So she was taken aback when he answered.

"Yes, I'm sure. We've been going pee next to each other in the boys' bathroom since kindergarten. I've seen his penis lots of times. No big deal. He's a boy, like me and Tim and Bret and—"

"Yeah, yeah," Tracy shushed him. "Okay, I get the idea."

They both sat quietly for a minute. Not a comfortable pause kind of quiet but more of a bad funk kind of quiet.

"But now he says he's a girl," Toby added in a tone that was more confused than indignant.

"Do you—do you think he really thinks that?" Tracy asked sceptically.

"I don't know," the little boy answered dejectedly.

Tracy shivered a little bit. He sounded so forlorn that she decided she'd let him use the colored pen set he was always trying to borrow from her. He did more with it than she did anyway. It was kind of weird what a good artist he was. After all, he was only seven but he could draw an animal with a pen with lots of little lines and it looked really good, like a real artist would do. Tracy could only draw a crooked cartoon figure, and she had to use a pencil so she could erase a lot even to do that.

So why should a little seven-year-old kid—a good kid who was polite and did okay in school and could even draw like that—get in trouble for saying what was so obvious?

Except that as of yesterday, it seemed like half the town was ready to call night day and sweet sour and a boy—a girl. It made Tracy's head spin.

And, Tracy wondered, what was Mrs. Blake telling her mom in the den? Was it about Toby or Susie or Mr. Pullman or what the meeting was about at school or what?

She had a lot of questions but, as usual, there was nothing she could do but wait until the adults were ready to spill the beans.

Except that at that moment her phone rang. The caller ID showed that it was Charlie. Tracy couldn't decide whether she was happy because Charlie was probably calling to tell her what actually had gone on at Toby's school that day or mad that, as usual, she had lost her chance to be the first one with the juicy gossip.

But maybe she hadn't—Charlie might not know about Toby's getting in trouble at school or why he got in trouble. Yet with her little brother sitting right there, she couldn't really tell Charlie about that. Toby would be mad if she told. And he would tattle to their mom and then she'd be in trouble, too.

Which was worse, not to know something or to know something you couldn't tell?

9

"Trace, do you know what your little brother did at school today?" Charlie blurted as soon as Tracy said hello.

Great, there went her chance to be the first one with a juicy bit of gossip.

"Uh, yeah," Tracy bluffed. "I know all about it."

"Well, Pepper told Sharon that Mr. Pullman took Toby out of class and made him sit in the principal's office for the last two hours of school and lectured him about not being a bully."

"What?" Tracy exclaimed. She was mad now and sprang to her little brother's defense. "He is not a bully."

"Well, he acted like one today," Charlie insisted. "He kept saying that Jessica—that's the kid who used to be a boy—was not a girl and she shouldn't go in the girls restroom. He made Jessica feel real bad and cry because he was so mean."

"Whoa, Charlie!" Tracy raised her voice. "It is not mean to say that this Jessica is not a girl because he's not. And Toby had every right to say so." She caught her breath and added triumphantly, "He has a penis. He's a boy."

"Oh Tracy," Charlie countered. "You'd better not say that at school or the kids will laugh at you. That is just wrong, you know. That's ignorant. Body parts don't mean you are male or female. It's what's inside that shows whether you are truly a boy or a girl."

"You're crazy."

"No, I'm not. Everyone knows that. Look it up on the internet," Charlie countered.

"That's utter nonsense," Tracy sputtered. "It's just—just balderdash."

"Just what?" Charlie sounded puzzled.

"Balderdash."

"What's that?"

"I don't know," Tracy answered. "But that's what my grandpa says when something is really stupid and dumb and—and *ignorant*," she finished angrily.

"Tracy," Charlie sighed, "you are hopeless. Listen, as your friend, I'm telling you, you'd better just keep your mouth shut at school. Believe what you want. I know your parents are real old-fashioned and kind of religious and stuff so it's not your fault. But until you figure this all out, you are better off just to keep your mouth shut, okay?"

Tracy did a slow burn as Charlie fell into her superior *I-know-this-stuff-and-you-don't-because-I'm-more-hip-than-you-are* mode. Charlie did that a lot. On everything from how to comb your hair to what diet you should eat. Charlie's latest idea was that everyone should eat a paleo diet, but she didn't count pizza as cheating on her paleo diet.

Charlie did what she wanted to do, and defined things as she wanted to define them. Then all the rest of the kids just kind of fell in line behind Charlie and Sharon and parroted whatever they said. Except for Tracy. And Zoe. But Zoe didn't count because she was an outlier.

And as for Tracy, Charlie always told her just to keep her mouth closed and look as if she agreed with the crowd and then she could go on home and believe whatever she wanted to. Because the kids at school wouldn't rag on her if she kept her mouth shut.

Tracy guessed she was a bit of a coward because usually that's exactly what she did. She kept her mouth shut at school. So what did it matter if the kids all thought they were eating paleo while they gorged on pizza? Tracy thought of it as her own private little joke and kept her mouth shut.

And what did it matter if the kids all swooned over some singer or movie star and said he or she was the greatest and they all went to see the movie he or she was in?

Tracy hardly ever went to the movies, and then it was usually just with her family. No sex or horror or blood and guts. Her parents didn't approve of those. Which left fewer and fewer movies that were acceptable. And the movies she went to didn't have the stars the kids were talking about in them. So she didn't mention it if she went. She just kept her mouth shut.

She was used to keeping her mouth shut and just letting the kids think that she agreed with them.

But this was different. Tracy wasn't sure she could keep her mouth shut on this one. This was crazy. It was as if the whole school was suddenly declaring the world was square or flat or whatever. What about the pictures from space? The earth was round, obviously. So if the kids started saying it was square, would she just keep quiet?

Maybe. Because she didn't really care whether the world was round or square. Well, actually she did care because it would mess up the whole solar system if the earth was square. But that wasn't the point.

The point was that this time the kids were talking about her little brother. Maybe they wouldn't rag on *her* if she kept her mouth shut, but they were ragging on her little brother. They were saying he was mean and ignorant. But he wasn't.

He was right.

Tracy wasn't going to let the kids talk like that about her little brother. She wasn't sure what kind of trouble that would get her into, but she knew it would be wrong to keep quiet this time.

"Uh, Charlie," she said abruptly, "I've got to go. I'll talk to you tomorrow."

When she hung up her cell, she saw Toby staring at her with questioning eyes.

"Don't worry, Toby," she mustered. "I won't let those kids say mean things about you. I promise."

But her heart sank as she said it. How much trouble would that promise cause?

10

When Mrs. Blake left, Tracy's mom bustled into the kitchen all cheeriness and business.

"Trace and Toby, go do your homework," she said. "I've got to get dinner going."

"Uh, Mom, what did Mrs. Bl—," Tracy started, but her mother interrupted her before she could get the words out.

"Hurry off now, Tracy." She fluttered her hands palms down as if shooing chickens into a pen. "Your father will be home in half an hour and then Josh comes after dinner. So you've got to get your homework done right away."

Toby was probably going to play electronic games on the computer in his room instead of doing his homework, Tracy thought. His homework was easy second grade stuff—work sheets he could finish in a few minutes once he put his mind to it.

But her homework was more serious, especially now that she was in AP math. She didn't really think she needed Josh coming over to tutor her anymore, except once in a while when she got stuck on a new math concept. But her parents liked Josh. They thought it was a good idea for him to keep tutoring her, to make sure she didn't get behind.

Usually Tracy didn't mind. Josh was kind of nice and he was comfortable to be around. Not comfortable like her brothers—they were comfortable like an old jacket that you could drop on the floor or sit on and it was still a perfectly good jacket. So you could ignore your brothers or have fun with them or fight with them and it was all okay in the end because they were your brothers.

40

It was easy having Josh around because he was comfortable too, even though it wasn't like with her brothers. He was more like a pal, a boy who was a friend. Not a boyfriend. She'd never had a boyfriend. Not unless you counted Billy in the first grade who used to bring her dandelion bouquets after school.

But she'd never had a boy who was a pal, a real friend before, either. Well, not since the fourth grade when she used to ride bikes with Carlos from down the street. But now Carlos was one of the popular guys at school. He didn't want to hang out with her anymore.

Yeah, Josh was nice. They got off the subject of math sometimes and just talked. Josh talked about things the kids at school never talked about, like global warming.

Not like Mr. Allen, her science teacher, did. Mr. Allen was always telling the class that the oceans were rising and the world was getting hotter and hotter and it was all the fault of the greedy developed nations (especially the United States) where everyone drove a car, like the ultimate evil—an SUV. Tracy thought it was odd that Mr. Allen talked like that when he drove an extended-cab pickup. After all, that wasn't exactly a gas-saver.

But Josh didn't just chant the media mantras like Mr. Allen. He gave real examples, like temperature cycles shown in records from the early 1900s. He showed her graphs with temperature data over time on his phone, and he even pulled a bunch of newspaper articles off the web from the 1970s.

Back then the world was actually getting colder, Josh said. Tracy laughed with him as he read headlines out loud that warned about the earth entering another ice age. "In 1969 experts wrote an article in Science and Mechanics, a respected magazine, claiming that a new ice age was coming. In 1972 Walter Cronkite, a famous television anchorman, also warned of a coming ice age."

"And look at the headlines on the covers of *Time Magazine*," Josh had continued. "*The Big Freeze* in 1973 and again 1977. *How to Survive the Coming Ice Age* for a cover in 1977, and *The Cooling of America* in 1979. In fact, scientific literature and conferences emphasized fear of a coming ice age."

Josh said while the media trumpeted ice age hysteria in the 70s, now the popular wisdom was that the earth was drastically heating up.

41

"*Global Warming* was a scare meme for a few decades. But then temperature charts showed an 18-year cooler interval from 1998 to 2015," Josh said.

He added that there was a so-called Little Ice Age from about 1300 to 1850 or so. It wasn't a true ice age like the one about 4500 years ago—just a 500-year period of global cooling. But after the Little Ice Age, a return to normal warmer temps made it *look like* the earth was heating up.

"What was the earth cooling from in 1300?" Tracy puzzled.

"The Medieval Warm Period. With temps like we have now—long before the Industrial Revolution of the 1800s created any *climate-changing pollution*," he drawled with irony.

"Wait—a previous *warm* period?" Tracy objected.

"Yeah, an interval of several hundred years in the Northern Hemisphere from around 800 to 1200 with more like our present temps. It was the warmest period since the Roman Warm Period."

"The *Roman Warm* Period? You mean there have been alternating cooler and warmer periods over the centuries?" Tracy asked.

"Yep, maybe 500 year cycles or so," Josh answered. "With blips like the cold snap in the 1970s or our recent 18-year cooler interval in the middle of a warm cycle," Josh explained. "Basically, what some scientists claim now as dangerous warming is within the normal variation in global temps. It's nothing man can really affect or change."

"So why the hysteria about global warming?" Tracy asked.

"I think the underlying aim of climate alarmists is political control," Josh said. "But to gain popular support they have to convince us of impending catastrophe. So when the recent 18-year cooling period was documented by reliable scientists, climate alarmists simply switched the *global warming* meme out for a more generic term, *Climate Change*."

Josh pointed out to Tracy how silly it was to buy into media scare stories and how contradictory ideas and claims could be amusing. It was fun to laugh with a boy over something like that.

About the only thing most of the boys at school thought was humorous was a stupid prank, usually some kind of trick that publicly embarrassed some kid. That was mean. A lot of the boys were like that. But her brother Nate wouldn't do something like that and she didn't think that Josh would either. He didn't seem to like that kind of humor at all.

So yeah, usually Tracy was fine with Josh coming over to tutor her even if she didn't feel she needed the help with her math.

But not tonight.

Tonight Tracy didn't want to see any boy. (Her brothers didn't count.) She wanted to find out what had happened at the meeting her parents went to at Toby's school and she wanted to ask her mom questions about the whole transgender thing.

But she didn't really even know what to ask her mom because she'd never thought much about this whole transgender thing before a day or so ago. Whenever the TV news had said anything about it, she'd just blocked it out, the same as she blocked out stock market reports. She just didn't care.

But all of a sudden she did care and she wanted to know things. Information. Starting with what happened in the meeting with Mr. Pullman today. What he said and what that meant and why he was saying it and what her parents were going to do about it.

Only while Josh was there, she couldn't ask her mom any of that. And she certainly couldn't talk about gender with Josh! She'd rather not even see him tonight. Maybe she could develop a headache or a stomachache and beg off for tonight. Except that never worked—her mom always saw right through it if she feigned illness.

It worked for Toby though.

Life was not fair. Toby could get away with things and now because of Toby her whole family was—

Wait, that wasn't fair either, Tracy thought. The whole mess wasn't because of something Toby did. It was because of something Jason did—then the teacher and Mr. Pullman.

So what was going on with this Jason kid?

11

By the time dinner was cleared away, Josh was ringing the doorbell. At least he used the doorbell, unlike Mrs. Blake, Tracy thought.

But Tracy still wasn't eager to see him. She was frustrated that she hadn't had a chance to ask her mom what had happened at the meeting with Mr. Pullman and what Mrs. Blake had said. And she felt uncomfortable to have to sit right next to Josh for a whole hour. She was nervous about how the whole transgender vibe at school was going to affect the atmosphere.

"Hey, Trace," Josh said as he came down the hall. "Man, it's cold out there."

"Yeah. Well, it's still January," she grinned tentatively.

"Did you go watch the Polar Bears on New Year's?" Josh asked.

He was referring to the hardy souls who dove off the boat dock at the city lake every year. There were a few younger adults who did it but most of the Polar Bear members were old and rather—well, portly, to put it nicely. Tracy guessed the added avoirdupois (body fat) gave insulation from the freezing water. But a few of them were skinny, really wiry. Tracy didn't see how they could stand jumping into that frigid lake. Yet they all cavorted around as if it were July. She'd seen it on television when she and her brothers watched the New Year's reports with her parents. But she'd never seen it in person.

"What was it like being there?" she asked.

"It was bizarre," Josh guffawed. "I was wearing my winter jacket with the sheepskin lining. The men were wearing swimming

44

trunks. Most of the women were wearing swimming suits too. But two ladies wore long formal gowns as a joke. One man wore a tuxedo jacket and speedos."

"Weren't they freezing?" Tracy wondered.

"If they were, they hid it well. They were all bravado and bluster, yelling that the water was fine and why didn't we all jump on in."

"How long did they stay in the water?" Tracy asked.

"About half of them only stayed in a few minutes, just long enough to be able to stake their claim as Polar Bears. But the rest of them were unbelievable. They looked like they were having a grand time and really didn't appear to be cold at all. But as soon as someone got out, he or she was wrapped in a blanket."

"Well, no one is ever going to talk *me* into doing something that weird," Tracy said adamantly.

With that Josh opened his math book and showed her a new problem his teacher had introduced that day. She forgot that she'd been worried about feeling uncomfortable about having to sit next to him for an hour with all this new emphasis on gender at school. That is, he'd always been a *boy* sitting next to her and that in itself made her kind of nervous because she wasn't used to that kind of extended one-on-one relationship with a boy who wasn't her brother or her cousin. But it was worse now with all the kids at school focused on what *made* you a boy or a girl, even more than normal. That was something that was already hard to forget at her age anyway.

But Josh was so easy to listen to that she forgot all that and became absorbed in the math steps he was showing her. That was pretty amazing she thought, because math had never been a particular interest of hers. But the way Josh explained it made so much sense that it became fascinating.

The hour passed quickly and then he was off with a wave. "See you tomorrow, Trace," he smiled as he went out the door.

"Yeah, see you tomorrow," she answered with an echoing grin. She was surprised to realize that she was humming as she closed and locked the door.

That hadn't been so bad after all, she thought. Josh hadn't mentioned the gender thing at all. In fact, he seemed unfazed by the rumors and tensions at school. He seemed totally—normal. Just like always. Just friendly and casual and talking about facts and ideas, not other kids. And he seemed calm.

Tracy took a deep breath. Maybe that's what she should do, just ignore all the uproar at school and focus on her subjects and then come home and enjoy her family.

Except that was the problem. It was someone in her family that was in the middle of the uproar. Or had caused the uproar.

Only he hadn't. It wasn't Toby's fault that all the kids were arguing about gender at school. It was that kid Jason at elementary school who said he was the wrong gender. Or he was changing his gender.

What on earth did that mean? What *was* gender anyway, Tracy stewed. It couldn't be biological sex because you were born a biological sex, weren't you? Of course you were! You were a boy or a girl. Except now the kids said maybe you weren't. But if a boy was really a girl, what *was* "being a girl" if it wasn't having a—well, you know, a girl's biological body?

Tracy's head began to hurt. As she started down the hall to the den, she hoped her mother had some answers for her. Some real answers that made sense.

12

Tracy waited impatiently while her mother got Toby off to bed. Usually he went without much protest as all three siblings knew the routine—who had what chores and what time their own lights-out was.

But Toby had needed a lot of extra reassurance tonight. He'd had endless questions about what his parents had decided about school for tomorrow. In the end his mom said she'd keep him home the next day until they sorted something out. So he finally became less anxious and let his mom tuck him in bed, something he usually would have told her emphatically that he didn't need any more because after all he was *seven years old* now.

"Mom, finally," Tracy sighed when her mother came into the den and sank down on the sofa beside her. Her dad was in the living room working on his computer, making up for the time he'd taken off work to go to the meeting with Mr. Pullman that day.

"Well, I'm here, dear. What would you like to know?" her mother asked.

"First please tell me about the meeting with Toby's principal today," Tracy said. "And what is going on with that Jason kid anyway? How could Toby's teacher say Jason is a girl now? What does that mean? I don't see why Mr. Pullman bawled out Toby. And what was Mrs. Blake's deal all about?"

It all came out in one pent-up breath. Tracy felt as if she'd been holding her breath for hours waiting for answers.

Mrs. McKenzie smiled a little as she remonstrated gently, "That's more than one question, girlie." She patted Tracy's knee and sighed.

"Okay, let's start with this afternoon and go backward. In the meeting with concerned parents today Mr. Pullman apparently felt he had to back up his teacher, although it was plain to see that he was uncomfortable with the whole transgender issue. He reported that district policy is to support students who report their gender as—well, as whatever they want to report it as. So despite the fact that he seemed a bit nonplussed about the policy—or at least he appeared embarrassed and a little befuddled trying to explain and defend it—he stuck to his guns that he had to discipline Toby for 'bullying' Jason-now-Jessica by calling him a boy."

"But Jason *is* a boy," Tracy broke in. "Toby told me that he's seen his—you know, his penis—lots of times in the boys bathroom when they were going pee."

Even though she had brothers, Tracy didn't like to say the word *penis* out loud. It felt like a violation of privacy or modesty. She didn't like to talk about personal body parts or body functions. It was embarrassing.

Actually, unless you were at a doctor's office, she felt that it *should* be embarrassing. Some things were *private*. Like going to the bathroom. She always made sure to lock the bathroom door so one of her brothers wouldn't barge in by mistake. Ugh, *she'd* never share the bathroom with a boy!

"Yes, Jason is a boy—a biological boy, but we'll get to that last," her mom reiterated. "What we found out today was a bit about how this all started."

"As you know Ms. Barton is Toby's second grade teacher," Mrs. McKenzie continued. "She is a recent university graduate. Transgender theory is rampant in the university setting. Professors are pushing it hard, and university students seem to be falling in line with the media mantras about gender identity."

"Gender identity? Wait, Mom," Tracy objected. "I haven't even figured out what gender is. What's gender identity? Is that something different?"

"Well, gender identity is tied up with gender expression and—"

"Mom!" Tracy wailed in protest. "Gender *expression*? What's that?"

"Okay, this is the deal," Mrs. McKenzie began again. "Toby's teacher is friends with Mr. and Mrs. Jalston, the parents of Jason. Jason's mom told Ms. Barton that she really enjoyed it when Jason was little and he snuck into his big sister Cindy's closet and tried on her clothes. It was so cute to see him prancing around in a skirt and trying on Cindy's girlie shoes. The whole family chuckled at that and took pictures. Sometimes Mrs. Jalston would even put make-up on Jason. He got a kick out of it and the whole family thought it was a great joke. Mrs. Jalston told Ms. Barton that this had been going on for four years, since Jason was three."

"Yuck," Tracy screwed up her face. "That doesn't sound cute to me. It sounds kind of sick."

"Well, Ms. Barton counseled Mr. and Mrs. Jalston that their son could very well be trying to tell them that he was actually a girl—a girl trapped in a boy's body."

"That's ridiculous," Tracy scoffed. "He was just being a bratty little kid who'd figured out a way to get a lot of attention."

"Maybe, Trace, but are you sure you aren't judging too harshly or jumping to conclusions?" her mom rebuked gently. "Why do you think Jason was so thirsty for attention? Was it the normal self-centeredness of a little kid, or was he emotionally vulnerable for some reason?"

"I dunno," Tracy shrugged.

"The problem is, the more attention Jason got, the more he wanted to 'play girl' so he'd be the center of his family's attention. And when this went on for four years, Jason actually convinced himself and his parents that he really *was* a girl—inside. He was just in the wrong body."

"But you can't be in the wrong body, Mom," Tracy protested. "Your body is—well, it's *you*. It's part of who you are. If you were in a different body, you wouldn't be you. You'd be... Oh, I don't know. But you wouldn't be you!"

"I agree."

"So does a boy's body have a boy in it, or if you're a boy do you get a boy's body when you're born, or how does it work?"

"Boys and girls—male and female—it all goes back to God's plan for reproduction," her mom responded. "Both a male and a female are necessary in order to propagate a species. That's called a *binary* system of the sexes."

"You mean like a bull and a cow have to have sex in order to make a calf. I know all that, Mom. I'm not an *infant*," Tracy sighed, rolling her eyes.

"Of course you're not. Just covering the basics, Trace. So the deal is, less than one to five percent of all critters (mostly things like snails and slugs and worms) are self-fertile. Most need both a male and a female to reproduce."

"Once in a while you will hear the term hermaphrodite," her mom continued. "That's an organism that can be self-fertile, an organism that does not need a male and female to reproduce. For example, many flowers and common plants like corn and peas. But higher animals and humans are never hermaphroditic. And it absolutely takes both a male and a female to make a human baby."

"Yeah I know, Mom," Tracy protested, "but a year or so ago all the kids at school were talking about a man that had a baby. It was on television."

"Do you think it was true just because it was on the news?" Mrs. McKenzie asked.

"Well, no, but all the kids said..." Tracy let the sentence drop off into the air.

"Do you think if *everyone says so* something must be true?"

Tracy squirmed a bit on the sofa. "No, but I didn't know what to tell them."

"That's understandable," her mom said. "All the news stories were claiming it was true. The problem is they were talking about someone who *looked* like a man but was really a woman. You see, the 'man' who got pregnant was a woman who pretended to be a man by cutting her hair in a man's style, wearing men's clothes, and even taking hormones that caused her to grow a beard. But she was still a woman. She still had a vagina, ovaries that produced eggs, and a uterus—which you know is where the baby grows inside the mother."

"Now this woman who claimed to be a man is called a *trangender man* or a *trans man*," Tracy's mom explained. "But a *trans* man is still a *biological* female."

"So this biological female—a.k.a. trans man—was in a sexual relationship with a biological man, a regular man," Mrs. McKenzie continued. "We've talked before about how babies are made. During sex, if a man's sperm penetrates a woman's egg, a baby starts to grow. So this is what happened when the woman who was a pretend-man, or *trans* man, had sex with her partner, a biological man. It was not a miracle—it was basic biology."

"Okay, I get that," Tracy said. "But then if having a penis makes someone a man, what about people like Charlie keeps telling me about? People who have surgery to have their sex changed? She said a man can have his penis cut off and take hormones so he grows breasts and doesn't have a beard anymore. So then is he a real woman?"

"Having a penis does not make someone a man just as having a vagina does not make you a woman—" Mrs. McKenzie began.

Tracy started to giggle. "Mom," she remonstrated, "you sound like Charlie! That's what she says."

"But wait, I haven't finished," her mom grinned. "You have a penis because you *are* a male. And you have a vagina because you *are* a female. That is, I'm talking about a real penis or vagina."

"What do you mean a real one? Are there fake ones?" Tracy asked with a flip grin.

"Yes, that's exactly what they are—fake, and non-functional. You see, *sex reassignment surgery* is a misnomer. Nothing can change a person's sex—not even surgery. For a man who thinks he can surgically change his sex to female, the surgeon mutilates him by removing his real penis, then creating a blind pouch to resemble a vagina. Incidentally, the man will have to dilate the pouch opening regularly for the rest of his life to keep it from closing up."

"Eww," Tracy grimaced.

"And for a woman who falsely thinks she can change her sex to male, a surgeon will take muscle and skin from her arm or thigh to fashion a fake penis. But it will just hang there. It isn't real and it's not functional."

Tracy didn't speak. Her horrified expression said it all.

"I've learned a lot of things in my nursing classes that have really helped me to understand this," Mrs. McKenzie continued.

"You see, nearly every cell in your body is marked—actually *coded* like a computer—as either male or female. Did you know that?"

Tracy shook her head side to side.

"Each cell with a nucleus has a chromosome pair that is the sex marker. For a boy, the cell has an X chromosome and a Y chromosome, an XY together," Mrs. McKenzie explained. "And for a girl the cell has two X chromosomes, an XX chromosome pair. By the way, how many cells do you think you have in your body?"

"I dunno," Tracy shrugged. "Maybe about a million?"

"More," her mom said.

"A billion?"

"More."

"A *trillion?*"

"Actually you have more than *thirty trillion cells* in your body. I have more than thirty trillion cells, Toby has more than thirty trillion cells—everyone has more than thirty trillion cells."

"Wow, that's a lot," Tracy sighed. "And you said each cell has two chromosomes that tell your sex?"

"That's right. Every girl has thirty trillion XXs and every boy has thirty trillion XYs. Tracy, *your* brain cells, muscle, heart and liver cells are all female. Every cell in your body (except for a few enucleated or non-nucleus cells like red blood cells) is marked with an XX chromosome pair—*coded* as *female.* So for little kids, we can simply say, 'Your eye, your earlobe and your elbow are all *coded* as boy or girl.'"

"From the moment of conception—when the sperm from the father and the egg from the mother unite—this XY or XX code governs the development of the baby in the mother's womb. An XY code is the key for the development of male sex organs like testes and a penis, while an XX code would prompt the development of a vagina, ovaries and a uterus."

"So you can see," Mrs. McKenzie continued, "why cutting off a penis and even surgically creating a fake vagina would not make someone a woman. It might change the appearance of an individual but that individual would still have thirty trillion XY chromosomes. The point is, there are not just male parts and female parts of your body. Your entire body is either male or female right *down to the cellular level.*"

52

"Wow, I never knew that." Tracy mulled it over in the silence that followed.

"But we can't see inside the cells when a baby is born, can we?" her mom asked. "Well, we can if we do a DNA test. But just to look at a newborn—or an ultrasound image of a developing baby—we can't see inside to the cellular level, can we?"

"No, of course not," Tracy agreed.

"But we look at an ultrasound screen or a newborn baby and we say it's a boy or a girl because..." Mrs. McKenzie let the sentence hang.

"Because we see a penis—or we don't," Tracy answered.

"You're right. So a penis is an external marker of the code that is in the baby's cells. Being born male means you are a boy—a biological boy, the male sex. And you can't change your sex no matter how much you abuse your body with surgeries or hormones, which can only change your appearance. And vice versa, a vagina is an external marker that a girl baby's cells have the female code. She's marked as the female sex. "

"Okay, so if you are a boy—the male sex—you are the male gender, and that is that," Tracy summed up, sliding down more comfortably in the sofa cushions.

"Umm, well—that should be the end of it," her mother sighed. "But nowadays there is an ideological push to un-couple the concept of gender from biological sex. That's where gender identity and gender expression can get complicated. But—look at the time, Trace. You have school tomorrow. This is enough for tonight. We'll talk more tomorrow."

Tracy bolted straight upright. "Wait a minute, Mom," she objected. "You haven't told me what Mrs. Blake was going on about or what you and Dad are going to do about Toby's school."

"And," she added in frustration, "that Jason kid said he changed his gender. You just convinced me you can't—because you can't change your biological sex. But Jason's parents and Mr. Pullman and the kids at school think you can. So what do *they* mean by gender?"

Mrs. McKenzie didn't say a word. She just pointed to the clock and cocked her head to the side. When she arched her eyebrows like that, it meant she wasn't going to answer.

Tracy gave her mother a perfunctory smile and got up to get ready for bed, but she felt unsettled and a bit angry. Not angry with her mother, just angry at all the unresolved questions making her anxious.

Tomorrow Charlie would be prattling on repeating all the popular wisdom about transgender this and transgender that and she still wouldn't know what to say to her. How could she tell Charlie that *trans*gender made no sense when she wasn't even sure what the *kids* meant by gender?

13

Tracy slid into her chair as the tardy bell rang. She was technically on time but Mr. Holmes glared at her anyway.

"Some of you have been lollygagging on your projects," he bellowed, looking directly at her. "I want a report from each one of you on your progress by the end of class."

Tracy shrank down behind her desk and glanced sideways at the M's, who sat two rows over to her left. In the one short conversation she'd had with the girls about their project she'd suggested they gather fashion pictures to illustrate their theme, How the Role of Women Changed in the United States During World War II. She would then write commentary for the pictures, which they would arrange on a large poster board. But she had no idea if the girls had even started, and she couldn't write commentary for illustrations she hadn't seen.

When she felt Paul from the desk behind her poking her on her waist, she glanced back. He moved his eyes down to the side and shoved a folder forward at seat level. Tracy palmed it from him and slid it onto her lap, surreptitiously opening it and looking down when Mr. Holmes turned toward the blackboard to write homework questions. It was stuffed with pictures cut out from old magazines and newspapers, pictures of women of all ages in a variety of fashions.

Tracy shuffled through images of fashion models and advertisements showing smiling young women holding up detergent bottles or laundry soaps to older women—about the age of her mother maybe—holding up sparkling necklaces or watches. They were wearing dresses in 1940s style, with square padded shoulders and pulled-in waists. But Tracy didn't see how that was going to help much to illustrate their project theme.

But toward the bottom of the pile she saw images of younger women holding electric drills, their hair tucked into bandanas that were folded like triangles, the ends tied above their foreheads. Other women were working on machinery with the sleeves of their overall suits rolled up above the elbows.

And finally, Tracy saw pictures of Wacs and Waves in uniform. The WACS (the non-combatant Women's Army Corps) and the WAVES (the women's branch of the United States Naval Reserve) in World War II were smart-looking young women who absolutely radiated confidence and joy.

She was so shocked by the fact that the M's had actually done something and so caught up in the images that she didn't hear Mr. Holmes until Paul poked her again.

"Would you mind sharing what is so fascinating, Tracy?" the teacher drawled sardonically.

"Uh, oh—I was just reviewing some of the materials for our project, Mr. Holmes. So I could write the report for you on our progress now, as you asked," she sputtered.

"Well, let's see something," he growled.

Tracy grabbed a picture of a WAC wearing a tailored uniform in light brown, with pointed v-neck collar, square padded shoulders, cinched waist and knee-length slightly flared skirt. On her head was a boat-fold cap, the front point coquettishly perched on her forehead. Tracy didn't think the girl looked ready to fight a war, but her Women's Army Corps uniform was certainly attractive.

Mr. Holmes walked down the aisle between desks and picked up the clipping. Tracy saw with relief that he began smiling as he looked at the picture. He completely ignored her as he scrutinized the image.

"Ah yes," he said. "These were the girls who helped win the war." He suddenly scowled at Tracy as if she had personally held back the war effort. Then he turned as Marline squeaked and held up her hand.

"Mr. Holmes," Marline burbled. "That's my picture. I got those pictures from my grandmother. She kept a whole scrapbook from her aunt, who actually worked in a steel factory during World War II."

"Really?" Mr. Holmes seemed intrigued. "Uh, yeah—you and Megan are working with Tracy, right? Well, well. That's—let's see, your grandmother's aunt. So she was a real Rosie the Riveter, eh? That's what they called those girls, you know—the ones who worked on building ships and so on for the war effort. That's four generations back to World War II. Fascinating. Good work, girls."

Mr. Holmes beamed at Megan and Marline. He seemed to have forgotten Tracy, which was fine with her. She let out a breath as Mr. Holmes dropped the picture back on her desk and turned away.

One crisis passed, she thought as she quickly scribbled a paragraph about fashion illustrating the changing roles of women during World War II.

But the ringing bell caused Tracy to tense again as she saw Charlie beckoning to her from the doorway. What was it now that her old chum was so eager to scoop her with, she thought wryly. Had someone else *transitioned*, as the gang was now describing the Jason-to-Jessica transformation?

Reluctantly she gathered her books and followed her classmates out into the hall, where Charlie grabbed her arm and dragged her along toward their next class.

"Did you hear about Deke?" Charlie hissed *sotto voce*.

"Deke? *What?*" Tracy couldn't believe her ears. Not Deke! He was a football jock, with huge biceps and neck muscles. He liked to flex his muscles as he walked down the hall to impress the girls. Not Deke. *He* couldn't have decided he was actually a girl.

"They're not gonna let him play in the championship play-offs even though he's like the star of the team," Charlie went on. "Coach is really mad."

"Why?" Tracy asked, unbelief making her voice small.

"You didn't hear? He crashed his dad's car and the police found marijuana in his car. He was high—just a little—and that's why he crashed. But his dad says he's grounded for like, forever!"

Tracy began to grin with relief. At least it wasn't a transgender thing. It was just marijuana. Kids were always getting caught with pot. They got kicked out of school for a few days and usually got grounded by their parents, of course. But it never lasted long. Within a week they were parading up and down the school hallways smirking and acting cool. Or lording it over the other kids like gang wannabees.

"It's not funny, Trace," Charlie scolded. "We really need Deke on the team."

Tracy swallowed her wry grin and responded with fake concern, "Wow, what are we going to do? We can't let our school down, but you and I can't exactly join the football team."

"Maybe we could," Charlie drawled. "I'll bet Zoe could. She'd make a pretty good blocker or tackler," she giggled maliciously.

Tracy couldn't help giggling along with Charlie at the image her statement brought to mind even though she felt bad to be laughing at Zoe's expense. "Uh, no," she murmured. "She's a girl, Char."

"Not that she seems to remember," Charlie shot back.

Tracy felt the conversation was shifting into uncomfortable areas and quickly redirected it.

"So what's going to happen to Deke? Is he in trouble with the police?"

"Well, yeah, a little. He'll get a ticket or something for the pot but the car isn't too badly banged up. He hit a small tree in Mr. Clember's yard though. His dad will probably just fix the car and pay for a new tree and forget it."

"Isn't marijuana still illegal here?" Tracy asked.

"Technically, sure. But a lot of kids smoke a joint now and then. No one cares that much."

"Have you ever tried it?" Tracy pushed.

"No, of course not. Not yet, I mean," Charlie added quickly. "But I probably will sometime. It's no big deal, you know."

"I heard it's not good for kids," Tracy objected.

"That's sissy talk, Trace," Charlie scoffed. "That's what your parents tell you because they don't want you to do it. But I'll bet all of them smoked a few joints back in the day."

"No, I don't think—" Tracy began.

"Oh, don't be a goody-two-shoes, Trace," Charlie snapped. "Your parents may be religious and all that now, but they were young once." She rolled her eyes suggestively.

Tracy felt her chest burn with irritation. She wanted to defend her parents but against what? Against Charlie's ignorant insults? She knew that the more she protested, the more Charlie would pile it on. Better to let it drop, she figured. Anyway, they were at their classroom and the bell was about to ring.

At least the scuttlebutt today was going to be all about Deke and his car crash and finding marijuana in the car. It was a relief that the kids were off the transgender theme for today anyway. It would give her a chance to find out more from her mother about whatever *the kids* meant by gender now anyway.

14

Nate and Toby were playing chess in the den after dinner that night, so Tracy dragged her mom off to her bedroom. Lara McKenzie sat with her legs crisscross on the rug and leaned against Tracy's bed. Tracy sprawled opposite her on her stomach, chin on elbows.

"How did it go at school today?" her mom asked. "Were there more discussions about gender and transitioning?"

"No," Tracy grinned. "Fortunately today the school was all abuzz about Deke crashing his dad's car because he was high on marijuana."

"Oh, that's too bad," Mrs. McKenzie sighed. "Is he all right?"

"Yeah, he didn't get hurt and the car damage is minor, I guess. But he got busted—by the police *and* his dad."

"I'm glad he's okay. I hope he learns a lesson from this incident," Tracy's mom sighed. "He could have been really hurt."

"Oh, he's pretty tough, Mom. He's the star of the football team, you know."

"All the more reason for him to stay away from marijuana. It impairs the reflexes, which is relevant to any sport," Mrs. McKenzie said. "Really, Trace—marijuana is a much more dangerous drug than people realize."

"Yeah, but Mom, all the kids say it's just a relaxer. It makes you feel really mellow. And it's not addictive."

"False, false, and false," her mom responded.

"What do you mean?" Tracy asked.

"First of all, from a medical standpoint—a physiological aspect—marijuana is not a relaxer. In fact, it's just the opposite. It increases heart rate and blood pressure. That's bad for your health, young or old."

"Second, it doesn't necessarily make a person mellow. Some people say they feel happy and peaceful when they smoke marijuana, but others have very negative emotions like sadness or anxiety. That's because THC, the psychoactive ingredient in marijuana, reacts with chemicals in the brain. For example, like the neurotransmitter dopamine."

"Uh, okay," Tracy said.

"And as to the claim that it's not addictive, did you know that 17% of adolescents who start using marijuana become addicted? Actually, for daily users it's 25-50% who become addicted. Plus, cannabis is a gateway drug."

"But the kids say that pot—I mean marijuana—is harmless and it's not addictive at all," Tracy objected.

"That may be what they say, but the data proves that many teens who smoke marijuana do get addicted, and *are* more likely to go on to use hard drugs than teens who don't."

"Well, most of the kids who smoke a joint after school are the kids you *expect* to become druggies anyway," Tracy sniffed.

"Maybe," her mom cautioned. "But maybe it's not that simple. Maybe kids don't go from smoking a recreational joint to using stronger drugs because they are *bad kids*. Instead, maybe they have damaged their brains by smoking marijuana and so have more difficulty making good choices."

"Wow, that's scary," Tracy said.

"Yes, it is scary." Mrs. McKenzie rubbed her hand across her brow sadly. "The truth is, marijuana can cause physical changes in the adolescent brain. That is, it can actually change the structure and chemical composition of the brain. And *that* can cause behavioral changes leading to cocaine or heroin addiction—or opioid addiction. The nursing course I'm taking has taught a lot about this."

"Of course," Mrs. McKenzie added, "as a kid I was simply told—same as we told you and your brothers—to just stay away from drugs. But now I know more serious reasons than getting in trouble for being fuzzed while driving or crashing a car."

"But—but the kids say at least smoking a joint is not as bad as smoking cigarettes," Tracy muttered. "Or vaping."

"Really?" her mom came back. "Did you know that marijuana has all the same toxins as tobacco? Which is why marijuana causes the same lung and heart diseases as tobacco. Besides that, marijuana has higher concentrations of cancer-causing agents than cigarettes."

"Did you know," her mom continued, "that smoking pot can cause a drop in your IQ? It impairs memory and concentration. That makes school harder—*life* harder. And it can impact your chances of getting into college. A school record that shows a suspension for a drug issue—even just for smoking a joint or two—can negatively impact your chances for college and jobs, too."

"Plus, kids should be thinking long-term about the future," Mrs. McKenzie added, stretching.

Tracy made a face at that.

Her mom laughed and went on. "For example, my nursing course just covered a section on birth defects."

"Mom!" Tracy objected. "None of the kids—"

"Just listen, girl. It's common knowledge that a pregnant female who uses cocaine, heroin or meth is more likely to have a baby with birth defects, but now studies show that birth defects are more common in babies born to a female who smokes marijuana. Even her male partner's drug use can have an effect, damaging his sperm. In a sense, making him less virile."

"Huh, the guys who smoke pot all act like they are super studs," Tracy pressed her lips together and narrowed her eyes to slits. "But—so you're saying they're actually *wimps?*"

Mrs. McKenzie rolled her eyes. Tracy laughed, stretched and sat up with her legs crisscross like her mom.

"But you were going to tell me about gender tonight, and about Mrs. Blake," she prodded.

"There's not much to tell about Mrs. Blake," her mom replied. "She basically repeated the Jalston's story of how Jason started wearing his sister's clothes. But Mrs. Blake added a lot of gossipy details. You know Mrs. Blake can be—uh, colorful—in her reporting."

"Yeah, I know," Tracy giggled. "Like the time she ran into the street screaming there was a cougar in her house and it turned out to be that big yellow tom cat from down the block. He'd snuck in to eat her Chihuahua's food."

Mrs. McKenzie smiled despite her attempt to look reproving. "Yes, like that."

"So what is gender?" Tracy persisted.

"It's exactly what you said the other night, Trace," her mother replied. "Your gender is your biological sex."

"But you said it was complicated. And then you said it had something to do with gender identity and gender expression. What do you mean?"

"Gender identity is just what it sounds like—what gender you identify as," Mrs. McKenzie said.

"Well, that's pretty silly," Tracy scoffed. "It sounds like a circle. I am a girl—a female, so my biological sex is female, so my gender is female, so I identify as my gender which is female."

"But Toby is a boy—a male, so his biological sex is male, he's the male gender, and he identifies as a male," her mom added. "But what if he identified as female, pictured himself as a girl? That's what's happening with Jason/Jessica."

"But that's a mistake," Tracy protested. "You just said that *your gender is your biological sex,* so you can't *identify* your gender as the opposite of—your gender! Of what your biological sex is. That doesn't make sense. You'd be contradicting yourself."

"I agree, but many people say—" her mother began.

"Uh-uh," Tracy laughed, wagging her finger as if to scold her mom. "You are always telling me not to fall for *everyone says.*"

"Exactly," her mother grinned. "But in this case, it's Facebook that is the authority. After all, *Facebook* wouldn't lie, would it?"

"Okay, Mom, I get it." Tracy knew her mom was ribbing her. "What does Facebook say about this?"

Mrs. McKenzie pulled Tracy's laptop off her bed and pushed it across the rug. "Go ahead and open a search engine," she said. "Then search for 'gender identity options' or something like that."

"Um, here's an article that says Facebook offers 58 options for genders," Tracy said, scrolling down a search page.

"Oh, that's old," her mom replied. "Keep going on down."

"Ah, here's one that says Facebook has 71 options for gender," Tracy mumbled. "Things like agender, androgynous, bigender, cis...

63

Wait, it's got cis female, cis male, cisgender, cis woman—this is crazy. What's cis?"

"*You're* cis," her mom laughed. "Or cisgender or cis female or—"

"What?" Tracy interrupted. "What are you talking about, Mom?"

"The LGBT folks have invented this term for people who believe that their biological sex is their gender. People who are comfortable in their own skin. In other words, the vast majority of people in the world."

"Well, I don't like being labeled by people like that. I'm just a girl, a female. I don't want to be called *cis* or *cisgender,*" Tracy huffed.

"I agree," her mom nodded.

"But what are these others? Non-binary, gender fluid, pangender. What do those mean?"

"Non-binary is a refutation of the two opposite genders, male and female. We've already talked about how male and female are necessary for reproduction. That's a *binary* understanding of human sexuality," her mom elaborated.

"Gender fluid means a person thinks they can slide around and change their gender whenever they feel like, I guess," Mrs. McKenzie continued. "And pangender—well, *pan* means *all*, so that might mean a person was all the options you can think of. I don't know whether to laugh or cry when I read these lists."

"Well, I do," Tracy exclaimed. "This is the most ridiculous nonsense I've ever seen! How can people honestly believe this stuff? I think they're just trying to get attention."

"You're probably right about a lot of them," her mom conceded. "But many are seriously confused. Mental and emotional confusion like that is called gender dysphoria."

"Gender what?"

"Dysphoria. It's means being uncomfortable or dissatisfied with—well, in the case of gender dysphoria, it means feeling uncomfortable identifying with your biological sex."

"So Toby's classmate Jason has gender dys—uh, dysphoria?" Tracy asked.

"Yes, that's what I would say," her mom replied. "And a person who is that confused about who he is needs help and compassion, real counseling to find out the root of the confusion."

"But Jason just wants attention," Tracy spouted. "He's just a brat."

"Now-now, girl," her mom remonstrated gently. "I agree with you that much of the problem seems to have arisen from the fact that he got a lot of attention for his antics in trying on his sister's clothes. But remember, he was only three when he started doing that. He can hardly be judged harshly for liking the attention. And now he is really confused. That is sad—he needs help."

"But then it's really his parents who are to blame for his confusion," Tracy said. "They're the ones who encouraged him by giving him attention for it."

"Again, I agree that it is the adults who are ultimately to blame," her mother responded. "For misdirecting their child. But again, we need to be careful and compassionate. Loving parents want the best for their child. But they may also be confused, brainwashed in a way, by popular trends. Were Mr. and Mrs. Jalston also misdirected, persuaded to accept transgender claims by media pressure and even many who claim to be medical experts?"

"Remember what you told me about the news report about the 'pregnant man'? These days it's not unusual for a television show or movie to feature a transgender character in the plot," Mrs. McKenzie added. "There is a real push to get the public to accept the idea that a person can be in the wrong body—be a man in a woman's body, for example. So some parents who want the best for their children may think they need to support them in their gender confusion, their desire to be the opposite sex."

"Well, that's just dumb," Tracy sighed. "Parents don't think they have to *support* their little kid's desire to run out into traffic, do they?"

"Good point," Mrs. McKenzie nodded.

After a beat Tracy went on, "Okay, so gender identity is what gender you think you are. But you said there's also something called gender expression. What is—"

At that moment a crash and howl from the den brought Mrs. McKenzie to her feet.

"What are your brothers up to now?" she muttered as she dashed from the room.

Boys, Tracy thought in exasperation. She loved her brothers but sometimes... Well, it was time to get her homework done anyway.

She pulled her backpack over to her desk and took out her math book, smiling a bit as she saw the notations Josh had made on a scrap of paper she had saved. She didn't need that paper anymore but she liked to look at Josh's writing. Maybe not all boys were as obnoxious as her brothers could be sometimes, she thought dreamily.

15

Tracy turned her back on Zoe as she pulled off her gym shorts. Ugh, why did she have to have her gym locker right next to Zoe's? That meant the two of them were squished into a little alcove of eight lockers, out of sight of the other girls. They were the only two girls in this period that had lockers in this alcove.

It felt a little more private if both girls turned their backs while changing back into their street clothes. It was so cold outside that even two laps around the track hadn't made Tracy break into a sweat. So she skipped the shower. Zoe did too, although Tracy thought that she really shouldn't have.

Zoe was such a loser, Tracy thought—then immediately rebuked herself for such an uncharitable thought. After all, as her mother said, she didn't know what Zoe's family was like. She told herself that Zoe was probably doing the best she could.

As she turned around, she noticed Zoe was wrapping a strip of cloth around her breasts, squashing them. What was that all about, she wondered? It was beyond odd. Had she forgotten to bring her bra, or was she embarrassed by her well-developed breasts? Tracy could only wish she was so endowed.

Most of the girls, like the M's Megan and Marline, were very proud of their developing figures. The M's groaned about how uncomfortable it was when they had to run around the track because their breasts bounced, but that was just another way to bring attention to their endowments.

Of course, the M's had name-brand black sports bras that held their breasts just fine. Maybe Zoe couldn't afford a sports bra.

Maybe that was why she was wrapping that cloth around her upper chest. Well, Tracy thought wryly, at least that was one advantage *she* had. With her more trim figure, she could run with no bounce at all.

Tracy turned her back again quickly and bent to put on her shoes. As she picked up her book bag, it occurred to her that Zoe was not likely to be running down the halls. So why was she wrapping her breasts tightly now?

Not her business, she told herself. She forced a half-genuine smile at Zoe, who was now buttoning her shirt, and squeezed past her toward the exit.

As usual, Charlie awaited her in the hall.

"Hey Trace, what's happening with your brother?" she asked.

Tracy felt a stab of annoyance. Charlie didn't really care about her brother, she thought. But if she could extract a tidbit of gossip from Tracy about Toby's situation, she could report it to the Sharon group.

"Nothing," Tracy shrugged nonchalantly.

"But you said—" Charlie rejoined.

"Isn't that a new sweater, Char?" Tracy interrupted her to shift the conversation. "I like that color. Where did you get it?"

Fortunately, Charlie took the bait and launched into a report on the shopping trip she had made the last weekend. Charlie often spent Saturday afternoons at the mall with a group of girls and sometimes boys. They window-shopped, maybe bought a few things with their own credit cards, ate in the food court, and went to the movies.

Tracy didn't have her own credit card.

But the good thing was, the trick worked. By the time Charlie realized that Tracy hadn't answered her question about Toby, they were at the place where they had to head down separate halls. Tracy was on her way to AP math.

As she turned to head toward her class, she heard a boy's voice call out, "Hi, Trace. See you tonight!"

Surprised, she turned her head just in time to see Josh striding off in the opposite direction. In a flash he was hidden by the shifting crowd of students.

Charlie had heard some boy call out Tracy's name but hadn't gotten around a group of taller kids in time to see which boy it was. She widened her eyes at Tracy and mouthed across the expanse between them, "Who was that?"

Tracy just laughed and went on her way. She knew that Charlie would be dying of curiosity to know what boy she was seeing tonight. After all, the boys were always after *Charlie*, not her.

Again Tracy felt the not-so-noble satisfaction of having one-upped her popular friend.

But all feelings of satisfaction dissipated when she walked into the math room. The teacher looked cross. He sat on the edge of his desk and slapped a sheaf of test papers across his knee. Oh-oh, Tracy thought, we're in for it today.

And so they were. The whole class had bombed the test. She thought she had understood the new math problems the teacher had presented the week before, but like the rest of the kids, she had missed a crucial step. So it was do-over time.

Which meant that when Josh came that night, their tutoring session was all business. No time for side excursions into interesting subjects like climate change or looking at things on his phone. They just stuck to the homework and worked problems, Josh prompting her when she forgot a step. The only good thing about the whole hour was that a few times as he reached for her paper to show her something, his arm brushed hers. It gave her a little thrill.

But as soon as the tutoring session was over, Nate grabbed Josh and they went off to the den together, their heads close as they looked at something on Josh's phone.

What was that all about? Nate was a year older than Josh and had never paid any attention to him until he started coming to tutor Tracy. And now they were pals?

Tracy felt a stab of jealousy. Josh was supposed to be *her* pal, not Nate's!

Feeling suddenly rejected and grumpy, she picked up her books and took them to her room. As she put them on her desk, her mom poked her head in the door.

"You okay, Trace? You look a little miffed," Mrs. McKenzie said.

Tracy wasn't about to admit—even to her mom—that she felt possessive about Josh.

69

"Uh yeah, I'm fine," she muttered. "But wait," she added as her mom started to pull her head back. "What is happening with Toby? You never told me what you and Dad decided. Toby's been going to his regular class, but he's been awfully quiet at dinner."

"Yes, he's still in the same class," her mom replied coming into the room. "Dad and I talked with him and he's still trying to make it work—just trying to ignore any transgender talk."

"But what about Jason? What is Toby going to call him?" Tracy asked.

"That's a problem. We suggested Toby try not to call him anything. He obviously is not comfortable calling him Jessica or 'she.' We'll see how it goes. If it gets too problematic, we'll see if we can have him transferred to the other second grade."

"But he's been with the kids in his class since kindergarten," Tracy objected.

"I know," her mom sighed. "That's why we've waited to make any decision about transferring. It would be sad to be in a different class from all his friends."

"It's just not fair," Tracy complained. "Jason should be the one to change classes. Or change schools. He could have gone to a new school as Jessica. It would be a lie, but the other kids wouldn't have to know that."

"That might have been a better idea, at least from our standpoint," her mother conceded. "But in reality the news of Jason's transition to 'Jessica' has spread throughout the district."

Tracy flounced over to the bed and plopped face down in irritation. Mrs. McKenzie came over and sat beside her on the bed, stroking her hair.

"I never thought you and your brothers would have to face something like this," she murmured sadly.

Tracy sat up. "Yeah, it's weird," she sighed. After a beat she added, "But you were going to tell me more about gender. Uh, gender expression."

"Okay," her mom started. "We agreed that gender *is* your biological sex, your birth sex. Male or female. Right?"

"Right," Tracy nodded.

"Not your *sex assigned at birth,* as the transgender activists like to say nowadays, but your actual biological sex. That's your gender."

"Right."

"And gender identity is simply what you identify as, which logically would match your biological sex."

"Absolutely," Tracy responded.

"So a mismatch between what is popularly called your gender—your biological sex—and your gender identity is called gender dysphoria. That's a mental and emotional confusion, which I think would be very painful. So we do need to be compassionate."

"Yeah, I know," Tracy agreed reluctantly. "But they need to get their heads on square, too."

"Well, their lives would be much happier if they were comfortable in the bodies God gave them," her mom replied.

"So what's that other thing—gender expression?" Tracy prompted.

"Gender expression is how you—well, *express*—show your gender. For example, if I tell you I know an individual who loves football, could you guess if that is a girl or boy?"

"No. Of course boys are into football, but lots of girls like to watch football, too—or even play football," Tracy said.

"But what if I told you this person also liked car magazines and was loud and burped a lot?"

"Oh, that's a boy," Tracy shot back, wrinkling her nose.

"More than likely," Mrs. McKenzie replied. "And how about a person with long hair who loves color-coordinated outfits and nail polish?"

"Girl."

"Activities or outward appearances that are commonly associated with one sex or the other are some ways we express our gender. But aren't there girls with short hair who like car magazines and don't polish their nails? They are still 'all girl'—completely female. So this gender expression deal can be tricky."

"Huh..." Tracy mulled.

"Take another example. Do Toby and Nate wear dresses?" Mrs. McKenzie asked.

Tracy snorted.

"Right, of course not," her mom grinned. "Males in our culture do not wear dresses. But what about in other societies, other cultures? Have you seen pictures of Arab men in various Middle East countries wearing long dress-like robes? They're called djellabahs. Women in those areas may wear a similar garment. And what about Pakistani men wearing shalwar kameez?"

"What's that?"

"It's like a sheath dress—or a long shirt with buttons on the chest. It's often worn with baggy pants underneath. Have you seen pictures like that?"

"Uh-huh, now that you mention it. On the TV news," Tracy answered. "But I've seen Indian women wearing a style like that, too. What does that have to do with gender expression?"

"In the US, wearing a sheath dress is something a female does, not a man. So in the US, a sheath dress is a way for a girl to express—show—her femininity. But in other countries and cultures, dress-like garments may be associated with men, or both men and women."

"Okay..." Tracy drew out the word doubtfully.

"So gender expression can vary by your culture. But let's take another example," Mrs. McKenzie went on. "In the 1920s in the US, females wore earrings but men definitely did not."

"Except for the occasional pirate," Tracy inserted mischievously.

"Ahem, right," her mother laughed. "But by the 1990s, many boys and men wore earrings—"

"Ugh, or nose rings," Tracy interrupted.

"Right. So in the 1920s, earrings were associated with female gender expression, the XX chromosomes. Wearing earrings was strictly a female deal. (Except for the pirates!) But this was not a biological association. It was a sociological or cultural association. Then by the 1990s, earrings were worn by many guys—that is, were associated with male gender expression also. That is, earrings became associated with the XY chromosomes in addition to the XX chromosomes. Guys felt just as masculine wearing earrings as girls felt feminine. The point is, gender expression can vary both by time and place. Just remember that these are cultural constraints, not biological."

"But gender expression also varies by individual choice, doesn't it?" Tracy added thoughtfully. "It seems like most girls I know wear jeans or pants. When it warms up in the spring, a few girls will sometimes wear a dress to school, but most of the girls just switch to shorts."

"True," Mrs. Makenzie agreed. "All these different clothing choices are acceptable ways for our local girls to express their gender identity as females. There is *no spectrum between being male or female*—no sliding scale between the two sex categories. But there is a spectrum *within the expression* of male preferences, interests and abilities, or expression of female preferences, interests, and abilities."

"Yeah, Mom—that *gender expression spectrum* is why you can't get *me* to wear dresses," Tracy grinned mischievously. "You know the only time you get me to wear a dress is for church or a wedding or such. And I sure wouldn't wear a dress to school in this weather."

"In your great-grandmother's youth, girls always wore dresses or skirts to school," her mother replied.

"Even in the winter?" Tracy shivered.

Mrs. McKenzie nodded. "The girls wore long woolen stockings or warm woolen underwear kind of like panty hose under their dresses or skirts."

"That doesn't sound very comfortable," Tracy objected.

"Well, it was the custom of the time," Mrs. Makenzie said. "So gender expression depends on three things—the time or era, the culture of a certain geographical place, and individual choice. But there are limits to proper individual gender expression."

"You see," she continued, "in the Bible, in the book of Deuteronomy the twenty-second chapter, it basically says that a man should not dress so as to *present himself* as a woman. That's called cross-dressing. The Bible says cross-dressing in the style of the opposite sex, especially to *pretend* to be the other sex, is not allowed."

"Okay..." Tracy nodded thoughtfully.

"The difficulty is," her mom added, "that exactly what cross-dressing means within a particular culture—what style is acceptable for a male or a female—is a cultural or sociological association, which as we said can vary by time and place. So what is allowable for gender expression is restricted by a particular society in a particular time. "

"Whew, it *is* complicated, Mom," Tracy breathed. "But I think I got it."

"Well, with that I leave you to your homework, sweetie," her mom responded.

Tracy pulled her book bag toward the desk as her mom left her room. She heard Nate calling good-bye to Josh at the front door. What had they been talking about all this time? She would ask her brother in the morning. Right now she had to get busy on her homework or Mr. Holmes would have her head tomorrow.

16

At breakfast Nate was wolfing down his food when Tracy casually asked, "So what were you guys talking about last night?"

"Umm?" her brother mumbled, his mouth full of egg and toast.

"You and Josh? In the den? Last night?" Tracy prompted. "What was so fascinating?"

"Oh, that," Nate shrugged, taking a gulp of orange juice. "He was just showing me pictures of the flying car."

"The flyin—" Tracy caught herself mid-exclamation. Her brother was always tricking her like that. Like the time he told her about the Chinese colonizing the far side of the moon, or about the machine that looked like a bicycle that could shift-change into a tiny helicopter, or the time he convinced her that there were robots trained as nannies to take care of newborn babies—changing their diapers and feeding them their bottles and even singing them lullabies. She had told the kids at school about the bicycle-to-helicopter deal and had been totally mortified when it turned out to be a complete hoax. Her brother thought it was hilarious, but she was humiliated!

Tracy wasn't about to get hornswoggled by her brother again and embarrassed at school by one of his jokes. So now she nodded sagely and replied casually, "Oh yeah, I know all about the flying car."

Her brother widened his eyes and actually looked right at her. "Really? I'm impressed."

Then he went back to concentrating on his food. But Tracy wasn't fooled. She knew her brother was pulling her leg. Good show, she thought, how he faked being impressed by her answer. But this time she was one step ahead of him.

School was not terribly stimulating that day. No surprise quizzes, no teachers having mini-tantrums about lazy students, no brilliant presentations of new information. Just same old, same old. Another day to stumble through and try not to fall asleep in the middle of class.

Even Charlie was boring—no titillating tidbits of gossip about marijuana or whose boyfriend dropped who or which teacher was planning to transfer to another school. Boring. Well, it was February. The weather was boring, too—cold but not freezing, grey but not raining.

Tracy trudged home in a funk. There really wasn't a reason for it. She wasn't in trouble at school or home and Charlie wasn't even mad at her. But she felt tired and glum and totally uninspired to do her homework.

As she dragged herself up the front walk, Toby came running down the sidewalk. He was early. It was her mom's day at nursing class and she had barely beat her little brother home. She wondered what he seemed all excited about.

"What's up, Tobe?" she frowned as she unlocked the front door.

"There's another one," he grumbled. "It's like a disease. First one, and now another. This time it's in the other class, though."

"Uh-huh," Tracy yawned. "Another what?"

"Kid. Another kid," Toby answered, pushing past her and dropping his book bag by the door. He shrugged off his jacket as he hurried on down the hall.

"Hey, Tobe," Tracy called after him. "Come back here and pick up your jacket. And put your book bag in your room."

She slammed the door a bit too hard and locked it automatically. Grumpily she took her own backpack to her room and hung up her jacket in her closet. Then she went to the kitchen, where she found Toby with his head in the refrigerator.

"Hey, close the refrigerator," she scolded. "You're letting all the cold air out."

"So? The furnace is working," he shot back.

"Excuse me?" Tracy growled. "Is that a polite way to talk to your big sister?"

Toby ignored her as he reached for the milk and an apple.

"Brrr," she murmured. "Milk? On this cold day? I want some hot chocolate."

She set the tea kettle on the stove, turned on the burner, and took the hot chocolate mix out of the cupboard. Then she sat across the table from Toby while waiting for the water to boil.

"Me, too," her little brother said, wiping a milk mustache off his lips.

"Me too what?" Tracy yawned.

"Me too hot chocolate please," Toby answered, pulling an old Ranger Rick magazine out of the stack beside the table.

"Milk and hot chocolate?" she laughed. "You're going to get fat, Tobe."

"Yeah, right," he shot back. "Look who's talking."

Yeah, Tracy thought. She and her mom had been baking a lot of cookies lately. It was the weather. Cold gloomy weather just naturally seemed like cookie-baking weather. And for some reason she always felt like baking after school on Tuesday afternoons. It had nothing to do with the fact that Josh came to tutor her in AP math on Tuesday evenings.

The result of all that baking was that despite the fact that Toby, who was skinny as a lizard, would probably never be fat, she herself had put on a few pounds. She could feel it when she zipped up her jeans in the morning.

The kettle started to hiss. Tracy got two mugs out of the cupboard and spooned hot chocolate mix into them. She added the hot water and stirred both cups, setting Toby's across the table.

"Thank you," he muttered automatically.

As she sat down again she asked, "Okay, what's like a disease?"

"Huh?" Toby asked, immersed in an article about raccoons. "Hey, we should get some raccoon poop!"

"Tobe, gross!" Tracy almost spat a swallow of hot chocolate out of her mouth. "Why would you say such a yucky thing?"

But she really didn't wonder why. Boys always seemed to like yucky things. Hmm, another way that male gender expression could be seen, she thought wryly.

"To keep babies out of the attic," Toby answered as if it was the most reasonable statement in the world.

"To keep what? Toby, we don't *have* any babies in the attic," Tracy objected.

"Well, if we did," he answered, taking a swallow of his hot chocolate.

"If we did what?" Tracy groaned in exasperation. "I swear, Tobe, talking to you is like trying to decode Yoda."

"If we had babies in the attic," he grunted, deep in the article. "Like Ryan did last year. Remember?"

"Ryan? Oh," Tracy sighed, finally figuring out what her little brother was talking about. "You mean *raccoon* babies? Like when Ryan's parents were trying to get the female raccoon and her babies out of their attic last spring?"

"Um-hmm," Toby murmured.

"So what does that have to do with raccoon poop?" Tracy prompted.

"It says right here," Toby gestured, "that male raccoons sometimes eat baby raccoons. So raccoon mothers don't want any males around their babies."

Tracy put it all together. "Oh, so you're saying that if we had something that smelled like a male raccoon, a female raccoon wouldn't want to have her babies in our attic?"

"Yeah. That's what I said. You have to put the male raccoon poop in the attic," Toby answered.

"So...okay, so how do you get male raccoon poop, smart guy?" Tracy grimaced.

"You buy it."

"From..."

"From a company that sells wildlife supplies."

"And then you have to crawl up in the attic and smear raccoon poop around?" A great job for Nate maybe, Tracy thought dryly.

"Sure, it's easy," Toby explained. "It comes in a big tube like a syringe. So you just squeeze it out. By a roof opening. Like the vent where the mother raccoon broke into Ryan's parents' attic."

The boy looked at his sister's face and laughed. "You don't have to get any on you, sissy."

"Well, you can do it then," Tracy grinned. "Not me."

They sat in silence for a minute before Tracy remembered Toby's reference earlier to disease. What, chicken pox or something? She didn't see any spots on her little brother's face or arms.

"Hey Tobe, what did you mean when you said it was like a disease?" she asked. "What disease?"

"That gender thing," he scowled. "I don't want to talk about it."

That gender thing? Did he mean that transitioning thing? Did he mean another kid—a kid in the other second grade class— had changed *genders?* Bizarre. That was the class her parents had thought they could transfer Toby to if he couldn't continue in his own class.

It wasn't a disease, Tracy thought scoffingly. You couldn't *catch* gender—what had her mom called it? Gender dysphoria. You couldn't catch gender dysphoria.

Could you?

17

Mrs. McKenzie had barely opened the front door when Tracy accosted her.

"Mom," she whispered. "Toby says another kid at his school, in the other second grade class, says he's—or she's—well, I don't know which because he doesn't want to talk about it."

"Slow down," her mother laughed. "You're as bad as Toby."

Tracy waited while her mother took off her coat and slipped out of her shoes, wriggling her toes. "Just let me put these things in my room," she said. "Where is Toby?"

"He's in the kitchen."

"Okay, I'll meet you there in a minute."

Tracy went back to the kitchen and turned the kettle back on, then got her mother's favorite mug and a tea bag out of the cupboard.

"Oh thanks, hon," Mrs. McKenzie said when she came into the room. "A cup of tea will warm me up. It's getting colder out there again."

"I wish it would snow," Toby sighed. "Real hard. So we'd have a snow day."

"We never get snow days, Tobe," Tracy laughed. "The sugar frosting of snow we get here doesn't count."

"It's not fair. Even our cousins in California get snow days," the boy lamented.

"Yes, but they live in the mountains, Mr. Weatherman," Tracy reminded him.

"Well, it's still not fair," Toby insisted stubbornly.

Tracy shook her head. It was silly for her little brother to say the weather wasn't fair.

"And Mr. Pullman's not fair either," he added grumpily.

"What do you mean, Toby?" his mother asked gently. "How is Mr. Pullman not fair?"

"He let another kid do it today—but this time it was a girl."

"He let another kid do what?" Tracy asked.

"But it was the opposite this time. Into a boy," Toby grunted. "In the other second grade."

"You mean a second-grade girl decided she's really a boy?" Tracy asked, rolling her eyes.

"Yeah, they had another *transition* party. She came to school today with her hair cut short like a boy. She was wearing girl jeans and a girl top, but then she went into the coat closet and came out in boys' clothes—jeans and shirt like us boys wear. And her mom brought a cake and punch and confetti and they said her name is now *Carter*. But it isn't—her name is *Yolanda*."

"Wow, that doesn't make sense," Tracy mulled. "I mean I kind of get the Jason-to-Jessica name, but what does Carter have to do with the Yolanda?"

"Trace," her mom interrupted, "that's not the point, is it? Let's get back to the point."

"Uh, yeah. See, Toby, a girl can't really change into a boy because every girl has thirty thousand—no, thirty trillion XXs in her whole body. And every boy has XYs. And you can't change those. So you can't change your sex from female to male or the other way around either."

Toby stared at his sister as if she were speaking Chinese.

"She's right, Toby," Mrs. McKenzie agreed. "But let's start from the beginning."

At that point Nate came in the front door with Josh. Tracy groaned. Not now! She didn't want Josh in the middle of this conversation with her mom and Toby, so she slipped out of the kitchen and waylaid the boys in the hall.

"Um, Mom is having a private talk with Tobe," she told them. "Let's go in the den."

"Sure," the guys said. They tossed their coats on the sofa as they entered the room.

Josh pulled his computer out of his backpack and opened a web page. "Here guys, look at this neat new picture they put up on the website."

Nate sat on one side of Josh and Tracy on the other. They craned their necks at the screen.

81

"Look at this one from NFT," Josh said. "That's New Future Transportation, Trace. It drives like a car but then the wings come out from the side and it can go straight up and fly like a plane."

"If it goes straight up, isn't that more like a helicopter?" Nate wondered.

"Maybe, sort of," Josh murmured. "Look at this image. Is that a round wing, sort of like a wheel? But this other picture looks more like a small plane cab with fold-back wings."

Wow, Tracy thought, they really were looking at flying car models after all!

"Hmm, it says it will be the size of an SUV but will be all electric and non-polluting," Nate added.

"The inventors say they want it to be the Model T of flying cars, like the Model T was the car for the common man in the 1930s," Josh said. "Not just for the rich."

"You mean there are other flying cars?" Tracy asked.

"Yeah, there's a Japanese group called Cartivator that is working on something called a 'Skydrive' flying car," Josh answered.

"Right," Nate agreed. "And some people in Uber and Google are working on people-carrying drones."

"But the NFT people say that their concept is superior because it's a one-vehicle destination deal," Josh put in.

"So you don't have to drive to the airport and then fly somewhere and *then* drive again to your actual destination, involving more than one vehicle," Nate explained.

"And the NFT flying car will be able to park in a regular house garage or on the street," Josh added.

"But—but won't there be traffic jams and fender benders in the sky then? It sounds scary," Tracy objected.

Nate and Josh laughed and flattened their hands, zooming them through the air like planes, narrowly missing each other. With appropriate noises, of course.

Tracy rolled her eyes but grinned. "Okay guys, I'm never flying with you!"

"Hey, I've gotta get going," said Josh, jumping up. "I'll be late. Bye, guys!"

"Okay, see ya tomorrow!" Nate responded.

"Bye, Josh," Tracy added. She punched her brother gently on the shoulder and walked back to the kitchen to see what was happening with Toby and her mom.

Mrs. McKenzie sat with her arm around Toby, who looked very subdued.

"I still think it's wrong," Toby muttered defiantly.

"You're absolutely right, hon," his mother said, stroking his back. "But we can't control these other people. At least we need to know for ourselves that God made male and female. He created humankind with a *binary* system—bi, meaning two sexes, male and female—for the purpose of reproduction. It takes both a mom and a dad to make a baby. That's the Bible and that's the science, basic biology."

Toby sniffed a little and Tracy suspected he had shed a few tears. "Well, at least I don't have to see Yolanda very often because our classes don't have recess at the same time."

"That's good. Keep your chin up, kiddo. Your dad and I are still checking out other schools."

Tracy gave her little brother a quick squeeze and walked down the hall to her room to start her homework.

He was right—it really wasn't fair. He was just a little kid seven years old. He shouldn't have to be in the middle of a stupid mess like this, she thought. She was really mad at Mr. Pullman, too. He shouldn't allow kids to pretend to change genders like that.

Between being mad at Mr. Pullman, worried about her little brother and down about the weather, Tracy was working herself up to a real funk. But then she remembered sitting next to Josh on the sofa. He was smart and polite and kind of cute and she admitted to herself that maybe she had a little crush on him, but even better, it felt comfortable, not weird at all, to just be friends. Like a normal friend you could just talk to. About ideas, not other kids.

Not like Charlie, who lived for gossip. Josh didn't seem to care about that kind of talk. Which made him a lot more interesting. Which was kind of neat.

So maybe she wasn't going to be in a funk after all. Her mom and dad would make sure Toby was all right at school and her classes were going okay and the weather would clear up and she had the nicest boy in school coming to her house and showing her stuff on his computer. Life wasn't bad at all!

18

Her head was in her locker looking for a paper she'd dropped when Charlie grabbed her arm from behind. "Trace, he's back again," she hissed.

Tracy swiveled her head to look at Charlie. "Who's back?"

"Deke. And he has his hand in a cast."

"A cast? What happened?" Tracy asked. "He's been suspended these last two weeks—since the accident. Did he break it when he crashed his dad's car?"

"That's what he says," Charlie answered. "But Sharon thinks he got mad when his dad grounded him and he hit a post on his front porch."

"Charlie," Tracy rebuked softly. "That's just mean. Why would Sharon say a thing like that?"

"Well, she says that Deke really has a temper. She used to be his girlfriend, you know." Charlie didn't bother to speak softly and the girl at the next locker turned to listen. "She went to visit him while he was suspended. She'd been at his house before and now one of the posts on the front porch was splintered like it had been hit hard. So she figured it out."

The girl at the next locker smirked as she turned to leave.

"Or she made it up," Tracy scoffed. "A woman scorned and all that. And now she comes up with a story that is not exactly to Deke's credit."

"But it does make sense," Charlie insisted. "Deke does have a temper."

"How do you know?" Tracy challenged.

84

"One time a group of us went to the movies. Some guy who was real tall sat in front of us and Deke really cussed him out," she rejoined defensively.

"Wow, that doesn't sound like someone I'd want to be in a group with, Charlie," Tracy said.

"Yeah well, he only came along a couple of times," Charlie admitted nonchalantly.

"Good riddance, Charlie. The drugs and the accident—and a temper too? You should be concentrating on school and your clarinet practice, girl. You're really good—and you said you want to get in all-city band next year, right?"

"You're right, Trace," Charlie sighed. "But Sharon and Wendy both have boyfriends and I like to go to coffee or pizza after school on the days I don't have band practice, and then on Friday nights..."

Hmm, Friday nights. Tracy knew what she would be doing Friday night. Playing a board game with her brothers or watching an old movie—a really old movie—on YouTube. Or washing her hair. Her mom said she was too young to be dating much yet anyway.

Mr. Holmes was in his usual form that day, which meant that Tracy had to feign rapt attention as he droned on with a list of kings and presidents from across the world. She really wasn't that interested in who was the present leader of Burkina Faso— where was that anyway? Somewhere in Africa. But the pictures he put on his laptop projector of Tuaregs, nomads from the Sahara in southern Algeria, were pretty interesting. They wrapped a long piece of dark blue cotton cloth around their heads and then their faces, just leaving a small slit for their eyes. It was supposed to keep the blowing sand off their skin, but it also gave them anonymity. Which was important because many of them were bandits. They also dressed in dark robes that came down to their feet. Mr. Holmes said that they were expert camel drivers and caravaneers, but some worked in the date palm fields of the mid-Algerian oases.

Between classes she caught a glimpse of Deke in the hall. He locked on her glance and smiled slightly. She automatically smiled back. Actually, she thought he looked subdued and maybe in need of a friendly smile. That would only be kind she thought, and nodded a little as she smiled.

The rest of the school day had no points of interest. How many weeks was it to Easter? Spring vacation usually fell just before or just after Easter. Her family was driving up to her grandparents for a few days then. Tracy was looking forward to that.

Zoe continued her weird chest wrapping after gym class. Tracy turned her back to give her some privacy, but she wondered what was going on with that girl. She seemed to be getting weirder and weirder. It looked like she was wearing her brother's shoes. Poor girl, maybe she just couldn't afford a good enough bra or new shoes. Tracy resolved to be kinder to her and gave her a big smile as they both turned to leave.

Home was as routine and boring as school had been. She did her homework and loaded the dishwasher and sewed a button back on a sweater she wanted to wear the next day. Then she took her shower early and climbed into bed to read. Her English teacher Miss Fellows had given the class an assignment to pick a biography or autobiography and write a report.

Tracy didn't like to read about political figures or movie stars. Most of those were boring, she thought. Too many dates and speeches. She wanted something with a little more adventure.

So she had picked an autobiography about a teacher who lived in the Big Bend area of Texas way back in the 1940s. The young woman in the book lived in a stone cottage and had to walk down to a spring to get her water. She taught in a one-room schoolhouse where geckos and lizards ran up the adobe walls. There was no electricity and she had to walk two miles to the tiny adobe hut in the village that sold a few canned goods to buy her food. Tracy was fascinated, wondering how well she would cope in such primitive circumstances.

Deke started smiling at her every day when they passed each other in the hall at school. That was a bit strange, but she really felt sorry for him so she gradually smiled more readily. He seemed to be kind of withdrawn instead of his usual macho self. Hmm, well whatever, Tracy thought. Maybe he'd learned a lesson.

But on Tuesday Charlie had news.

Deke wasn't just suspended from the football team—now he was off the team for good because they'd found pot in his locker when the school did a spot check. Tracy didn't think the school should be allowed to do that—just look in your locker if they wanted to. It felt like an invasion of privacy. Not that she had anything terribly private in her locker, but still!

Anyway, Deke was suspended from school again. She couldn't understand why he would be so dumb as to smoke pot in the first place and then have marijuana in his locker when he should have figured the vice principal would be watching him. She almost felt bad for him, but it wasn't any of her business.

Charlie, on the other hand, was really stoked, milking every detail of the gossip going around school. Sometimes Tracy thought her best friend was just plain annoying.

But today was Tuesday, so Tracy brushed off Charlie's excited retelling of the day's gossip and hurried home from school to bake chocolate chip cookies. They were Josh's favorite.

Toby came trudging in as she got out the mixing bowl and flour. "How was school today, Tobe?" she asked.

"Fine," he shrugged. He poured himself a glass of milk and got a package of cheese and peanut butter crackers out of the cupboard. "What are you making, Trace?"

"Chocolate chip cookies."

"Oh yeah, it's Tuesday, isn't it?" He grinned mischievously and reached for a Ranger Rick magazine. "Be sure to make enough for me, too."

Tracy pretended she was going to throw the dish towel at him but she was glad to see he was showing a little of his old teasing spark.

"So how are the kids in your class?" she asked casually.

"You mean Jason, don't you?" Toby scowled. "He's crazy. He has a new outfit every day, like he thinks he's a model or something. The girls hate him. They won't talk to him and they won't go in the bathroom when he does. Ms. Barton is always ragging on the girls to be nice to 'Jessica' but they don't like him at all."

"Yeah well, my sympathies are with the girls," Tracy said.

"Yeah, me too," Toby responded. "I just pretend he's see-through. So I can't see him. I ignore him."

"That sounds like a good way to handle it," Tracy said thoughtfully. In fact, she couldn't imagine how she would handle a situation like that. It would be so weird, so crazy and uncomfortable. Her poor little brother! He was being really brave, she thought.

The house filled with the aroma of baking and Tracy made sure the kitchen was spotless after dinner. She knew how much Josh liked her chocolate chip cookies, and she expected him to eat four or five of them as soon as he sat down at the kitchen table.

But he didn't.

He sat at the table looking pensive, not even taking out his math book. Finally after a long silence—at least sixty seconds, Tracy thought—she spoke.

"Uh, Josh? You seem awfully quiet tonight? Don't you want a cookie?" she prompted.

"Oh sure," he answered absently. Then he shook his head and grinned. "Sorry, Trace—I was just thinking about Deke."

"Deke!" Wow, Tracy couldn't imagine Josh having anything to do with Deke or his friends. What could he possibly mean?

19

"It's just too bad Deke started hanging out with those kids he met down by the movie theater," Josh said.

"What kids?" Tracy asked.

"Oh, a group of tough guys. They're the ones who got him started on pot," Josh sighed.

Tracy raised her eyebrows, wondering how he knew all this.

Josh saw her sceptical look and continued, "My cousin knew some of those guys. They're a year older than Nate."

"Your cousin?"

"He moved to another town last year," he said. "Actually, my uncle moved the family because he wanted to get my cousin away from those guys. They were a real bad influence."

Tracy was quiet for a minute. "You mean with the pot?"

"I think they're using more than pot now," Josh said.

"Hmm, my mom says it's a gateway drug," Tracy contributed.

"Yeah, but marijuana itself is bad enough," Josh answered. "Besides, Deke told me he really tried to stop, but after he'd used pot for a while, he just didn't feel good if he didn't smoke a few joints every day."

The two sat in silence for a minute. Then Tracy shifted in her chair and spoke softly.

"I didn't know you and Deke were friends," she said hesitantly.

"We aren't. Not exactly pals, that is. But his yard backs up to my cousin's old house. My aunt and uncle moved before the house sold," Josh explained. "Then it became my job to go over and cut the grass and trim the bushes. It's only two blocks away from my house so I just push the mower over there. My uncle's house still hasn't sold. A couple of times when I went over late to clean up leaves, I found Deke in the yard smoking. He figured since the house was empty, no one would care if he hopped the back fence. So we talked a bit."

"Umm," Tracy murmured, unsure what to say.

"The thing is, when he isn't focused on trying to convince all the kids what a super star he is, he's actually a pretty nice guy. We talked about his dad's jeep. And the stars. He's interested in the constellations and knows all about the stars. That's something I wanted to learn, so sometimes I'd go over there late and we'd look at the night sky together."

"Wow, I never knew Deke thought about anything but football—and girls," Tracy sniffed.

"Yeah, he gave that impression, but actually I think he's lonely. His dad yells at him a lot. I never met his mom. The thing is, he tried to quit smoking pot—he told me so."

Josh was quiet a minute before he continued. "You know that a lot of teens who start smoking pot become addicted, don't you?"

"My mom said about 17%. But the kids all say marijuana *isn't* addictive," Tracy objected.

"Research disproves that. The kind of pot kids are smoking now is a lot more potent than the joints that were around in our parents' and grandparents' day, you know."

Tracy wrinkled her forehead. "Really? Like, how? What do you mean?"

"In our grandparents day the pot the kids got was natural, straight from the marijuana plant. But now a lot of the stuff kids buy on the street is actually synthetic marijuana, like a packet of K2 or Spice or something. It may *look* like crushed marijuana leaves so you think it's natural marijuana, but it's not. And that can be a huge problem."

"Why?"

"Because synthetic marijuana is often made with other stuff, like maybe Wild Dagga, often called *Lion's tail.*"

"What's that?"

"Another psychoactive plant. It's a broad-leafed bush like marijuana but it's actually from the mint family. The leaves are

90

smoked by some people in South Africa or Asia because it gives a mild high. Some people claim its orange flower has medicinal benefits. It's often used in making synthetic pot because it's cheaper," Josh answered.

"But why is synthetic pot more dangerous than natural marijuana?" Tracy objected.

"Hmm, I'm not sure," Josh conceded. "But the article I read—here, I'll pull it up."

He tapped and scrolled and turned his phone so Tracy could see the screen. "Hmm, it says synthetic pot is often contaminated with other substances like heavy metals and pesticides, or mold and salmonella. Sometimes even with opioids or rat poison."

"Rat poison! Yuck!" Tracy exclaimed.

"That's one of the reasons kids end up in the ER—or worse," Josh added. "In fact, it says here that there are several hundred different kinds of synthetic cannabinoids, and they all stimulate the same receptor as the THC in the cannabinoid marijuana. But they also may stimulate other psychoactive receptors in your brain."

"What does that do?" Tracy asked.

"That's the problem—it depends on what you're actually smoking or ingesting in some way," Josh said. "And how are you going to tell? It all *looks* like crushed marijuana leaves."

"So what happens to kids who use synthetic pot?"

"Let's see." Josh leaned over closer and pointed to the text. "It says synthetic pot does give a high, maybe even a stronger high. Some kids experience euphoria, but for others it increases anxiety or paranoia and may even trigger psychoses."

"Wow." Tracy moved her head closer to see the screen better. "It says it increases the heart rate—my mom told me that. But also it sometimes triggers a heart attack or stroke," she read.

"Or seizures," Josh added.

"But more commonly—lots of vomiting. Yuck!" Tracy looked up, grimacing.

"Geesh, look at this," Josh pointed. "It says that for various cannabinoids, sometimes the butane that is used to extract the THC isn't completely removed, and some pot smokers have had the butane ignite in their lungs, causing damage."

"Lungs on fire—whoo!" Tracy exclaimed. "You'd think that any kid who read this would be smarter than to try synthetic pot."

"But the problem is, synthetic pot doesn't always come in nice little packets. It *looks* like regular marijuana. Another problem is that there's little regulation or health inspection for cannabinoid harvesting or synthetic production overseas, so the stuff is cheaper to import than using US sources."

"Yeah, but we have port inspections and—" Tracy began.

Josh shook his head. "It's hard for customs officers to detect synthetic marijuana because it doesn't have the same smell as real marijuana. So the market is being flooded with synthetics. Which is another reason why you can't be sure what you are getting on the street."

Tracy was about to add a comment when she realized how close she had moved to Josh to see his phone. His arm was on the back of her chair and her head was almost touching his. Suddenly shy, she pulled back and shuffled her math book and papers self-consciously.

"That's—that's..." she stammered.

"So that's the story of Deke," Josh filled in. "Poor guy. I hope he gets his head on straight."

Tracy nodded solemnly.

"Okay, let's look at that math problem the whole class flubbed again," Josh grinned, breaking the mood.

"You heard about that?" Tracy asked in surprise.

"Oh yeah, all the AP math classes heard the sad tale."

Tracy play-punched him on the shoulder and opened her book. But with Josh sitting so close, it was hard to concentrate on formulas for the rest of the session.

20

"Now he's gone."

Tracy jerked in surprise and pulled her head back out of her locker.

"Charlie," she sighed, "can't you ever come up and just say hi normally? Do you have to sneak up and scare me like that?"

Charlie grinned mischievously. "But it's so much fun to see you jump. Anyway, I have news."

"Yeah," Tracy rejoined. "You said. He's gone. So who's gone?"

"Deke, of course."

"Deke? He's gone and he's still all you can think about?" Tracy teased, giving her friend a playful shove with her shoulder.

Charlie looked moony-eyed. "He's such a hunk."

Tracy rolled her eyes. "Okay, I'll bite. Where did he go?"

"I dunno," Charlie shrugged. "All I know is that he's been checked out of all his classes. Not just suspended, but checked out."

Tracy could hardly suppress a Cheshire cat smile. She figured she could find out from Josh what had happened to Deke, and then she could be the one with the juicy gossip. That would drive Charlie to distraction. But for the present, she feigned disinterest.

"So are you going to the band try-outs?" Tracy asked. "That's in two weeks, isn't it?

"Uh, yeah," Charlie answered, her eyes straying to a group of football players coming down the hall like the prow of a boat parting the waves.

"So—where are the try-outs this year?" Tracy prodded.

"Hiya, Pete," Charlie called, smiling a lopsided smile and lifting one eyebrow, as if she shared a secret with Pete.

Pete nodded back in the same way.

"Okay, Char," Tracy nudged her as the boys swept on past. "What's going on?"

"Wouldn't you like to know?" Charlie teased.

"Yes, I would," Tracy grinned back. "So give it up, girl."

"Oh, I might just be a little busy this weekend, is all."

Charlie shrugged as if it was nothing, but Tracy could tell she was excited.

"Come on, Charlie—tell me," Tracy begged.

But just then the bell rang the warning note which meant they had less than a minute to get to class and into their seats. Charlie waved gaily as she peeled off from Tracy at the intersection of the halls and headed down to her regular math class as Tracy turned to go to AP math. Well, she'd just have to find out later what her friend's weekend plans were, Tracy thought as she scurried into class.

The teacher handed out quiz papers, a re-do of the test the whole class had flubbed the week before. This time Tracy tackled the problems confidently, feeling sure that Josh's tutoring had prepared her to ace the test.

When she handed her paper to the teacher a minute or two before anyone else, he scanned it quickly and gave her a thumbs up. Relieved even though she had been confident, she headed back to her seat.

As she turned she saw one of her classmates slipping a crib sheet under a book. Startled, she walked back to her seat and sat down quietly.

Tracy wasn't sure what she should do. She didn't really know the girl—Alicia--that she saw cheating. This was the only class Tracy had with her. She had always seemed rather distant or withdrawn. Actually, Tracy had always felt a bit intimidated by her. Alicia had beautiful clothes, conservative but with a certain flair, and manners as if she came from a different era or foreign country. She had some indefinable quality that Tracy would have characterized as class.

But now this.

Cheating was not a class act, Tracy thought, her estimation of the girl crumbling. But neither was ratting on a classmate, she told herself. So what should she do?

Maybe somebody else saw the crib sheet and *that* student would tell the teacher. Sort of the mirror image of the old SODDI excuse used by defense lawyers: "My client did not murder this man. *Some other dude did it.*" But in this case, Tracy thought wryly, it would be *Some other dude should do it.* She didn't want to get involved—let some other kid rat out Alicia.

Or maybe the teacher himself saw it. It wasn't her problem, Tracy decided. She would just pretend she hadn't seen anything.

But that left a sour taste in Tracy's mouth. She wasn't sure whether she was more upset because she saw the cheating, or whether by not saying anything she felt as if she were covering it up—in essence participating in it.

But that was silly. She hadn't done anything wrong. It really was none of her business, she convinced herself. She would just keep quiet. After all, she didn't really even know Alicia.

On the other hand, Tracy toyed with the idea that maybe later in the day, when she and Charlie were having lunch, she would ask Charlie about her. In a round-about way of course, so Charlie wouldn't be able to worm out of her what it was all about. She would just say that there was this girl in her AP class called Alicia and give me all the dirt on her!

No, of course she wouldn't say that. She would just say she was curious about this nice girl in her AP class named Alicia who seemed like she might have lived overseas somewhere. And then Charlie would sensibly shoot back, "Well, why don't you ask her?" And Tracy would say, "Oh, I'm shy" or "I haven't had a chance" and Charlie would snort and say, "Yeah, right. You're a terrible liar, Trace. So what's the real story?"

There it was again. It seemed as if Charlie had the ability to talk to anyone and to find out anything about anyone in school and to lie if she felt like it and nobody cared because everybody liked Charlie. Tracy felt like the opposite, like an invisible shadow to Charlie's floodlight personality. And Charlie was right—she could never get away with a fib. It wasn't fair!

95

Well, that was silly, Tracy thought. There was nothing unfair about being honest. Oh, how did she get herself into such tangled mental gymnastics? She was sure Charlie never did. In fact, she suspected Charlie never second-guessed herself about anything. Surely a happier way to live, Tracy thought glumly.

At any rate, she didn't say a word to Charlie about Alicia at lunch because Charlie was bubbling with excitement. She had decided to let Tracy in on the secret of her weekend plans.

And what she told her made Tracy forget all about Alicia and AP math and cheating on a quiz.

21

"You can't be serious!" Tracy hissed.

"Of course I'm serious," Charlie shot back. "Why not? It will be tons of fun. Hey, I'm *in*, girl. Pete's okay," she shrugged. "He's kind of cute, you know. And it's Deke's house! We'll have a blast."

"I just don't think it's a good idea, Charlie," Tracy muttered. "You don't know those other kids, the older ones you said Sharon said will be there." She was thinking of the older group from the movie theater that Josh had told her about. What if they were coming?

"Don't be such a worry wart, Trace." Charlie played with the straw in her soda. "Sharon will be Deke's date, of course." Charlie scrunched up her nose in disgust. "But at least Deke will be there."

"Yes but—but you said his parents won't be there," Tracy objected.

"Big deal," Charlie shrugged. "My parents go off for the weekend lots of times and leave me and Marcia alone."

"But your sister Marcia is nineteen."

"Yeah, and she usually goes out with her friends and then I can do whatever I want without big sis tattling," Charlie winked.

"Charlie," Tracy rebuked her. "It's not a good idea and you know it. Deke has already shown—well, a lack of good judgment at the least, and you don't know what other boys or girls will be there, and you said they're older, and—"

"Oh, stop it," Charlie said crossly. "You're just jealous because you're not invited."

"That's not true. Honest, Charlie. I'm really worried about you. Please don't go," Tracy pleaded.

"Fat chance," Charlie hissed. "And button it up, girl. Here comes Sharon."

Charlie smiled as Sharon sailed up to their table and plopped down on the bench opposite.

"News?" Charlie asked, acting nonchalant.

"We pick you up at your house at eight tomorrow night," Sharon answered. "Just leave a note for your sister so she won't call the police or something when you don't get home til late."

Sharon flicked her eyes up and down and then looked sideways out of half-closed eyes. "*Real* late," she added slyly. Laughing, she stood to go.

Tracy felt her stomach tighten. She did not like that girl. There was just something about her, something wrong. She'd never heard anything really bad about Sharon, but she always seemed to want to give the *impression* that she was—was... Tracy didn't know how to put it, but it felt like trouble. Like Sharon *liked* flirting with trouble.

As Sharon breezed on down the row of lunch tables, Charlie grinned and called conspiratorially after her, "Got it!"

There was no need for Tracy to say anything, because as far as Sharon was concerned, Tracy was invisible.

Suddenly Charlie grabbed her backpack and stood. "Gotta go, Trace," she said, taking off after Sharon.

Tracy sat alone at the table, feeling both deflated and worried. Deflated because she was obviously second choice at best for Charlie. And worried because after all, Charlie was her best friend and Tracy feared she was walking into trouble.

Hmm, her best friend. Tracy thought about that. Why did she always say that Charlie was her best friend? This year Charlie had changed so much. Frequently in the last few months she hadn't even waited for Tracy to go to the lunchroom together. When Tracy got there from her last class before lunch, which was way on the other side of the school, Charlie would already be seated with Sharon or Wendy or some of the other girls and boys that hung out at Starbucks or the pizza place after school. Then Tracy would just have to look around for an empty seat. No big deal—a quick sandwich and they'd all regroup in the courtyard. But still.

Tracy sighed in exasperation and took a bite. She and Charlie had been best friends since third grade, she reminded herself. They met at the locker every day and exchanged phone calls after school and occasionally even went to the mall on weekends together. They had a lot of history. They really were best friends. Weren't they?

And her best friend was about to do something really stupid, Tracy thought. So of course she told her so. But Charlie didn't listen, and knowing Charlie, once she made up her mind, there was no changing it. So what could Tracy do?

Nothing. Not a single thing, Tracy told herself. She wasn't Charlie's mother or her big sister. In fact, Charlie was older than she was. Just five months, but still. And Charlie had never listened to her, not even the time they were on a field trip and she *told* Charlie that the pretty red leaf she was picking was poison oak. Charlie was really sorry that time! She was out of school for two weeks, with the most horrible case of itchy oozy blisters. Her face was swollen like a balloon and her hands were crusty oily mitts.

So that was it. Just forget it, Tracy told herself. It was not her problem. Charlie wouldn't listen. Tracy wasn't even sure she was her friend anymore. At least not much of a friend. It was her own responsibility what she did on the weekend anyway.

Tracy stuffed her sandwich papers back into her lunch bag and slung her backpack onto her shoulder. She dropped her trash in the waste can as she left the lunch area. There was seven minutes left before the next class so she headed for the courtyard. But when she spotted Charlie ensconced in the middle of Sharon's clique, she turned to the side and slid down a side corridor.

That was her mistake. Because she bumped right into Zoe. And Zoe wanted to talk to her.

22

But Zoe didn't really want to talk to Tracy after all.

"You—you want to talk to my mom?" Tracy stuttered, surprised by her request. "Uh, sure—yeah. I'm sure she'd say it's okay."

"After school today?" Zoe pressed.

"Yeah, but she has class today so she won't be home for a while after school. Uh, maybe you could come later or after supper," Tracy stalled.

Zoe looked stricken. "I don't mean to be... I mean, I don't want to be a bother."

Tracy felt bad as she saw Zoe shrink into herself. "Or you could come home with me and wait. If you want to."

Zoe looked up hesitantly. "If you're sure that would be okay," she said awkwardly. "So, uh—should we meet in the courtyard after school?"

"Yeah," Tracy shrugged. "Sure. See you there."

As she hurried off to her next class, Tracy felt mixed emotions. One part of her felt glad—a little noble maybe—for having done what she felt her mom would have wanted her to do, responding kindly to this somewhat obnoxious girl who seemed to be in such a muddle all the time. But the other part of her was mad at herself for agreeing to meet her in the courtyard, where all the kids would see her walking off with Zoe.

Tracy could just imagine how intrigued Sharon and the others would be. The gossip always flew madly as they tramped off to the pizza parlor, and today the kids would have a heyday making up stories about her and Zoe being together. She wondered if Charlie would stick up for her or would join in the rude jokes she was sure Sharon and Wendy would come up with. She hated to think of them mocking her.

Well, it was whatever it was, Tracy sighed. She'd given the invitation. She could hardly avoid it—it had seemed cruel in the moment to put Zoe off, whatever her problem was. So she'd agreed.

Why had she agreed to meet her in the *courtyard*, of all places? If only Zoe had suggested the gate to the maintenance area! None of the kids gathered there. But it was too late. She was committed.

Tracy was distracted during the rest of her classes. She kept thinking about the dreaded meeting in the courtyard, in full view of the Sharon group. And she kept wondering what on earth Zoe wanted with her mother.

When the final bell rang, Tracy slowly stuffed her notebook and papers into her backpack, purposely being the last student to leave the room. She stopped in the restroom on the way to the courtyard and then walked slowly, hoping Sharon's group would have gathered and left before she got there.

But luck was not with her. This would be the day that the boys were playing hackey sack and the girls were all standing in a semi-circle cheering them on. She caught a glimpse of Charlie clapping as Pete kicked the hackey sack up with his toe and then did an impressive twirl to catch it on his heel, sending it up again.

She was only distracted for a few seconds as she watched the group but that was long enough time for Zoe to sidle up beside her. Startled, she pulled back and frowned, then caught herself and forced a smile.

"Oh, you scared me, Zoe," she breathed in apology.

"Sorry." Zoe looked abashed, almost frightened. "I'm sorry. I didn't mean—"

"No, it's fine," Tracy broke in hurriedly, faking a little laugh. "No big deal. I do that a lot. My brothers are always sneaking up on me just to see me jump."

Zoe gave a tentative smile. "So it's still okay to go to your house now? To see your mom?"

"Sure, come on," Tracy answered. She jerked her head toward the nearest exit from the courtyard. "Let's go this way."

The path she indicated was not the shortest way to the street, but it kept the two of them from having to cross the middle of the courtyard in full view. Tracy hoped the group with Sharon was too busy with their hackey sack game to have noticed her leaving with Zoe.

The two girls walked in silence most of the way home. Tracy tried to start a conversation several times but Zoe answered in monosyllables. She debated inwardly whether that was just Zoe—after all, Tracy had never tried to have a conversation with her before and Zoe never said anything in the classes they shared—or whether Zoe was just thinking about what she was going to say to Mrs. McKenzie.

Toby came skipping up as Tracy was unlocking the front door to her house.

"Hi, Trace," he said. "Who's this?" He asked it casually as if his older sister was in the habit of bringing new girlfriends home from school all the time.

"Oh. This is Zoe from school," Tracy answered stiffly.

"Hi, Zoe," Toby said, sticking out his hand. Zoe reciprocated awkwardly and the two of them shook hands. Then, apparently having used up his good manners for the day, he pushed through the door in front of the girls, dropped his backpack in the middle of the entrance, and ran down the hall toward the kitchen.

"Toby, come back here and pick up your backpack," Tracy called after him. "Toby!"

When she turned to close the door, Tracy saw Zoe was laughing. Surprised, she raised her eyebrows.

"Little brothers," Zoe chuckled, as if that was explanation enough.

"Yeah," Tracy shook her head in agreement. She kicked Toby's backpack out of the way and motioned for Zoe to put her book bag and jacket on the hall bench.

"Come on down to the kitchen," she gestured. "There are some cookies left from last night. Or there were. We'd better hurry before Toby eats them all!"

23

As they walked to the kitchen, Tracy felt somehow ashamed of herself for how she had always dismissed Zoe at school as a dork or a pest to be ignored. When she smiled and chuckled, Zoe seemed like she might be all right. Like a regular girl. Or she would be, if she *looked* like a girl. Which she didn't, with those clunky shoes and shapeless clothes that looked like she'd raided her brother's closet.

But a little brother's clothes wouldn't fit her, Tracy frowned. She realized she didn't know anything at all about this girl.

How could she know anything about her? Zoe was like a stick figure person at school—never talking, never smiling. Except, Tracy remembered, Zoe did smile back when she herself had started smiling at her as the two girls finished changing clothes after gym class. But it wasn't like a real smile. Zoe's smile then had been too tight—a tiny twinge of the lips that disappeared almost as soon as Tracy saw it.

But today Zoe seemed almost human, Tracy thought. Oh, that wasn't kind, she rebuked herself. Of course she was human. Maybe she just needed someone to be a little friendly.

As the girls entered the kitchen, Tracy saw to her surprise that Toby had gotten out three cups and turned on the hot water.

"Have a cookie, Zoe," he said as he pushed a plate of oatmeal raisin cookies down the table. Then he buried his nose in his Ranger Rick magazine as if having Zoe drop in after school happened every week.

"Uh, thanks," Zoe said, sitting in the chair next to him.

Shocked that Toby seemed unfazed by Zoe's manner and appearance, Tracy took the hot chocolate mix out of the cupboard. Maybe it was time to figure out just who Zoe was, she thought.

"So, do you have a little brother, Zoe?" Tracy asked.

"Two," Zoe answered.

"Oh. How old?"

"Ten and twelve."

That would not account for the clothes, Tracy thought. "And older brothers?"

"Three." Zoe answered, again not volunteering any additional information.

"Three? Any sisters?"

"No. Just me."

"And your older brothers?" Tracy pressed.

"Only one lives at home. One is a lot older, but he's a half-brother. And the other one has moved out. My brother Brett lives at home though."

"Brett? Wait—what's your last name again?" Tracy responded abruptly. "Isn't it Hudson?"

"Yes."

"So your brother is *Brett Hudson?*" Tracy was stunned.

Zoe nodded, somehow looking more miserable.

Brett Hudson was a star athlete, the absolute opposite of clumsy Zoe. Charlie would call Brett a hunk. He was a senior. And he was supposed to be smart, too.

Charlie would die to know that *Brett's sister* was in her house, Tracy thought. She had never made the connection between Zoe and Brett, and she doubted that Charlie had either. There were a lot of Hudsons in town. *Charlie would never link the out-going Brett with the flat personality of Zoe,* Tracy guessed.

But then Tracy realized her sudden perk of interest when she learned of the connection to Brett was a mistake. Zoe was probably well aware of the contrast to her popular brother, and the implication hurt. "Uh—it's just—well, I never knew Brett was your brother," she stammered to explain.

After an awkward silence Tracy continued,

"So—that's quite a large family. What does your dad do?"

"He's a supervisor at a plastics plant."

"Ah." That didn't sound like a promising subject. Tracy let the question drop. "And your mom?"

"I don't have a mom. I mean, she died when I was five."

"Oh, I'm so sorry," Tracy said, instinctively reaching out and touching Zoe on the arm. "That must be hard." After a pause she continued, "So you're the only girl in the family."

Zoe nodded uncertainly.

A picture was forming in Tracy's mind. A household of boys, the boyish clothes and clunky shoes. No mom. No feminine influence for Zoe, the only girl.

The front door opened. Tracy looked at the clock in surprise. It wasn't time for her mother to be home and her dad had taken Nate to the dentist.

Who had opened the door?

24

"Mom?" Tracy called, her voice tinged with caution.

"Yes, hi kids," Mrs. McKenzie called back cheerily.

"You're early," Tracy said when her mother came into the kitchen.

"We didn't have lab today because they had to repair an electrical problem," her mom replied. "The renovations at the college keep interrupting the lab classes. Ah, who is your friend?"

"This is Zoe, from high school," Tracy said.

"Welcome, Zoe." Mrs. McKenzie took both of Zoe's hands in her own and smiled into her eyes.

Zoe blushed a little and smiled shyly. Tracy was intrigued. Even with her mom's first greeting, Zoe—the clunky angry withdrawn nobody from school—had seemed to soften a bit.

"Zoe wanted to talk with you, Mom," Tracy said.

"Oh good," Mrs. McKenzie replied easily. "That will give us a chance to get acquainted."

Zoe's shoulders seemed to loosen as Mrs. McKenzie patted her on the back and turned toward the hot water pot. "Just let me make myself a cup of tea," she smiled.

Toby looked at the three females, rolled his eyes and sauntered out of the room to find a quieter place to read.

For the next five minutes the conversation retread the same ground that Tracy and Zoe had already covered. But with Mrs. McKenzie guiding it, it seemed natural and easy. Tracy could see by her body language that Zoe was progressively relaxing.

Her mom was really good at making people feel at ease, Tracy thought. She hoped she could be like that someday.

"So—did you want to talk with me about something in particular?" Mrs. McKenzie asked gently. "Would you rather it was just the two of us? Tracy can go to her—"

106

"Um, no. Tracy should stay," Zoe interrupted, almost as if she was afraid to be alone with Mrs. McKenzie.

Tracy kept her mouth shut and watched. She sat at the end of the table. Her mother sat opposite Zoe without speaking but smiling encouragingly as she cradled her cup of tea.

"It's just—well, it's just—I told you about my brothers," Zoe began.

"Yes, three at home—but *five* all together," Mrs. McKenzie emphasized.

"But I'm a girl!" Zoe blurted angrily.

"Absolutely," Mrs. McKenzie murmured calmly.

Tracy was taken aback by Zoe's sudden outburst, but her mother seemed unperturbed.

"It must be kind of tough being the only girl in such a gang of brothers, uh?" Mrs. McKenzie asked with a twinkle.

"But—but the thing is..." Now Zoe colored and looked shame-faced. "Well, the thing is, the school nurse says maybe I'm— *I'm not.*"

"Not? Not what, Zoe?" Mrs. McKenzie prodded kindly.

"Not—*not a girl.*" Zoe hung her head and scrunched her shoulders together.

Tracy was frozen in shock. *What?* Of course Zoe was a girl. After all, when they changed clothes next to each other before and after gym class, you couldn't help but see—well, you know. She could tell Zoe was a girl.

"You certainly look like a girl to me," Mrs. McKenzie said cheerily, still smiling. She reached across the table and took both of Zoe's hands in her own and squeezed them gently.

Zoe looked up barely raising her head but her shoulders relaxed a little. There was a glimmer of hope in her eyes as she asked, "I do?"

"Of course you do, Zoe," Mrs. McKenzie laughed. "You know in my nurses' training we have to learn about the different symptoms that men and women have for a heart attack, for instance, or other illnesses. We have to learn about the different ways that medicines affect males and females so that we don't overdose someone. In fact, researchers say there are over 6500 genes they have identified that are expressed differently in men and women."

"There are?" Zoe and Tracy exclaimed in surprised unison.

"Yes. And I can see several male/female differences just by looking at you, Zoe." Mrs. McKenzie walked around the table and took the chair Toby had vacated. Sitting beside Zoe, she cupped Zoe's chin in her hands.

"Look at that pretty triangle-shaped jaw," Mrs. McKenzie said, titling Zoe's head up as if appraising a model. "Boys' jaws are more square, but you have a nice girly shape to your jaw. A cute little heart shape from your cheekbones to your chin."

Zoe's eyes widened. Tracy was entranced watching her mother.

"Hmm, look at your neck," Mrs. McKenzie continued, her hands gently brushing Zoe's skin. "You have a long slender neck—a lovely neck. Most men have shorter, thicker necks than women, although on skinny little boys this is sometimes not as apparent as it will be when they are older."

Tracy realized she had slipped her hands up to her own neck, checking its length. Suddenly self-conscious, she dropped her hands to her lap.

"Now for females, having a longer neck is both a good and a bad thing," Mrs. McKenzie added wryly. "A long slender neck is lovely, a thing of female beauty. But on the other hand, females get much worse whiplash than males. Do you know why?"

Tracy and Zoe shook their heads no in unison.

"Imagine a ball on a flexible stick," Mrs. McKenzie began, using her hands to illustrate. "A solid wooden ball on a long skinny flexible stick. Now jerk that stick forward and back quickly—and stop! What happens to the ball? *Whiplash!*"

"Think of the heavy ball as your skull. Now, girls have a long skinny stick for a neck," Mrs. McKenzie continued. "But boys have a shorter, thick stick for a neck. So right away boys have an advantage because there isn't as much *flex* with a short thick stick as with a long skinny stick. For girls, more flex means a harder rebound jerk—and worse whiplash."

"But there's another reason women get worse whiplash than men. Feel the top of your jaw bone, right under your ear—here."

Mrs. McKenzie positioned Zoe's fingers under her ear. "Do you feel a little bump there? It's called the mastoid process and it's a handy place to attach neck muscles. For females, it's not a very big bump. But for boys—older boys and men—it's a more prominent bump. So boys are able to attach thicker stronger muscles to the mastoid process than girls can." She paused, then added wryly, "As I said, another reason women get worse whiplash than men. And another difference between males and females."

"There's also a bump on the back of your skull. Just above where it connects to the spine—here—called the external occipital protuberance. It's larger in males than females. There—can you feel it?"

Mrs. McKenzie took Zoe's hand and moved it to the back of her skull.

"I'll check out the jaw and skull bumps on my brothers tonight," Zoe chuckled, her eyes twinkling.

That was the second time Tracy had heard Zoe laugh today. She couldn't believe it.

"We haven't talked about the shape of your skull or how your skull bones are lighter and thinner than a boy's skull bones. Or your eyebrow shape. You see, we haven't even gotten below your neck and look at all the ways I can tell that you are a lovely female!" Mrs. McKenzie smiled.

Zoe seemed to glow a little at Mrs. McKenzie's words. Tracy sat in stunned silence, watching the change in the girl.

After a moment, Mrs. McKenzie asked gently, "Do you know why the school nurse said you might be a boy?"

Zoe squirmed a little in her chair and looked down. "It was probably my fault," she murmured.

"Why do you say that?" Mrs. McKenzie queried softly.

"Well, I didn't know what to do when I was—you know, having menstrual pain." Zoe blushed. "So I went to talk to her. She was really nice and had me come back to talk to her several times. One time I said it was *a pain being a girl,* and I didn't feel very feminine anyway. I mean, no one ever curled my hair and I usually wore my big brother's clothes after he grew out of them because— well, because we *all* wore hand-me-downs. My dad doesn't have a lot of money, and with so many kids in the family... So the nurse told me, 'Well, maybe you're not a girl.'"

"How did you feel when she said that?" Mrs. McKenzie asked.

Zoe sighed and the glow left her face. She answered in a flat tone. "Surprised. Shocked really. And kind of depressed. But mostly I just felt confused." Tears welled at the edges of her eyes as she went on, "It sounded crazy, but the nurse said some people are born in the wrong body."

Zoe looked up, suddenly almost hysterical. "She said I could be *a boy in a girl's body!*"

25

Tracy was taken aback by the mercurial change in Zoe's emotions, but her mom seemed unperturbed.

"The school nurse told you that you could be a boy in a girl's body?" Mrs. McKenzie repeated in a neutral tone.

"Yes," Zoe answered, her jaw set. "But she said that it was a mistake and it could be fixed."

"Fixed?" Mrs. McKenzie prodded.

"She said I was a bit late, that some kids start taking medicine when they are ten or eleven, but it wasn't too late. I could start taking some kind of block so I would stop—you know—all the things that happen as girls grow up."

"Um-hmm," Mrs. McKenzie murmured. "Puberty blockers to arrest the development of female secondary sex characteristics, like menstruation and developing breasts and a softer rounder body and so on."

"Right. She said I could sort of turn back the clock on all that, except the breasts."

Now Zoe looked half defiant, even angry, and half pleading. Why? Tracy couldn't follow Zoe's kaleidoscope of emotions as she interacted with her mom.

"But she showed me how to bind my breasts and said when I'm sixteen I can get rid of them," Zoe added.

"Have your breasts removed by a double mastectomy. Yes," Mrs. McKenzie nodded calmly.

Tracy's eyes widened in horror and she unconsciously folded her arms over her own modest breasts.

"So—did you start taking puberty blockers?" Mrs. McKenzie asked kindly.

111

"No! I hate medicine," Zoe blurted emphatically. "It scared me. The whole idea scared me. And the nurse scared me, too. I didn't know what to do but I didn't want to take that medicine."

"So what did you do?"

"I just—I tried to be more like a boy. But—but that didn't feel right either," Zoe sputtered.

"Why? How did that not feel right?" Mrs. McKenzie asked.

"I dunno. It—well, it just didn't make me feel any better," Zoe answered in a tiny voice.

Mrs. McKenzie stroked Zoe's hand gently but she spoke firmly. "I'm very glad you came to see me, Zoe. That was an intelligent thing to do. You came to get more information. Maybe a different opinion. So you could decide for yourself what you thought after you had more facts, right?"

"Uh, yeah," Zoe mumbled.

"Now, I'm only a nursing *student,*" Mrs. McKenzie continued. "But I can tell you what the research and well-qualified doctors report, all right? I can give you some facts to help you think about this. Does that sound good?"

Zoe nodded hesitantly.

"First of all, you were brave to speak up for yourself and say you did not want to take the medicine. Second, let me tell you a little more about these puberty blockers, okay?"

"Puberty blockers arrest the development of secondary sex characteristics—that's for both boys and girls, by the way," Mrs. McKenzie continued. "But they have other side effects. They weaken the bones and stunt overall growth. Worse, puberty blockers along with cross-sex hormones started at or before age thirteen can make boys and girls infertile. In other words, you probably could never have a baby, even if you changed your mind after you had taken puberty blockers for a while. Is that a decision you want to make at this age?"

Zoe looked devastated. "But I *like* babies. Like my neighbor's cute little baby..." Her voice broke and her shoulders shook. "No one ever told me—I mean..."

Mrs. McKenzie slipped her arm around the girl and held her gently. "Of course, how could you know? No one ever told you," she said softly. "But your instincts were good. You didn't want to take the medicine without more information. Other possible side effects from taking puberty blockers are weight gain, disfiguring acne, high blood pressure, breast cancer, liver disease, heart problems—"

"Weight gain and acne!" the girls echoed softly, their eyes wide with horror.

"Yes, these medicines totally disrupt the normal maturation of your body. And that's dangerous."

"Furthermore," Mrs. McKenzie continued, "why would you want to mutilate your body with a double mastectomy? You would have ugly scars on your chest instead of lovely soft breasts. And if you continued in your transition to pretend to be a boy— we'll talk more about why it is impossible for you to become a boy in a minute—then later you would have to begin taking cross-sex hormones. You would have to take *that* medicine for the *rest of your life.*"

"Is—is that medicine dangerous too?" Tracy asked, speaking up for the first time. Zoe didn't look as if she could speak anyway, and Tracy wanted to know the answer.

"Yes, Trace," her mother replied. "Cross-sex hormones *are* dangerous. Taking cross-sex hormones leads to metabolic imbalance and immunity problems. Then come cancers, cardiovascular problems like high blood pressure or heart attack. Or stroke, which could leave you partially paralyzed. And as if that's not enough, there's more risk of diabetes and other physical problems. Plus depression, because *transitioning* to the opposite sex does not solve the problems that caused the psychological discomfort a person had with his or her biological sex in the first place."

"You mean, all that medicine and turning your whole life upside down and people aren't any happier?" Tracy asked.

"Apparently not," Mrs. McKenzie replied sadly, "because the lifetime attempted suicide rate—at least, for the *claimed* suicide attempts—for a trans man or trans woman is twenty-two times higher than for the general population. That's the same rate as for gay, lesbian or bisexual people, for psych patients, and for bullied people. The rate for *completed* suicide among trans people is nineteen times higher than for the general population."

"Whoa!" Tracy breathed in shock.

No one spoke for a long moment.

"I know this is a lot of information to dump on you all at once, Zoe," Mrs. McKenzie said gently. "But you need to know the facts. I think you want to know the facts. Am I right?"

Zoe cleared her throat and sat up straighter. "Yes, I do. I want to know exactly what any medicine I have to take does. But why did you say I could only *pretend* to be a boy?"

26

"Do you know what a chromosome is?" Mrs. McKenzie asked.

"Uh, sort of," Zoe shrugged.

"Me too, sort of," Tracy echoed.

"Almost all of the cells in your body have a nucleus. And in every cell with a nucleus, there are forty-six chromosomes, or twenty-three *pairs* of chromosomes. One chromosome of each pair comes from your father, and one from your mother."

"Okay," the girls nodded, glancing at each other.

"Now these chromosomes contain all your DNA—that is, the DeoxyriboNucleic Acid with all your genetic material, all the genes that say if you will be tall or short, blond or black-haired, and so on. And also, your sex—male or female."

"Um-hmm," the girls murmured.

"But what determines your biological sex? What determines whether the fertilized egg is a baby boy or a baby girl?" Mrs. McKenzie asked.

"One of those twenty-three chromosome pairs in every nucleated cell of your body determines your sex, so let's concentrate on that one sex chromosome pair," she continued. "Female DNA shows an XX sex chromosome pair in every cell. But a female egg cell has only *one-half* of each chromosome pair. So for the egg cell, the sex chromosome just has an X."

The girls frowned slightly as they concentrated on Mrs. McKenzie's explanation.

"But the father," Mrs. McKenzie went on, "has an XY sex chromosome pair in every one of his cells with a nucleus. Like the female egg, the sperm has only half of each chromosome pair. So in the sperm, the sex chromosome can carry an X or a Y. If the sperm that fertilizes an egg has an X, the baby will have an XX chromosome pair—the second X coming from the mother—and the baby is a girl. But if the sperm has a Y, the baby will have an XY chromosome pair—the X again coming from the mother—and the baby is a boy. So it's the sex chromosome from the father that is the wild card. It's the father that determines the sex of the child."

"It's kind of confusing," Zoe said slowly, "but it makes sense that both the egg and the sperm can only have *half of each pair* of chromosomes from the parents."

"Yeah," Tracy added. "Otherwise the baby would have—how many?"

"Let's see, forty-six and forty-six is..." Zoe began.

"Ninety-two chromosomes in every cell!" the girls finished in unison, giggling. "A monster!"

"Right," Mrs. McKenzie grinned. "Just remember, if the father contributes a Y chromosome, the baby is a boy. *Y means male.* That helps to explain a lot of questions that sometimes come up later."

"But as we said, if the father's sperm fertilizes the mother's egg with an X chromosome, the baby is a girl," Mrs. McKenzie continued. "And then every nucleated cell in that baby girl's body will have an XX."

"So on the *sub-cellular level* all throughout your body, you are either male or female," Mrs. McKenzie summarized.

"Yeah," Tracy added excitedly, "and Mom said we have trillions—*thirty trillion,* Mom?—cells in our bodies!"

"Thirty trillion?" Zoe looked shocked. "Thirty trillion XXs?"

"Exactly," Mrs. McKenzie nodded solemnly. "That's why we say your eye, your ear, and your elbow are *coded* female. Kind of like a computer code. You are a girl. You can't change the code. It's in most every cell of your body."

"But don't cross-sex hormones change the code?" Tracy asked.

"That's a common misconception," her mother replied. "No, cross-sex hormones can change some physical aspects of appearance.

More testosterone can make facial hair grow and the voice deepen, more estrogen can make breasts swell, and so on. Cosmetic surgery and a change of clothes and changing the balance of sex *hormones* in a body can make someone have a convincing *appearance* of being the opposite sex from what they were born, but that does not change *the DNA on the sub-cellular level.*"

"From the moment of conception, a baby is either male or female," Mrs. McKenzie concluded.

"So I could never be a boy even if I wanted to be," Zoe said slowly. "So I don't have to choose."

"That's right, sweetie," Mrs. McKenzie replied smiling. "When it comes to your biological sex, you don't have to choose—you are a girl! And that's a wonderful thing to be."

"But—but I still don't *feel* very girly," Zoe began hesitantly.

"Maybe you just need a little help with that," Mrs. McKenzie grinned. "Maybe I could help?"

"Oh, would you?" Zoe responded. "I mean, what would you do?"

"Would you like to go shopping together to find some pretty new clothes?"

"Oh, could we? I don't know how to pick clothes," Zoe said shyly. "And maybe—" she touched her hair—"what about my hair? Can you help me?"

"Absolutely."

Just then they heard the front door open.

"Oh dear, that's your father and Nate back from Nate's dentist appointment and I don't have dinner ready. You girls will have to help me, okay?" she laughed. "Zoe, you will stay for dinner, won't you?"

"Well, I—I guess I could call my dad and ask."

"Please do. We'd love to have you."

Tracy scurried to clear the cookie plate from the table and was getting the silverware out when her cell phone rang.

It was Charlie.

117

27

"I can't talk right now, Charlie." Tracy bent her head so her hair fell forward and held her phone close to her mouth.

"Why not? I need you to come with me to the mall tonight," Charlie said. "The black jeans I planned to wear to the party tomorrow night don't fit right and—"

"I can't, Charlie. Not tonight," Tracy sighed.

"Why not?"

"We have company."

"So? Can't you get away?" Charlie pleaded. "You know how important this weekend is to me."

"I still don't think your date tomorrow night is a good idea," Tracy responded sharply. "But whatever, Charlie. It doesn't matter. I'm busy. You'll just have to figure it out yourself."

"Wow, and you always said you were my best friend," Charlie snapped sarcastically.

"Don't be like that, Char," Tracy hissed at her cell. "I'll tell you all about it tomorrow."

"Wait! What's the big mystery?" Charlie shot back quickly. "Who's so important you have to stay home instead of coming to the mall with me?"

But it was too late. Tracy had closed the call with a flick of her thumb. As she turned around, she saw Zoe watching her anxiously and realized she had heard the whole conversation.

Tracy shook her head from side to side and rolled her eyes. "Yeah, that was Charlie. But don't worry, Zoe. I won't tell her anything. I mean, I won't tell her what we talked about."

Zoe responded with a weak smile and turned as Nate came tromping into the room.

"No cavities, Mom," he grinned. "Oh, hi Zoe. What's for dinner, Mom? I'm starving."

Her brother hi-fived Zoe as he pushed past his sister toward the refrigerator.

"Uh-uh-uh," Mrs. McKenzie said. "Don't start snacking. Dinner will be ready in ten minutes. I baked the chicken this morning and we're heating it and the vegetables right now."

"Just getting a drink, Ma," Nate winked. "See, sparkling cider. Want some, Zoe?"

"No, thanks. I'll wait for dinner, Nate," Zoe smiled.

Tracy was in shock again. Nate acted as if he'd known Zoe forever. As if she were an old pal. But how could he?

"How's Brett?" Nate threw over his shoulder as he headed for the hall. "Did he ever finish painting his room?"

"Fine," Zoe answered. "And yes, he did."

"Awesome," Nate called back as he left the room.

So that was it, Tracy thought. After all, Brett was only one year ahead of Nate. A lot of juniors hung out with seniors. But her brother had never mentioned Brett before.

Zoe saw the confusion on Tracy's face. "Nate comes over to visit my brother sometimes," she said simply.

"Oh. I didn't know," Tracy replied awkwardly.

After a pause Zoe added, "He really liked what Brett did in his room. The paint, I mean."

"Tracy, will you call everyone to the table," Mrs. McKenzie interjected. "We're ready to eat."

When they were all seated, Mr. McKenzie said a short prayer to thank God for the food. Zoe closed her eyes and bowed her head but she peeked to see if everyone else kept their eyes closed. They did. They acted as if it was completely normal to pray before eating. She wasn't used to that.

As she passed the chicken to her mother, Tracy continued the conversation.

"Nate, you liked the way Brett painted his bedroom wall? Why, was it some weird color or something?" she added, giving her brother a playful kick under the table.

"No, Lizard Legs," Nate replied.

Tracy kicked him again, harder this time. Nate had started calling her Lizard Legs when she was a skinny six-year-old. Her middle name was Elizabeth, easily shortened by a teasing older brother to Liz—or Lizard Legs. Which was not shorter, of course.

Zoe laughed. "Brett is a cartography nut."

"Uh, cartography?"

"Map making. So he painted the big wall of his room like an ancient map," Zoe explained. "In excruciating detail."

"An ancient map?" Tracy looked blank. "Of what?

"Of Tibet."

"Tibet?" Tracy asked in surprise. "Why Tibet?"

"Because of his other obsession," Zoe answered.

"You mean it was like a treasure map or something?" Tracy puzzled.

"No," Zoe laughed.

Zoe didn't say it, but Tracy heard the intonation. It sounded to her ears like, "No, silly girl." She had always thought Zoe was dumb, but it felt like the shoe was on the other foot now.

"Because of the mountains," Zoe added.

"So he painted a bunch of mountains on his wall?" Tracy pursed her lips, thinking. "Oh—isn't Tibet where Mount Everest is? Or is it Nepal?"

"Both. Mt. Everest is on the border between the two countries," Zoe nodded. "Nepal is to the south, closer to India. But Brett didn't paint it like you're thinking. Not like a photograph."

"Okay, I'm totally confused," Tracy sighed. "He painted the mountains of Tibet but not like the mountains of Tibet?"

"I told you he is a cartography nut," Zoe explained patiently. "He likes maps. A lot. So he reproduced an ancient cartographer's depiction of the highest mountain in the world. If it is."

"If it is? What do you mean?"

"It might be Everest—or it might not be."

"Wait—you're saying Mount Everest might not be the highest mountain in the world?" Tracy objected.

"That's right, it might be only the second highest mountain in the world," Nate chimed in, taking a huge helping of mashed potatoes.

"But Mr. Holmes said—" Tracy began.

"Good old Mr. Holmes," Nate interrupted. "Trace, trust me, you don't want to believe everything that old dino—uh, everything that teacher says," changing his words mid-sentence as he saw his parents' disapproving looks. They would not brook disrespect for a teacher, no matter how firmly they disagreed with him. "He was saying that two years ago when I had him, too. He could just google it," he scoffed.

"Google what?"

"What is the highest mountain in the world?" Zoe and Nate singsonged in unison.

"So if it's not Mount Everest, what *is* the highest mountain in the world?" Mr. McKenzie asked. His face showed his amusement and interest.

Nate gestured to Zoe to answer the question.

"It depends on how you measure it," she began.

"Or what country you live in," Nate winked.

"True," Zoe answered. "You see, some people say it is Mount Chimborazo. That's a volcano—"

"A stratovolcano, actually," Nate put in.

"In Ecuador," Zoe nodded at Nate. "It's in the Andes Mountains."

"What's a stratovolcano?" Toby piped up.

"It's a volcano that's built up of alternate *stratum* or layers. A layer of ash, then a layer of cinder, then ash, and so on," Nate explained.

"Very interesting," Mr. McKenzie commented. "So how tall is Everest?"

"Over 29,000 feet," Zoe said. "Right, Nate?"

"Actually 29,029 feet," he nodded. "At least, that's the figure commonly accepted, although some people say it's a few feet less or more. Maybe 29,035 feet high."

"And how high is this Chimbo—uh, Chimboramo, was it?" Mrs. McKenzie queried.

"Chimborazo," Zoe corrected. "It only rises 20,548 feet above sea level. That's more than 8,500 feet shorter than Everest. But—" She gestured for Nate to take over.

"But the earth bulges at the equator, and Chimborazo is almost right on the equator. So if you measure from the center of the earth, Chimborazo is actually *two miles taller* than Everest."

"But that's not all," Zoe added. "There's another mountain that is claimed to be taller than either of these."

"What?" Toby sputtered, his mouth full of chicken. "Dueling mountains. Rad!"

"So what is this third mountain?" Mr. McKenzie prompted.

"Mauna Kea, or the White Mountain," Zoe said.

"In Hawaii, of course," Nate added. "On the Big Island. Which, naturally, is called Hawaii Island."

"And how tall is this mountain?" Mr. McKenzie asked.

"Mauna Kea is actually less than 14,000 feet above sea level," Zoe began. "But that's the catch." She held out her hand to Nate to continue.

"Yeah, see if it's measured from its base on the ocean floor, it beats both Everest and Chimborazo," Nate said. "Almost the height of Everest—about 29,000 feet—of Mauna Kea is below sea level. So altogether it's about 33,500 feet high. Right, Zoe?"

"Right. Definitely taller than Everest at only 29,000 plus."

"Or Chimborazo at only 20, 500 plus," Nate echoed.

"Geesh, how do you guys remember all those numbers?" Toby grunted.

"I was wondering the same thing," Mrs. McKenzie said. "You kids are amazing."

"Well, as I said, Brett is a cartography nut," Zoe replied as if that explained it.

"He's full of odd and interesting bits of information," Nate added.

"But you said Brett painted a map of Mount Everest on his bedroom wall, Zoe." Tracy persisted. "Like with roads and stuff?"

"No roads," Nate scoffed. "Just elevation lines."

"Elevation lines?"

"Contour lines. You know, those wavy lines that go in a circle around a mountain on a map? Each line shows a certain rise in elevation or height," Zoe explained. "So you can see where the land is getting higher."

"Oh," Tracy nodded slowly. "That's, uh—yeah, that's interesting."

Actually she thought it sounded a little strange, a wall painted with squiggly lines that sort of went around in a circle. But Zoe and Nate obviously thought it was *rad,* as Toby would say.

"This is all fascinating," Mr. McKenzie said. "But I have some reports to finish. So if you will excuse me..."

As he rose from the table, he turned to his wife and kissed her lightly on the cheek. "Thank you for a good dinner, dear."

Tracy saw Zoe watching her parents carefully, as if trying to absorb every detail of the dinner. Funny, Tracy thought. It was all just the usual stuff, a normal family dinner. She wondered what dinner was like at Zoe's house.

"I've got homework," Nate yawned, "so excuse me too, please." He picked up his dad's plate as well as his own and carried them to the sink counter. "Bye, Zoe. Say hi to Brett for me."

As he headed toward the hall, Zoe said hesitantly, "I really need to be getting home."

"Oh, let me drive you, dear," Mrs. McKenzie offered. "Tracy, would you take care of putting the leftovers away?"

"Sure, Mom. Bye, Zoe. See you at school tomorrow."

It was only when she heard the front door close that Tracy realized what she had said. *See you at school tomorrow.* Why did she have to say that?

Now things were going to get complicated. Charlie would want to know what was going on, but Tracy couldn't tell her about Zoe and the whole thing with the school nurse or her mom's offer to take Zoe shopping. And Tracy knew that Charlie was going to blabber on and on tomorrow about Sharon and Deke and Pete and the others, which Tracy really didn't care to hear. And then Zoe was going to walk up and act all friendly, and Charlie was going to freak.

But Zoe actually seemed nice, Tracy thought. Like a normal person when Nate was around. He treated her like anyone else—just like her mom did—and Zoe seemed to mirror their expectations.

Well, all except for the hair and clothes. That definitely wasn't normal for a girl their age. Maybe if her mom took Zoe shopping...

On the plus side, Zoe certainly made more interesting conversation than Charlie did! So maybe if she looked different...

Ugh, but Zoe acted so weird at school. Tracy was afraid she would still be embarrassing to be around. And Charlie would never accept Zoe as a friend.

So that was it. Charlie or Zoe?

But that was no contest. Even if Charlie was being a pain right now, she was still her closest friend. Since third grade. So what was she to do?

Zoe would have to go.

28

Friday morning. Quiz day. Most of her teachers seemed to think Friday was a great day for a pop quiz. Which meant that most of the kids *expected* quizzes on Fridays. So the good students studied on Thursday nights and the less interested students got ready for the weekend. Or at least, that's the way it seemed to Tracy.

Which meant that after Zoe left, Tracy had spent the rest of Thursday evening reviewing formulas and concepts in math and re-reading notes from Mr. Holmes' class. She didn't need to review her English homework. English had always been easy for her. For Spanish she flipped through a few verb charts and listened to a review tape. She despaired of ever being able to roll her r's properly but Mr. Ramirez was fairly tolerant of her Anglo pronunciation.

Charlie accosted her the moment she set foot in the hallway by her locker that Friday morning, which was also not a surprise. Tracy knew that Charlie would be seething with curiosity about who had been at her house last night.

"Oh, Brett Hudson's sister came by." Tracy dropped the words casually, as if it were not the spectacular news that she knew Charlie would think it was.

"Brett Hudson's sister?" Charlie shrieked *sotto voce.*

Tracy giggled to herself. Yep, she'd gotten the reaction she wanted. And Charlie was being—Charlie. She wondered if there was anyone else on the planet who could shriek in a whisper.

"Yeah," she yawned. "Did you get the black pants you wanted at the mall?"

"Yes—no, wait! Go back," Charlie exclaimed. "Brett's sister? How did you meet Brett's sister?"

125

"Oh, I've known her for quite a while," Tracy drawled, dragging out the suspense. It was such fun to tease—or torture—Charlie this way. "Were there any good sales at the mall?"

"Stop talking about the mall," Charlie scolded. "*Who* is Brett's sister?"

The warning bell rang. Tracy slammed her locker shut and turned quickly. "Oh, I have to run, Char. I think we're having a pop quiz in first period. Talk to you later."

With that Tracy was off, leaving Charlie standing open-mouthed and scowling in the middle of the hall.

Lunchtime was a different matter. Tracy was afraid she would not be able to duck Charlie's questions in the cafeteria. As she walked toward the cafeteria in the crowded hallway she saw Zoe just ahead of her and Charlie ten paces beyond that, separated from them by a group of upper classmen.

It was showdown time, Tracy thought. Today both Zoe and Charlie would gravitate to sit with her in the lunchroom. But then Charlie would act so dismissive to Zoe that the poor girl would be deflated.

Unless I speak up for Zoe, Tracy thought. Or unless I stop Charlie from being rude to Zoe by spilling the beans right then that it is actually Zoe who is Brett's sister. But she knew that getting Charlie to change her attitude by pulling the Brett card right in front of Zoe would hurt her feelings, and that just seemed wrong.

Tracy dreaded the next five minutes.

But as Zoe passed the English room the door opened and Miss Fellows beckoned first to Zoe and then behind her to Tracy. "Girls, will you help me with these banners? I can't seem to get them straight."

Zoe glanced back, surprised and pleased to see that it was Tracy who was behind her and that Miss Fellows was addressing them both. The girls smiled, shrugged and stepped into the English room.

It took almost fifteen minutes to get the banners hung correctly. Miss Fellows was always so friendly that neither girl minded taking the time to help her. And the added benefit, from Tracy's point of view, was that by the time they got to the cafeteria—Zoe and Tracy naturally walking together—most of the kids had finished eating and had adjourned to the courtyard for gossip, hacky sack and other games.

And neither Charlie nor Sharon were anywhere to be seen.

"Thanks for letting me come to your house yesterday," Zoe said. "I really enjoyed getting to talk to your mom. She's so nice, and she knows a lot of stuff I needed to know."

"Yeah, she's a pretty neat mom," Tracy smiled. "And I enjoyed it too. I learned things I didn't know about this whole transgender thing. And I learned more about you, too. We'd never really talked before."

Zoe smiled shyly but didn't say anything. Surprisingly, Tracy felt okay with that. With Charlie, there wasn't a moment of quiet. It was machine-gun chatter all the time—usually gossip about someone. It was kind of relaxing just to sit and chew for a moment without being alone.

But Zoe broke the silence after a minute. "Did your mom tell you she said she could take me shopping tomorrow?"

"No," Tracy replied. "I was doing homework when she got home, and then my aunt called. She lives in California with my cousins. They were still talking on the phone when I was ready for bed, so I just waved goodnight to her."

Why didn't her mom mention it this morning, Tracy wondered? Then she re-played the morning chaos as she and her brothers made their lunches and swallowed eggs and juice. Their dad was discussing some financial thing with their mom, and even Toby's dog Flounders was in a hyper mood. But then Flounders was usually in a hyper mood. So much for his laid-back golden lab genes, she thought wryly. The dog kept tearing around the kitchen between everyone's legs, trying to entice them to play fetch with the slobbery ball clenched in his grinning jaws.

Uh yeah, that's why her mom didn't mention it this morning, Tracy chuckled to herself.

"So anyway," Zoe continued, "you'll come too, won't you?"

"Yeah," Tracy shrugged, reaching for her juice box. It wasn't as if she had anything better to do this Saturday. It was supposed to be a drizzly day. The last thing she wanted to do on a Saturday was rattle around the house by herself, but if Charlie dropped by she would be a total bore. All Charlie would want to do would be to talk about her date the night before with Pete. Better to be gone—out with her mom and Zoe. "Yeah, sounds like fun."

"Your mom said you had to clean your room Saturday morning but after lunch would work," Zoe said timidly.

"Um yeah," Tracy muttered, swallowing. "Clean my room, change my sheets, vacuum the den or clean the kitchen. The usual Saturday morning chores. At least it's not my week to poop scoop in the back yard," she added. That was never a glorious task, but in a drizzle it was even worse. Picking up mush with the poop scooper.

After a minute Tracy asked, "What about you? What do you do on a Saturday morning?"

"Pretty much the same," Zoe answered. "Except I have to clean the bathrooms too. The boys never do that and it can get really gross."

"Yuck," Tracy responded vehemently. "At least my brothers have to clean the bathrooms. They're the ones who make a mess."

"That's for sure," Zoe grinned.

Tracy liked the feeling that Zoe understood what it was like having brothers, older and younger. Charlie didn't have any brothers, just the one older sister.

"Give me your cell number," Tracy said as the warning bell rang. "So I can call you tomorrow to tell you when we'll pick you up."

"Oh, your mom has it," Zoe answered. "I'll give it to you in gym class. We'd better run to class now."

As they dropped their trash in the receptacles at the cafeteria door they almost ran into Charlie, who acted as if she didn't even see Zoe.

"Tracy, where have you been?" Charlie gasped between giggles. "I've been looking all over for you. Sharon just said the funniest thing."

Charlie slipped her arm through Tracy's and pulled her down the hall. As Zoe melted away, Tracy cast an apologetic glance after her, worried that she would be offended by Charlie's obvious disdain for her. But Zoe showed more spirit than Tracy expected.

She winked.

29

Charlie was off with Sharon the minute the last bell rang and Zoe was nowhere to be seen, so Tracy crossed the courtyard alone and started for home. But as she left the school grounds, an old jalopy at the curb beeped. Curious, she turned to look as the front passenger window rolled down..

"Hey, Tracy—want a ride?" Zoe called.

Tracy peered beyond Zoe to see who the driver was but his head was turned away from her. All she could see was the back of his baseball cap. She couldn't make out who the boy was. She was hesitant to ride with a boy she didn't know, even though she trusted Zoe. Well, she thought she trusted Zoe. But then she really hardly knew her.

As she stepped closer to the car, the driver turned his face toward her.

"Josh!" she exclaimed. "Uh, I didn't know you had a car. Or a license."

"Yep, all legal. Even if I am only fifteen."

"But how could you get a—" Tracy began.

"Get in and I'll tell you," Josh urged, grinning.

Josh should be okay, Tracy thought. He was always so careful at school so he was probably a careful driver. He was super smart so she was sure he knew all the driving rules.

But Josh bumped into things all the time around school. Well, that was when he was walking, she thought. Like when he had his nose in a book or was looking up data on his phone. Tracy assumed that while driving he wouldn't stick his nose in a book or look at his cell phone! Nate had told her there was a big fine for using a cell while driving.

Nate was old enough to drive but he didn't have a car. Sometimes her dad let Nate take the car for a few hours on the weekend but he laid down strict ground rules. No more than two friends in the car at a time. No funny business. No fender benders or tickets. And Nate had to pay for the gas.

"Come on, Tracy," Zoe smiled. "Get in the back."

Hesitating, Tracy opened the door. "Uh, can you take me right home, though? I usually have to ask permission to go in someone's car. But I'm sure my parents would trust you, Josh."

"No problem," Josh laughed. "I'm going home myself after I drop you girls off."

Tracy threw her backpack into the car and climbed in.

"Seatbelt," Josh prompted.

"Oh, yeah. Of course," Tracy muttered, buckling up.

"I live just a half block down from Josh," Zoe volunteered.

"Oh." That answered the question Tracy was dying to ask but felt would be rude—like, *how on earth did you end up in Josh's car, Zoe?* She felt embarrassed to admit to herself that she was a little jealous. Josh was supposed to be her friend, and then it turned out he was *Nate's* friend, and now Zoe's too?

"But—uh, how did you get your license early, Josh?" Tracy asked as he eased the car into traffic.

"It's a special permit," he replied. "My mother can't drive. She needs physical therapy twice a week but my dad has to work. So I got a hardship exemption for an early license."

"I didn't know there was such a thing," Tracy said. After a pause she added, "I'm sorry. I didn't know your mom was ill."

"Oh, she's not sick," Josh answered. "It's not like the flu or anything. Her right side is weak so she needs physical therapy."

"That's—" Tracy began. *That's too bad* didn't seem like the right thing to say. She wasn't sure what to say. She wanted to ask why her right side was weak but didn't.

"We help at home," Josh continued. "My dad and I. We take turns doing her home physical therapy. But she needs the specialized help that the physical therapists at the hospital can do a couple of times a week."

"Physical therapists are amazing," Zoe added. "I'm interested in becoming a physical therapist someday. But they have to take years of schooling. First a bachelor's degree and then in this state, also a master's degree."

"That's like six years of school past high school, isn't it?" Tracy asked.

"Yes," Zoe nodded. "You have to learn a lot of anatomy."

"What makes you think physical therapists are so amazing, Zoe?" Tracy puzzled.

"They do so much good," Zoe responded enthusiastically. "They really help people. When Brett got hurt in football last year, he was bummed because the doctor told him he might not be able to play anymore. But the physical therapist helped him not only regain his strength when his bones healed, but also sort of realigned the ligaments that had gotten torn and twisted. Brett really likes football, so that meant an awful lot to him."

Tracy vaguely remembered that the star football player had been injured in a game last year. She hadn't paid much attention at the time. She wasn't that much into school sports. Her idea of sport was tussling with her brothers on the back lawn or going on long bike rides, solo.

"Brett is hoping for a football scholarship so he can go to college, isn't he?" Josh added.

"Yes," Zoe replied. "Although he could probably make it on academics if he wanted to. He's actually smarter than you, Josh," she finished, punching him lightly on the arm. Josh responded with an affectionate grin.

Tracy was taken aback. She still felt awkward around Josh even though he had come to her house on Tuesday nights for weeks now. But Zoe seemed completely comfortable. As uninhibited as Tracy was around her own brothers.

Maybe that was because Zoe had a lot of brothers herself, Tracy thought. Or maybe Josh and Zoe had more of a relationship than she had thought. Like boyfriend and girlfriend. A stab of jealousy flashed through her heart and Tracy blushed in shame. Even though the two in the front seat could have no idea of her thoughts, she was embarrassed.

But she was being silly, she mused. Zoe had wondered if she was a boy. If she felt like a boy, she wouldn't *like* a boy. Not in a boyfriend way.

Except then Tracy remembered the two boys she saw once in a while in the hall at school. It was embarrassing. Holding hands was bad enough, but at the lockers they would even kiss. Most of the kids ignored them. Some of the boys whistled or hooted and some of the girls postured as being *very tolerant*. But most of the kids thought they were either stupid or nauseating and just tried to pretend they didn't see them.

Tracy's train of thought was interrupted by Josh slamming on the brakes. Her seatbelt tightened as she was pushed forward by the sudden stop. Josh and Zoe were also thrown forward but again, the seatbelts made the sudden stop anti-climactic.

"What was that all about?" Tracy asked a bit crossly.

"Didn't you see the cat?" Zoe responded, twisting in her seat to look behind her. "A mama cat with a kitten in her mouth."

"Sorry, Trace," Josh said. "I just couldn't bear to hit her. And I checked my rearview mirror. There were no cars behind us."

"Where is she going in that empty field?" Zoe muttered. "Look, she's coming back now without the kitten."

"She's not going to leave the kitten there all alone, is she?" Tracy added.

"Okay, I can tell you girls are going to worry all night unless we stop and check this out," Josh grunted. He pulled ahead to the curb and stopped.

"Should we go check on the kitten?" Zoe suggested.

"No. Just wait and watch a few minutes," Josh cautioned. "I'll bet she has more babies."

Within a few minutes the mama cat had transported two more little kittens across the street in her jaws. Then she settled down beside them in the straggly grass of the vacant lot.

"Now what? That's it, mama?" Josh muttered as if talking to the cat. "That's not a great place to nurse your kittens."

"Oh, no!" Tracy and Zoe exclaimed in unison as a mangy looking dog came tearing across a nearby front yard. "He'll kill those kittens!"

The girls were out of the car and running across the street as Josh jumped out of the car. He ran the opposite direction—toward the dog—yelling and waving his arms. The mutt lowered his body, ready to spring, and growled deep in his throat. Josh feinted a lunge forward and yelled again. At that, the dog tucked his tail between his legs and backed off.

"The mama is too thin," Zoe called back to Josh.

"She can't keep the kittens here," Tracy added.

Keeping an eye on the dog, Josh walked back to the car and opened the trunk. He dumped miscellaneous tools out of a beat-up cardboard box and shook it to get dirt and dust out of it.

"Here," he said, crossing the street to the field. "Put them in here. I hope they don't have fleas."

"What are we going to do with them?" Zoe asked.

"We can't take them to the pound—" Tracy added.

"Humane society," Josh corrected automatically.

"—because they have too many cats and..." Tracy let the sentence hang.

"Can you take them?" Josh asked her.

"With Flounders?" Tracy doubted. "He's a sweet dog, but he gets a little crazy with cats."

"Actually my little brother has been asking for a cat," Zoe spoke up. "Of course, this is more than one cat, and I don't know if my dad will let us keep them. But I could take them home and ask."

"We can help find homes for the kittens when they are a little bigger," Josh added.

"Well, that's settled then," Tracy said, picking up a kitten and placing it gently in the cardboard box.

Zoe and Josh each picked up a kitten also. When they were all in the box, the mama immediately jumped in as if being adopted by these kids had been her plan all along.

A few minutes later Tracy was waving from her front sidewalk as Josh's jalopy disappeared down the street. As she walked up to the porch, her thoughts rambled over the day's events.

The morning had begun with a coup for her by distracting Charlie from finding out who Brett Hudson's sister was.

Then Miss Fellows had saved her from lunchroom drama since Charlie was gone by the time she and Zoe got there.

And to Tracy's surprise, Zoe showed spunk when Charlie did finally appear and ignored her.

Then Josh's jalopy was another surprise.

That led to her suspicion that Josh and Zoe might have some relationship that justified the jealousy she felt on seeing how comfortable they were together.

But now as Josh and Zoe drove away together she felt only comradery with them. The three of them together had effected a rescue and had a mission—to find good homes for not just the mama cat, but also the kittens.

"Hmm," she mocked herself as she walked up the front steps. "Who has the shifting emotions now? Before yesterday I thought Zoe was weird. A half hour ago I was jealous of her. And now I think she may become a better friend than Charlie has been all this year."

30

When Charlie sidled silently up to her at her locker Monday morning, Tracy knew something was wrong.

"Good morning?" she drawled sarcastically. Then, when Charlie responded with no more than an anemic grimace that could hardly be called a smile, Tracy added, "What did you do with Charlie? You are obviously a fake, not my best friend."

"Am I still your best friend?" Charlie asked wistfully.

"Huh?" Tracy snorted. "Of course! What's got into you?"

Suddenly it looked as if Charlie was going to burst into tears.

"Hey, what's wrong?" Tracy prompted, concern furrowing her brow. "What happened?"

"Oh, Tracy," Charlie wailed in a whisper. "It was awful."

"What was awful? What are you talking about?"

"We can't talk here," Charlie sniffed as the warning bell rang. "I'll tell you at lunch. Meet me in the band room, okay? No one will be there at lunchtime."

Tracy watched in puzzlement as Charlie blinked her eyes hard and rubbed a finger at a tear that slid down her cheek. Then she straightened her neck and set her mouth in a fake smile, waving Tracy off as she started down the hallway.

What on earth was wrong with Charlie, Tracy wondered. She had never seen her like this. Charlie was always the ebullient one, irrepressible, full of life and laughter. But certainly not this morning, Tracy mused wryly.

The only class Charlie and Tracy had together before lunch was English, but Charlie wasn't there. Had she skipped class today? That could get her in major trouble if she got caught. But she'd been doing that sort of thing recently, since she'd been hanging out with Sharon more. Tracy hadn't figured out how they got away with it. If she tried something like that, she always got caught.

There was no time between classes to find Zoe and tell her she wouldn't be in the lunchroom, so Tracy surreptitiously palmed her phone onto her lap in fourth period and sent a text: *can't make lunch. explain later in gym.* It was against the rules to use her phone during class, but that was a minor infraction—not like skipping class. All the kids texted during class and she didn't want Zoe to think she had stood her up. Anyway, she didn't get caught.

As soon as the lunch bell rang, Tracy headed for the band room. Charlie wasn't there. No one was there.

Tracy was surprised the room was not locked. The band room was wide open even with expensive instruments lying around. Most of the instruments were in hard black cases, but a few trumpets and other wind instruments lay on a side table. A drum and cymbal set stood at the back of the room next to the marimba, where a variety of hard- and soft-headed marimba mallets lay on the wooden bars.

When Charlie did not appear after three minutes, she shrugged and dug into her book bag for her sack lunch. She perched on the edge of a small riser at the back of the room and bit into her cheese sandwich. Her mouth was full of half-chewed bread and cheese when Mr. Jamulka, the band teacher, opened the door.

"Well, hello!" he called cheerily as he entered the room. "Who have we here? A new band student?"

"No-schorry, jus-swaiting-formai-fwen," she mumbled, blushing as the sticky cheese garbled her speech.

"Uh, what was that?" the teacher grinned, waiting for her to clear her mouth.

"Sorry, waiting for my friend," Tracy repeated.

"And your friend is..." Mr. Jamulka prompted.

"Charlie. Charlotte Smeldan?" Tracy added as she saw the teacher's questioning look.

"Oh of course, Charlotte Smeldan in third period," Mr. Jamulka nodded. "We also have a Charlie Anderson in fifth period, and a Chuck Gainer in last period."

"Ah," was Tracy's only reply. She felt it was inadequate but wasn't sure what else to say.

"Charlie Smeldan is a very talented clarinet player," the teacher said. "I hope she keeps up with her practicing. She could make All City next year."

136

"Yes, she is good," Tracy agreed enthusiastically.

"But she wasn't in class today," Mr. Jamulka added absentmindedly as he walked over toward his desk. "Hmm, where did I put those papers..."

He shuffled some papers on the desk and selected a clipped stack. He whistled cheerfully as he thumbed through the stack. After a moment he looked up as if surprised that Tracy was still there.

"Oh, you're welcome to stay but I doubt Charlie will be coming. As I said, she wasn't in class today," he added.

"I'll wait if you don't mind," Tracy answered.

She kept checking her phone but Charlie never responded to her texts. She was worried. Now she knew that Charlie had skipped at least two of her morning classes.

It was more than likely that Charlie had gone somewhere with Sharon and Wendy, probably off campus, Tracy figured. But she didn't want to leave the band room in case Charlie ran in at the last minute.

Tracy waited the entire lunch period but Charlie never appeared. Mystified and a bit miffed, Tracy finished her lunch and headed for the restroom.

The M's—Megan and Marline—were primping in front of the mirror in the restroom. Tracy gagged on hair spray as she squeezed by them on the way to a stall.

"Geez, Meg," she grumbled, "think you've used enough of that stuff? You could kill a cow with it."

"Oh, I'll share," Megan tittered, sending a cloud of spray after Tracy.

"Yuck, Megan!" Tracy wailed in protest.

The M's cracked up laughing but the warning bell spurred them to pack up their lipstick, eye shadow and eyelash liner. A girl named Sondra emerged from a stall, her eyes dilated unnaturally. She scraped long fingernails across the latest tattoo on her upper arm, which looked like a cross between a warped flower and an atomic explosion. The M's rolled their eyes behind Sondra's back and sashayed out of the bathroom together. Tracy washed her hands and hurried after them.

As she took her shorts out of her gym locker, she heard Zoe come in behind her. Turning, she grinned at her new friend.

"Hi, Trace," Zoe grinned back. "Thanks for taking me to the mall Saturday with your mom. That was such fun."

Tracy stood still looking at Zoe, her mouth open in an expression of mock shock.

"You can close your mouth now," Zoe laughed.

"You look absolutely gorgeous," Tracy said. "Really, that haircut is adorable and you are beautiful in those new clothes."

Zoe blushed, her face alight with pleasure. "This sweater is a pretty color, isn't it?"

"You look so feminine," Tracy added. "No question whether or not you are a girl now!"

"Yeah," Zoe sighed happily. "It feels so good to look like a girl—"

"A very pretty girl!" Tracy interjected.

"—and I owe it all to you and your mom," Zoe finished.

"Well, to my mom, anyway," Tracy demurred. "But I sure had fun watching you try on all those outfits at the mall."

"Your mom knew just what to pick for me to try," Zoe marveled. "She's so good at that. She could be a fashion consultant."

"She's pretty good at most everything," Tracy bragged on her mom. "Except sewing. She can't sew worth beans. She'll tell you that herself. Grandma taught me how to sew on buttons and mend a seam or take up a hem. My mom says she's hopeless when it comes to sewing."

"Huh, that's funny," Zoe said, pulling on her gym shorts. "I got your text. What was the deal at lunch?"

"I was supposed to meet Charlie in the band room at lunch but she never showed up. In fact, I haven't seen her since before first period," Tracy answered.

"Hmm," Zoe murmured. "You knew she went to Deke's house Friday night because she had a date with Pete Adams, didn't you?"

"Yes. Why?"

"Well, I guess there was some trouble at that party," Zoe said.

"Trouble? What kind of trouble?" Tracy responded anxiously. She wondered why she was just hearing this now. Zoe hadn't mentioned anything on their Saturday mall outing.

"I'm guessing some kids got drunk, maybe there were drugs," Zoe shrugged. "That doesn't surprise me. Brett says he's heard some of those kids have gotten a bit wild on weekends. He stays away from that crowd."

"Oh no, I warned Charlie not to go on that date," Tracy sighed. "I've been nervous about Sharon as an influence on Charlie for some time, but I didn't know about Deke's problems until recently, and I don't know anything about Pete."

After a pause, she added sceptically, "But I didn't hear any gossip floating around today about Deke's party."

"It's been pretty well hushed up," Zoe answered. "Josh didn't say anything when he came to the house Friday night."

"He was at your house Friday night?" Tracy snapped.

"Yeah. He dropped off a book he'd borrowed from Brett," Zoe yawned. Apparently she had not noticed the irritation in Tracy's response.

Tracy was startled by this admission of an additional tie-in between Zoe and Josh. First it was Josh and Nate, and now Josh and Brett? Were they chums, too? And Zoe hadn't said a thing about Josh being at her house Friday night in all the hours she and Tracy had spent together on Saturday!

There was no more time to talk as the gym teacher was blowing the whistle for the girls to line up in the gym. It was still too cold to play volleyball outside in their shorts, but the gymnasium was big enough for two girls' games to be going on at one end of the building and boys' physical education to be in full-swing at the other end. The noise level with that many young people engaged in physical activity at once made any further talk between Tracy and Zoe impossible.

As they were changing back into their street clothes after gym Tracy was silent, absorbed in her own thoughts.

"Ugh, it was so cold and wet this morning. Do you think it has warmed up at all outside?" Zoe mumbled, pulling her sweater over her new bra.

The last thing Tracy was worried about right now was the weather. Zoe looked so pretty today. How often did Josh go to her house? Had he just gone to return a book or was that an excuse to see Zoe again? After all, they apparently had been friends for quite a while.

Tracy flushed with shame at the stab of jealousy that flooded her heart. But Zoe was bent away from her pulling on a new boot so she didn't notice.

Now that she had gotten to know her a bit, Tracy really liked Zoe. She told herself it was perfectly reasonable that a boy who lived a half block down from Zoe would visit her brother Brett from time to time. Tracy assumed they had some interests in common, although what a geek like Josh could have in common with a jock like Brett eluded her.

"Do you want to ride with us again after school?" Zoe asked absentmindedly, admiring her new very feminine faux suede boots. "It's too cold to walk."

"Uh, sure," Tracy responded automatically.

It was true that the weather had turned bitterly cold over the weekend. Spring weather was so fickle in their part of the state. Why not take a ride when you could, Tracy thought? Then she wondered if it would be uncomfortable to be in the car with both Josh and Zoe if he was *interested* in her.

Tracy could understand that a geek like Josh might have liked Zoe, who was obviously smart, as a pal before her weekend transformation—even when she had seemed so awkward and had worn her older brother's cast-off clothes. But now the new Zoe was suddenly so pretty and confidently feminine. She even walked differently in her new boots. So now Josh might be doubly interested in her.

Zoe muttered something about seeing her after school and left to head for her next class. Tracy didn't really catch what Zoe had said because she was too busy wrestling with her emotions—ashamed of her jealousy, telling herself she was being silly, but at the same time resenting the familiarity Josh seemed to have with Zoe and her brother Brett.

You are not being nice, Tracy admonished herself. After all, she had no claim on Josh, and she should be glad if a boy like Josh found her new friend Zoe attractive.

That's what she told herself. But it didn't help. The truth was, she was jealous.

140

31

Zoe waved Tracy over as she crossed the quad after school. "There's Josh," she said, nodding toward the jalopy pulling around from the parking lot to the curb in front of the school.

The girls hurried forward together.

"So whatever happened to Charlie today?" Zoe asked Josh as she opened the car door to slide into the front seat.

Tracy was startled. Why on earth would Zoe be asking Josh that? After all, *she* was Charlie's closest friend, and she didn't know where Charlie was or what was going on. Sharon or Wendy would seem more likely than Josh, of all people, to know the scoop on Charlie. But Tracy hadn't seen them all day. In fact, she suspected the Sharon/Wendy duo were somehow responsible for Charlie's disappearing act.

"She went home at the beginning of second period," Josh answered casually. "Said she wasn't feeling well."

Now how did he know that, Tracy huffed to herself. After all, Josh was not in any of Charlie's classes.

"I'm not surprised," Zoe said sympathetically.

What was going on, Tracy thought sullenly. Both Josh and Zoe were acting as if they had inside information on Charlie and *she herself, Charlie's best friend ever since third grade,* hadn't a clue.

"Uh, what are you guys talking about?" Tracy snorted, sliding across the back seat and fastening her seat belt.

"She told the nurse she felt flu-ish," Josh said, "but I'll bet it was just the after effects of the party."

"It sure is a good thing she left early," Zoe added kindly.

"What—how do you know she left early?" Tracy snapped. "And what after effects? *After effects* from what?"

"Oh, the booze and probably the edibles," Josh answered, glancing briefly over his shoulder at Tracy as he put the car into gear.

"Wait a minute," Tracy said sharply. "What is this? The gossip of the day in all the halls? I didn't hear anything."

Zoe turned her head around, frowning with concern. "Oh no, no one else knows. When Josh stopped by to drop off Brett's book Friday night, he said he couldn't stay because he was driving Charlie home. That's all."

"She was really shaken up, poor kid," Josh added in an avuncular tone.

Huh, like you're a ton older than we are, Mr. Smart Guy, Tracy snorted inwardly. Geesh, she'd thought Josh was so neat and now he was acting like—like— Well, like he was all-wise and mature, as if he wasn't just one year ahead of them in school.

No one spoke for a few minutes as Josh maneuvered out of the tangle of parent's cars outside the four-year high school. But at the first stoplight, Tracy's curiosity got the better of her pride. Even though she was afraid her questions would make her sound naive or ignorant, she just had to know what they were talking about.

"Okay, guys. What did you mean about booze and food at the party? And how did you get mixed up with Charlie, Josh? *You* weren't at the party, were you?" Tracy asked.

"Ha, no! Those guys wouldn't want me at one of their parties. Not even Deke—not when he's with his drug buddies. And even if he did, I wouldn't go," Josh laughed.

"For sure," Zoe echoed. "Brett says the same thing."

"So what was the deal with the booze?" Tracy pushed.

"Charlie said some of the kids were drinking. Some of the girls got a little drunk, and the boys were rowdy and aggressive."

Tracy wasn't sure what that meant exactly but it sounded unpleasant at best, or even scary.

"Were they smoking pot?" she asked in a small voice.

"I don't know," Josh said. "I didn't want to ask Charlie a lot of questions. She looked pretty unhappy. She just walked the two blocks from Deke's house to mine and knocked on the door and asked me for a ride home. So of course I took her. I stopped on the way to return the book I'd borrowed from Brett since I'd promised to get it back to him Friday evening and I wasn't sure how long I'd have to stay with Charlie. I was worried about her. I wasn't sure she was going to be okay."

"What do you mean?" Tracy followed up with alarm.

"Well, she was pretty wobbly. She said she'd only eaten half a cookie but she felt awful. She said no one was home—her parents were out of town and she didn't know where her older sister was. I wasn't sure I should leave her alone. Actually, I was planning to call and ask if your Mom could help if she seemed really sick, but when she got home she said she felt better and she just wanted to take a shower and go to bed. So I just dropped her off."

"Maybe she just needed some food," Zoe said.

"Maybe," Josh shrugged. "But I'm afraid it was the food that made her sick."

"The cookie?" Tracy scoffed. "It wasn't like she ate spoiled seafood salad or something."

"The cookie was probably an edible," Josh replied.

"An edible?" Tracy echoed. "What do you mean?"

"You know, like the brownies," Josh answered, pulling around a car stopped to pick up a boy with a trumpet case.

Tracy and Zoe exchanged puzzled glances.

"Josh," Zoe sighed, rolling her eyes. "What kind of brownies or cookies make you sick?"

Josh looked startled, as if he was surprised that they didn't understand. "Brownies or cookies with pot, of course. Marijuana."

"Oh, I've heard of that, sort of," Tracy fibbed lightly. "But—like, what exactly does that mean?"

"You can buy pre-packaged brownies or cookies with marijuana in them. Or bake them yourself, I guess," Josh answered.

"Like how?" Tracy asked.

"Uh, I don't know exactly," Josh replied. "Maybe with shredded marijuana leaves or powder, I guess."

"So, is that real bad?" Zoe pressed.

"Yeah, it can be. In fact, I was reading statistics the other day about the increase in emergency room visits for teens because they'd consumed edibles with pot," he said.

143

Hmm, yeah—he'd been reading statistics. Now that sounded like the Josh she knew, Tracy thought wryly.

"But pot is illegal," Zoe objected. "So how are kids getting it for parties?"

"It's illegal in *this* state, but in more and more states it's legal for both medical and recreational purposes. So kids have their cousins or friends in those states get it for them, or they visit and buy the pot products. The article I was reading said that increases in marijuana-related ER visits, traffic deaths and even pet poisonings have skyrocketed in the studied state almost sixty percent in a two-year period. But emergency visits for out-of-state visitors to medical marijuana states have gone up twice that much."

"But—but isn't marijuana tightly controlled in states where it's legal?" Tracy objected.

"Not according to what I read. One article I googled quoted a doctor who said the marijuana industry is 'subject to minimal regulation,' as he put it. Even for medicinal marijuana, apparently there is little guarantee of the accuracy of THC levels published on packaging at dispensaries. And if edibles are baked at home, it's anybody's guess what the THC levels are."

"So, what's the deal about THC levels?" Zoe asked.

"The marijuana grown today is much more potent than what was grown in our grandparent's day—or even our parent's youth," Josh explained. "That means as much as four times higher THC levels."

"What is THC anyway?" Zoe persisted.

"It's the psychoactive component of pot," Josh said. "It's Tetrahydrocannabinol."

Geesh, that's Josh, Tracy thought. *I could never remember that name.*

"That sounds like cannibidiol," Zoe mused.

"Canna-what?" Tracy sputtered.

"Cannabidiol. But actually, cannibidiol doesn't have THC," Josh countered. "Or it has a different kind, or something."

"Huh?" Tracy and Zoe said together.

Josh sighed. "See, the THC in regular marijuana is a hallucinogen, meaning it can produce a high—euphoria—or even hallucinations. But cannibidiol is a specific component of the marijuana plant. Cannibidiol (CBD oil) modulates the psychoactive

144

effects of the THC in it because it fits into CB1—a protein receptor in the brain and central nervous system—at a different place from where regular THC docks in CB1. It's complicated, eh?"

"Yeah," Tracy sniffed, shaking her head. Sometimes Josh was impossible to follow. "Let's get back to Charlie. You said she ate half a cookie?"

"Yeah, she swore that's all she ate and she didn't drink anything but a Pepsi," Josh said. "She opened the can herself—the Pepsi can—so it wasn't adulterated with anything. So it must have been the cookie."

"You mean the cookie must have had marijuana in it?" Zoe added.

"Exactly."

"But just half of one cookie? Come on, how much pot could be in that?" Tracy objected.

"I don't have any idea," Josh answered. "All I know is, Charlie was a mess. She was really upset and kind of shaky."

"Poor girl," Zoe breathed.

Tracy wanted to keep asking questions but she didn't want her friends to think she was a total ignoramus. Like what CBD oil was used for, if it had any medical benefits, or if using it was risky— just another way to push legalization of marijuana? But she was also distracted by something poking at the edge of her brain, some question she couldn't quite put her finger on.

Then she remembered what it was that was bothering her. How had Josh, who had no classes with Charlie, known she had gone home second period today when no one else seemed to know that? And how did he know what she had told the nurse?

32

"Here you go, Trace," Josh said, pulling to the curb in front of her house.

"Uh, yeah. Thanks for the ride," Tracy responded automatically. She was still distracted wondering how Josh suddenly knew so much about Charlie. She wanted to ask but was afraid it would look like she was cross-examining him, which is exactly what she did want to do.

"See you tomorrow," Zoe waved as the car pulled away.

Tracy felt her stomach tighten with anxiety as she watched her friends pull away. They *were* her friends, weren't they? There they went off together again, while she stood alone on the sidewalk. And her best friend—Charlie, *her best friend*—well, *they* seemed to know more about her at the moment than she did.

What was happening? She felt like each one she had felt was her special friend had banded with the others. And now they were deserting her, going off in their own new circle and leaving her out.

Turning, she saw Toby running down the sidewalk toward her. A cold wind spurred her to trudge on up to the front door. She had just stepped inside when Toby tromped in without wiping his boots and shucked them off by the hall bench.

"Toby!" Tracy snapped. "Pick up those wet boots and put them on the drip mat."

Toby looked up, startled by her harsh tone. "Okay, okay," he said wearily.

Tracy had expected a smart-alec reply. Her little brother's lack of fight took the steam out of her frustration. She had never seen him look so depressed.

"Oh, I'm sorry, Tobe," Tracy sighed. "You do need to put your boots on the mat, but I shouldn't have been so cross. Uh, how was school today?"

"Fine."

"No, *really*, Toby," Tracy said gently, tousling his hair as he dragged his book bag toward the kitchen. "How was school?"

"Pretty much the usual," he shrugged. Then he added with sudden explosiveness, "But if I have to talk to Jason now I just call him Jas since he says he's a girl named Jessica 'cuz Jaz sort-of sounds like Jess and then I don't get in trouble and I mumble it so they won't notice 'cuz I'm *not* gonna call him *Jessica!*"

Toby's outburst came out all in one breath.

"Hmm, pretty clever, Tobe." Tracy smiled fondly as she studied her little brother. "And how is that working?"

"It's *been* working," Toby sighed. "But today I got busted. Mr. Pullman came into the room and he said, 'What did you say, young man?' in a real mean tone. I pretended to have a sore throat and said *Jas* again, and then Mr. Pullman said, 'I want to hear you say *Jessica* loud and clear.'"

"Oh no!" Tracy cried, her eyes wide with concern. "What did you do?"

Toby sank into his chair, leaned forward and buried his head in his arms on the table. Tracy sat beside him and put her arm around his shoulders.

"Toby?" she said gently. "Tobe, what did you do then?"

"I wouldn't do it," he muttered, his voice muffled by his arms. "I just wouldn't do it."

"So..."

"So I had to go sit in the secretary's office for the last hour of school. And Mr. Pullman said he was going to talk to my parents."

"What do you think he's going to do?" Tracy asked.

"He'll probably give me a suspension," Toby said, hanging his head. Suddenly he looked up, his eyes twinkling. "Hey, maybe he'll kick me out of school. That'd be great!"

"But—but you have to go to school," Tracy objected.

"Maybe Mom can homeschool me," Toby answered. "I saw her looking on her computer about homeschool stuff. That'd be great. I wouldn't have to get up early or anything."

147

"How would Mom have the time to homeschool you when she's still taking classes and working two mornings a week at the senior clinic and—"

But Toby was no longer listening. He bounded out of his chair whistling and slid over to the refrigerator to find a snack. Tracy was glad to see that his depression had lifted, but she felt as if his worries had been transferred to her.

If her little brother was kicked out of school, how would her mother ever be able to handle another responsibility added to her schedule?

Tracy had the uneasy feeling that she would suddenly be forced to assume more responsibilities herself, just to keep the family going.

Well, why not? Her friends seemed to be getting along like gang busters without her, Tracy thought. She might just as well stay home like Cinderella and scrub floors while they went off to play together.

Tracy left Toby in the kitchen and went to her bedroom. She dropped her book bag beside her desk and hauled her laptop over to the bed. Sprawling across the top quilt, she brought up a search engine. She didn't want to expose more of her ignorance on the subject of marijuana and edibles. She could research it herself.

The first article she read shocked her. It was about a nine-year-old kid in New Mexico. Her parents had medical marijuana in the form of gummy bears. The girl thought the gummy bears were regular candies, and she took some to school to share. Three children each had one gummy bear. They felt sick, dizzy and nauseous. The fourth child had three or four candies and passed out on the floor.

The problem, it turned out, was that eating a marijuana gummy bear may give you two to 100 times more THC than smoking a joint would.

Tracy was disappointed that the article didn't give much detail about the long-term effects of such a potent dose of THC. Especially she wanted to know how to tell if something was a regular candy or was laced with THC.

Another article on the net talked about a mom who got a call from the emergency room. Her seventeen-year-old son had been admitted for an overdose. The mother was in shock—no way her son, a straight-A student, would experiment with drugs! In fact, he'd just written college-application essays about the dangers of drugs and drinking. But he was in the emergency room. What was going on?

It turned out the boy had eaten half a cookie at a high school football game. An hour or so after he ate the half cookie, the boy began uncontrollable vomiting. The article—again frustratingly—didn't give a lot of detail about what happened to the kid, except to say that someone called the paramedics and he was rushed to the ER, hooked up to heart monitors, and so on.

The article kept referring to the boy's pre-frontal cortex not being fully developed. What did that mean, and what did that have to do with anything?

Well, the kid survived anyway. And since he had good grades and hadn't been in trouble before, the high school principle didn't give him a suspension. Apparently a suspension in high school could go in your permanent record and affect college admittance. But the thing was—

Tracy's thought was interrupted by a rapid knocking on the front door. *Now who could that be,* Tracy wondered. Nate had his own key, as did her mom, of course. But neither of them would be home yet. *Probably that nosey Mrs. Blake,* Tracy figured, *come to find out bits of gossip about Toby's problem at school today.*

Annoyed, she pulled herself off the bed and shuffled down the hall, muttering, "Hold your horses!" as the knocking repeated.

Just before she unlocked the door it occurred to her that it might be Mr. Pullman.

If it was, she wouldn't open the door.

33

Tracy pressed her eye up against the peephole and gasped. Another eyeball was right up against the glass from the outside, trying to look the wrong way into the house. An eye with dark black lashes.

"Charlie!" Tracy exclaimed, pulling the door open. "Where have you been? Why didn't you answer my calls or texts? I've been calling and calling."

Charlie sort of fell through the door and pushed it closed behind her. "Oh, Trace," she wailed. "It's been awful."

"What's been awful? What happened?" Tracy asked.

Suddenly Charlie quieted and looked around cautiously. "Nothing. Nothing happened," she said defensively.

"Uh, okay," Tracy began. "But—"

"Who's home?" Charlie whispered. "Can we go to your room?"

"Uh, sure." Mystified, Tracy led the way.

As Tracy was closing the door to her bedroom she noticed with concern that Charlie was trembling.

"Hey, hey," Tracy said comfortingly. "Here, sit down and tell me what's going on."

The girls sat on the rug and leaned back against the bed.

"It was awful," Charlie sniffed. "I should have listened to you."

"What was awful, Char?" Tracy prompted softly. "Why didn't you call me?"

"I couldn't. I couldn't find my phone."

Oh yeah, Tracy remembered. The Smeldans didn't have a landline. Charlie, her parents and her older sister all had their own cell phones, but their house didn't have a landline connected to the phone company anymore. A lot of people didn't have landlines anymore. Tracy's house still had one—something to do with her dad's job—but more and more people only had their cells. So if Charlie was home alone and had lost her phone, she'd have no way to call.

"When did you lose it?" Tracy asked.

"I don't know. At the party, I guess." Charlie started crying softly. "Oh Trace, you were right. I never should have gone."

"There, there," Tracy murmured, slipping her arm around her friend's shoulders. "It's all right."

"But it wasn't all right. It was awful!"

"Charlie, *what* was awful?" Tracy's frustration was undercutting her sympathy. "Was it the cookie?"

Charlie looked up in surprise and stopped crying, dabbing her eyes with the back of her hand. "How did you know about the cookie?" she sniffed.

"Josh said that—" Tracy began.

"Josh!" Charlie flared. "Has he been gossiping about me?"

"No, no," Tracy soothed. "No, Josh hasn't said anything. Except you didn't turn up in the band room at lunch and I was worried in the car on the way home so he said you'd only eaten half a cookie."

Now Charlie looked confused. "Josh took you home from school?"

Suddenly Tracy realized how much had happened—how much had changed—since Thursday afternoon. Of course, Charlie had no idea about any of that. It was just too much to catch her up on right now, especially with the whole Zoe saga.

"Yeah, it was too cold to walk," Tracy shrugged evasively. "But start from the beginning, Charlie. Tell me what happened Friday night."

Charlie slid back closer to the bed, sitting up straighter. "Okay, here it is," she sighed. "We went to Deke's house—you know, Sharon and Wendy and her boyfriend Alex and Pete and I, and there were a bunch of other kids already there. Most of them older, like Deke's age."

"Nobody was smoking pot," she continued. "I was glad to see that. But there was some drinking. Not that much, you know," Charlie added quickly, "just some beers."

"Mmmm," Tracy murmured encouragingly. She was thinking what her folks would say about kids drinking *just a few beers*. Parental explosion, to put it mildly.

"So anyway, there were some plates of cookies. There was music and we danced a little and talked. Then some of the girls started getting really silly."

"I'd eaten part of a cookie when I first got there but I didn't really like the taste so I didn't finish it. The guys were acting all macho and a few of the girls got really drunk. I'd never been to a party like that before and it made me uncomfortable. But then—"

Charlie stopped talking and just looked down at the rug.

"Charlie! Don't leave me in suspense," Tracy sighed. "What happened then?"

"Well, it wasn't just Pete," Charlie grimaced. "It was all the guys. They started getting, like really aggressive."

"What do you mean, aggressive? Were they fighting?" Tracy prompted.

"No, not that kind of aggressive," Charlie said in a squeaky voice. "Like, you know—aggressive," she shrugged.

"Oh, you mean like..." Tracy let the sentence hang, embarrassed to continue.

"Yeah. Like Pete kept trying to put his hand—you know— and I told him not to and pushed him away but he kept doing it so I got mad. And I was feeling really sick. So all of a sudden I just got up off the sofa and walked out of the room. I could hear Pete laughing and calling after me, something about the bathroom was at the end of the hall. But I went down the hall the other way and snuck out the front door. Then I realized I wasn't far from Josh's house and I knew he could drive now so I walked over there and he took me home."

There was a short break as Charlie let out a half sigh, half moan. Then, *"And that's all that happened!"* she suddenly exploded.

"Oka-ay," Tracy responded mildly, surprised at Charlie's flare of anger.

The two girls sat in silence for a few minutes, Charlie sniffing occasionally and Tracy twisting a lock of her hair nervously. She wondered how Charlie knew about Josh's driving license. Had Nate known when he got it? When did Josh get it? And why would Charlie know it when *she* didn't know it until Friday afternoon herself? More important, Tracy still had a lot of questions about the party but she didn't want to upset Charlie further by quizzing her right then.

"I walked over here Saturday afternoon but nobody was home," Charlie said.

Charlie's voice was so soft and mournful that Tracy felt her stomach twist with sympathy for her friend, even if she still didn't quite understand exactly what Charlie was so upset about.

But she held back from being open with her friend about last weekend. It was all so complicated. How could she tell Charlie that she'd been at the mall with her mom and Zoe Saturday afternoon while her dad and brothers were at some game or other? She was afraid that if she dropped the whole Zoe story on Charlie right now she'd—she'd— Well, Tracy wasn't sure what she'd do, but it seemed kind of cruel to tell Charlie that she and Zoe were having a great time trying on clothes while Charlie was alone, agonizing over her previous night's horrid experience.

"Uh, we were all out," Tracy said simply, evading the long explanations that she was afraid any other answer would entail. "Why did you come over?"

"Well, I wanted to talk to you, silly!" A sad smile lifted half of her mouth. "You are my closest friend, after all. Aren't you?"

"Since third grade," Tracy grinned, giving her friend a quick squeeze. "So what did you want to talk about?"

"Well, this." Charlie set her lips in an annoyed twist. "The party and stuff."

"Yeah...so how long were you at the party?" Tracy asked.

"I dunno," Charlie sighed. "Maybe an hour. It was dark when we got there because Sharon and Pete and all took forever to come pick me up. And when I left I was pretty wasted so I just don't know."

"What do you mean *wasted?*" Tracy repeated.

Charlie grimaced. "Bad word choice. I wasn't drunk. All I had to drink was a Pepsi or a Coke or something, straight from the can. But I felt kind of drunk in a way—dizzy and unfocused, and my stomach hurt really bad."

Charlie put the palms of her hands on her stomach and pushed in, grimacing and looking unfocused. "I wonder what happened to Sharon and Wendy at the party after I left."

"You haven't talked to them?"

"No, I can't find my phone, remember? And I left school at the start of second period today. My stomach was killing me, like bad nausea. The nurse couldn't get ahold of my parents. As *usual,*" she added bitterly. "I knew Josh had to leave about that time on Mondays to pick up his mom for physical therapy. But the nurse said she couldn't legally send me home with Josh. She couldn't send me home with non-family, and an underage driver at that. She did ask Josh if he'd be willing to stop at my house on his way home to see if my mom was there. But then my mom actually called and said she'd gotten the nurse's text on her phone and she'd pick me up. Of course, she took forever to get to school. I don't know where she was all that time. Shopping, probably. That's all she ever does, is shop."

Charlie's voice petered out at the end and ended in a little whimper. Tracy rubbed her arm sympathetically, doubly glad she hadn't mentioned what she and Zoe were doing Saturday afternoon. Feeling somewhat self-righteous, she convinced herself she was protecting Charlie's fragile emotional state by not telling her. But a sneaky little voice in her ear kept objecting that she was actually protecting *herself* from what she feared would be Charlie's angry reaction to her shopping.

But at least one mystery was finally solved, Tracy thought. Now she knew how Josh knew that Charlie had gone home second period. It still irked her that her friends seemed to know a lot more about each other's activities and whereabouts than she did, when she had thought each of them was her private friend.

Maybe there was no such thing as a friend of her own. A friend who was closer to her than others. It was beginning to look that way—at least for her. In fact, although Charlie kept saying she was her best friend, she seemed to have more to do with other kids than with Tracy.

Now it wasn't just jealousy souring her heart. A little worm of resentment was wriggling around, stirring up discontent.

Tracy knew her feelings were petty and immature. To top it off, it occurred to her that worrying about when one of her friends knew that another of her friends had gotten a driver's license might not be as significant as Charlie's regrets about what went on at the party!

Tracy scolded herself inwardly and tried to put herself in Charlie's shoes. But again, it wasn't working. She was jealous of the friendships both Charlie and Zoe seemed to have with Josh.

Huh, Tracy mocked herself inwardly, *what's so great about Josh?*

But even as she thought it, she pictured the freckles on his cheeks, how he held his phone at a funny angle as he worked magic with apps and data searches, and how he always bumped into the edge of the table when he came into the McKenzie family kitchen. Every. Single. Time.

Why had she ever gotten a crush on such a nerdy guy? But there it was. He was—well, he was *Josh.*

34

"Why did you say it like that?" Charlie looked annoyed.

The girls had moved to the kitchen table when they heard Toby and Flounders bang out the back door into the yard. Tracy set out milk and cookies and pushed the plate across the table.

"Why did I say what like what?" Tracy answered, blanking on Charlie's meaning.

"Have a cookie—like it had some special meaning," Charlie grumped.

"Oh come on, girl. I didn't mean anything. Just—have a cookie."

"Sorry, Trace. It's just—it's just—" Charlie bit her lip. "Look, I don't know what was in those cookies, but kids were doing things, you know, that I never thought I'd see there or I'd never have gone to that party. And this morning I overheard something in the nurse's office about one kid in the hospital. I'm afraid there's gonna be worse things that come out..."

"You mean, like someone could die?" Tracy asked, her eyes wide.

"No. Maybe *wish* she were dead," Charlie answered.

"Oh. *Oh,*" Tracy echoed with a feeling of foreboding.

"Yeah," Charlie responded with a significant look. "And when they find out I was there, they'll tar me with the same feather, even though I didn't do that stuff."

Tracy was too embarrassed to ask Charlie exactly what she meant. But suddenly she sat back in her chair. "Wait—you said you didn't know what was in the cookies?"

"No. Why? Do you?"

"I think so."

Tracy brought Charlie up-to-date on some of the information she'd learned about edibles, conveniently neglecting to mention Zoe at any point, or even Josh.

"Gee, I never heard Sharon or Wendy talk about anything like this," Charlie muttered. "I don't think they had any more clue than I did. How did you—?"

"Search engine," Tracy blurted, turning a little red at the half-truth.

"Oh, yeah," Charlie sighed, staring unfocused at the cookie plate. Despite her earlier reluctance, she reached absentmindedly for a cookie. The girls munched automatically.

Charlie broke the silence. "You asked if the girl in the hospital might die? Could that happen?"

"Naw, I don't think so," Tracy reassured her. "Wait, I'll bring my computer here."

Tracy was back at the table in a minute and opened a search box, typing in *marijuana edibles risks*. The screen flicked to a long list of articles.

"Here look, I remember this article talked about one kid who did die, but it was because he jumped out of a twelve-story window," Tracy mumbled, scrolling on down. "The doctors called it marijuana intoxication, like being drunk."

"You mean like being so-out-of-his-head drunk he didn't know what he was doing?" Charlie asked.

"Yeah," Tracy shrugged. "Or he knew he was jumping out of a twelve-story window but thought he had super powers or something. But most of the articles talked about nausea and stomach pains like you had, or have, and—*Wait, now I get it,*" Tracy exclaimed.

"Get what?" Charlie sighed.

"It's the frontal cortex angle. Some articles talked about how in teenagers—maybe even up to age 25, my mom told me—the frontal cortex is immature. That's the part that is supposed to help us make decisions, weighing the risks versus benefits of an action before deciding to do something. So if the frontal cortex is fuzzed by marijuana or alcohol intoxication, a kid can't make a rational assessment of the risks of an action. He might think he can ace jumping out of a twelve-story window."

157

Charlie looked bleary-eyed. "Okay, fine. There were no twelve-story windows at Deke's house. Just two-story. You could break a leg maybe but—"

"But that's the thing. Whatever happened at that party, maybe the kids—or especially the girls—wouldn't have done it if their frontal cortexes had been firing properly—if they'd been thinking straight."

"Ah, I get it," Charlie nodded. "The girls wouldn't have let the guys get out of line if their brains hadn't been fuzzed by alcohol or marijuana?"

"Right," Tracy came back. "But it's worse than that. My mom told me that teenage brains can be permanently damaged by marijuana use. Meaning even after a kid is no longer 'intoxicated' their decision-making process might not work very well. So they might keep on making poor choices."

"Gee, that's scary," Charlie responded.

"Some of the articles even talk about an 8 point drop in IQ," Tracy added.

"Oh-oh, the M's didn't have the highest IQ's before the party," Charlie grimaced wryly.

"The M's were there?" Tracy asked, her eyebrows shooting up with surprise.

"Yeah, with two guys I'd never seen before. A lot of girls were with older guys. Hey, even Sondra was there."

Charlie's voice trailed off. Her last statements did not sound judgmental. She sounded worried about the girls. Tracy pondered that for a moment, thinking maybe her friend had more depth than she had given her credit for in a while.

After another gloomy silence, Charlie sighed, "We'll find out soon enough, I suppose, what happened to the other kids at the party. I just hope the fact that I left early means I won't be featured in the gossip. But show me more stuff on your computer about edibles, okay?"

Tracy slid the computer closer to Charlie so they could both see the screen. "Look, it says here that edibles have a lot higher dose of THC, the psychoactive ingredient in marijuana, than old-fashioned pot. But the high comes on much slower than from *smoking pot,* so kids don't realize how much THC they've ingested. That's how they overdose."

"Yeah," Charlie pointed. "Right there it gives an example of a high school kid who ate half a cookie, but didn't feel anything for an hour. That's exactly what happened to me!"

"Good thing you didn't like the taste of the cookie because that kid ate the rest and landed in the ER. Because when the high finally hits, it's a lot stronger than from just smoking pot."

"And there—no, scroll back up a bit—there! See that? It says a big reason kids are switching to edibles—in addition to the stronger high—is that you can't *smell* the pot in edibles." Charlie leaned back in her chair and grinned. "I wondered why no one was smoking. Deke had figured out how to get away with having pot at his party but his parents wouldn't smell anything when they came home."

"His parents weren't even there?"

"No, Deke said his dad has really been coming down on him, trying to make sure he stays away from drugs. But his parents went away for the weekend, something about a marriage counseling seminar. His mom's been talking divorce but his dad is pushing her to stay."

"What a mess," Tracy muttered, finding it hard to even conceive of her parents abandoning her brothers and herself for the weekend. Or talking about divorce. She scrolled on down, skim reading. "Ah, here it is. Josh said this. Or was it my mom? Anyway, look—it says that about 17% of teens who try marijuana for the first time become addicted."

"Seventeen percent! That's—gee, there were about forty-five or fifty kids at the party—"

"What? How big is his house?" Tracy interrupted.

"About twice as big as yours," Charlie answered absently. "Pete said Deke kept the party small so they wouldn't get in trouble."

"Small?" Tracy scoffed. "That's a small party?"

"Shush, I'm trying to figure something out here. Fifty divided by seventeen is... Oh, Trace," Charlie broke off, wailing. "I couldn't do math in my head *before* I ate that cookie! Help me out here!"

"You don't want to divide here. For the percentage, you need to *multiply* fifty by 17%, or 0.17."

"Oh yeah, I always forget," Charlie groaned. "So..."

"So eight and a half."

"So eight, you mean."

"Huh? What are you talking about, Char?"

"You can't have half a kid. Say fifty kids at the party. If seventeen percent try the marijuana and get addicted, that's eight kids." Charlie broke off as a look of horror crossed her face. "Oh Trace, *what if I'm addicted?*"

"Oh relax, Char," Tracy comforted her. "I don't think you get addicted on the first try. I think it just means some people keep trying it and they get addicted."

Charlie looked sceptical but relieved. Tracy hoped her answer was right. She really had no idea but she had to say something to calm her friend down.

"It also says that currently in the US about 3300 teens try marijuana for the first time *every day*. That would mean—"

"—over five hundred kids—"

"—getting addicted to pot every day!" Charlie finished.

As the girls sat in stunned silence, sobered by the numbers, the back door slammed open and Flounders shot in. Toby followed, almost tripping over Flounders as he zigged and zagged in front of the boy.

"Gee, what's the matter with you guys?" Toby grunted. "You look like you swallowed a porcupine."

The girls glared at him for an instant, locked eyes with each other, then burst into laughter at this typical Toby-ism. You never knew what Toby would come up with next. Mr. McKenzie said Toby must have inherited an old-time cowboy gene from his great-uncle Zachary. The laughter broke the girls' tension.

"Hmm, something like that, Tobe," Tracy said, pushing the cookie plate toward him across the table.

At that moment the front door opened, more quietly than Toby had opened the back door, but with its usual scraping sound. Rapid footsteps and the sound of a book bag being dropped advertised the progress of someone down the hall. Nate, of course.

"Charlie! I didn't expect to see you here," Nate said as he entered the kitchen.

Charlie had an almost frightened look on her face as she answered. "Yeah, I—I just stopped by to see Tracy," she stuttered.

Nate grinned and punched Toby lightly on the shoulder as he passed the girls on the way to the glasses cupboard. "Well, don't eat all the cookies," he said casually. "Leave some for me."

A split second later a puzzled Nate turned to see why the girls had dissolved into hysterical giggles.

"Crazy girls!" he muttered softly, getting a glass of juice. But he was grinning as he shooed Tracy out of his usual chair.

The girls decamped to the hallway where Charlie grabbed her jacket and said she'd better get on home. Tracy objected that her mom would be home soon and could give her a ride, but Charlie insisted a fast walk in the cold would help to clean the crud out of her system. So Tracy gave her a hug and saw her to the front door.

"You keep your chin up, Charlie. It's all going to be all right. You'll see. You left that party in time," she said encouragingly.

Charlie's grin was a bit lopsided but at least she was smiling as she started off at a brisk pace. Tracy stood watching her until the cold made her shiver. She shut the door and leaned against it.

Well, now she knew what was going on at that party. By tomorrow half the school would know as the magic of cell phones and gossipy tweets and texts zipped and zapped across the ether. For the sake of the kids who had been there she hoped there weren't pictures. But somebody would inevitably post some. Maybe even videos. Things the kids who had been there might hope no one would ever see.

Suddenly Tracy's problems and her silly jealousies seemed very small. She just hoped—for Charlie's sake and all the other kids at that party—that any further news would not include juicy tidbits that could stain young lives forever.

35

As soon as Charlie left, Tracy went to her room. She picked up her cell and stood in the middle of her rug like a statue. Now what? What she really wanted to do was call Zoe and tell her everything Charlie had said. Zoe, the girl whom she had always tried to avoid before three days ago! But now she felt that her new friend Zoe was the one person she could trust to listen and care about her old friend Charlie. Other than her mom, of course. How weird was that?

But at the same time, she didn't feel free to do that. Calling Zoe would be gossiping big time, maybe just being catty. On the other hand, Tracy tried to justify the idea of sharing this new information with Zoe because she knew Zoe already knew some things about the party and had expressed sincere concern for Charlie.

That was also ironic, she snorted to herself. Here Charlie was supposed to be her best friend but the girl that Charlie had always dismissed as a loser was expressing more compassion for her than Tracy honestly had.

But the crux of the matter was that while Charlie hadn't sworn her to secrecy before spilling the beans about the party, Tracy knew that Charlie probably assumed their conversation would be confidential. After all, they'd been guarding each other's secrets since they were eight years old.

Until this last year. This last year their friendship had consisted more of Charlie dropping two-minute monologues about the latest news from Sharon and Wendy before waving off Tracy—the person she still insisted on calling her best friend—to run off with her new crowd.

Oh whatever, Tracy thought. After all, she was pretty sure that Zoe didn't even have her own cell phone. The number Zoe had given Mrs. McKenzie seemed to be for a cell shared with her younger brothers, like a household cell. She knew from something Josh said once that Brett, at least, had his own cell phone, but he was older and a VIP on the football team.

Tracy couldn't imagine having to share a phone with either of her brothers. Well, Toby didn't have his own, which he thought was cruel and unusual punishment since most of the kids in his class had their own cell phones. But Mr. Pullman didn't allow the kids to bring their cells to school before fourth grade anyway, which meant that in the second grade Toby didn't stand out as weird for that reason at least. Her parents just said he was too young to have his own phone, and after all they did still have a landline.

In times past Tracy would have called Charlie to share news tidbits about other kids at school, but of course not only did Charlie not know where her phone was at the moment, Tracy couldn't pass on to *Charlie* gossip that Charlie had shared with her in the first place!

With a sigh Tracy set down her phone, pulled out her books, positioned her laptop and began her homework.

It was her turn to put the dishes in the dishwasher after dinner that night. She thought it might give her a chance to talk with her mom after her brothers and dad left the kitchen. But her mom started talking about an exam she had coming up in her nursing classes. She said she'd really have to hit the books tonight.

"Okay, I've got this, Mom," Tracy said. "You go ahead and study."

She had finished the kitchen clean-up and was heading down the hall when she heard a familiar tattoo on the front door. Josh? What was he doing here, she wondered. It was Monday night, not Tuesday. And why did he sometimes ring the bell, sometimes knock like that?

When she opened the door, she just stood there looking at him. What now?

"Uh, Trace—you gonna let me in?" Josh grinned. "It's cold out here."

"Oh, uh—yeah," she answered brilliantly, stepping to the side so he could pass.

"You like my little friends?" Josh asked with a twinkle in his eye. He held up two large plastic dinosaurs, each one a full ten inches tall.

"Sure. Did you come to play?" Tracy deadpanned.

"Yep," Josh shot back. "Where're Tobe and Nate?"

A muffled roar from the back of the house provided a clue. "Check the boy's rooms," Tracy said, waving Josh on down the hall.

Shaking her head and grinning, Tracy sauntered into the living room. Her dad sat in his usual recliner with his laptop, frowning slightly as he worked the keyboard. Her mom sat cross-legged on the sofa, books spilling across the cushions on both sides of her, her laptop balanced on a large throw pillow across her knees. Both of them were deep into whatever they were doing. Tracy didn't want to disturb them.

She didn't have that much homework to finish and she felt too restless to read, so when she heard strange sounds coming from Toby's room, her curiosity got the better of her. She knocked on his bedroom door.

"Enter if you dare."

Toby sounded as if he were talking underwater. When she opened the door, she saw why. Her little brother was faced away from her, on his knees with his feet toward the door. His rump was high in the air but one ear was pressed to the rug. He was peering into a cave-like opening in a twenty-inch tall paper-mâché hill. Nate and Josh were on the far side of the room, sawing the sides of an old dishwasher cardboard packing box into jagged peaks.

"What's going on in here?" Tracy asked, stepping into the room.

Suddenly Toby's hand shot forward into the cave. Then he whirled and stood, simultaneously roaring and shoving one of Josh's plastic dinosaurs in her face.

Despite herself, Tracy jumped. "Okay, Tobe—you got me," she laughed. "But what on earth?"

"We're making dino-land, Trace," Toby answered. He pulled a small plastic bin loaded with six- to eight-inch tall toy dinosaurs out from under his desk. "Josh brought his old *Stegosaurus* and *Spinosaurus* over for me to borrow, too. They're the giant dinos!"

164

"We should paint tropical-looking vegetation on these backdrops," Josh said, unfolding the heavy cardboard packing box.

Tracy saw that the boys had slit one corner of the box top-to-bottom so they could pull the sides out straight. Then they cut the top flaps off. They used a butcher knife to saw 'mountain peaks' into the top edge of the unfolded sides. The dino-land backdrop stood against the wall under the bedroom windows. Large rocks placed on the bottom flaps kept the cardboard from falling over.

"Where did you get the rocks?" Tracy asked idly.

"Stones," Josh muttered absently.

"Boulders!" Toby interjected with glee. "Huge pre-historic boulders!"

"Geesh, what's the difference between a rock, a stone and a boulder anyway?" Tracy muttered, a tad annoyed.

"Technically, stones are smooth and rounded," Nate said. "But rocks can be jagged."

"So what's a boulder?" Tracy asked.

"Some people say boulders can be as small as a housecat," Josh replied. "Others say they have to be bigger than a man."

"A boulder is a large, smooth detached rock. Usually too big for a person to move easily, sis," Nate responded.

"Sounds like an exact science to me," Tracy chuckled sarcastically. "Where do you guys learn all this stuff?"

"Remember Mr. Thompkins, the boys camp leader two years back? He was a geology buff," Nate answered.

"How would I know Mr. Thompkins? I was over at girls camp," Tracy shot back.

"I saw you," Josh interjected quietly.

"Where?" Tracy puzzled. "I never went over to the boys camp side. And you aren't in our church."

"But Pine Crest Summer Camp is for kids from a lot of the churches around here. I saw you at the campfire service the last night of camp," Josh said. "You know, with all the kids together."

"Oh yeah, that's right." Tracy replied as if disinterested, but her heart skipped a beat. Josh said he *remembered her there from two years ago*. Well, maybe Nate had pointed out that she was his sister.

Or maybe Josh had *noticed* her.

165

36

Tracy came out of her reverie to tune in to a new argument.

"You can't put a superhero in with dinosaurs, Tobe," Nate scoffed.

"Why not? Noah was kind of a super hero," he countered. "Maybe this is how Noah really dressed."

"Yeah," Josh chimed in, picking up another action figure from Toby's desk. "Let's put this guy by the *Triceratops*."

"Well if that's your attitude," Nate gave in with a chuckle, "here, is this Bat Girl or Japheth's wife?"

"You guys are all crazy," Tracy muttered. "You're only like two hundred million years off."

"Says who?" Toby challenged.

"Look, lil bro," Tracy drawled, rolling her eyes. "I may not know the exact date the dinosaurs lived, but at least I know they were long gone before Noah."

"Well, our *school texts* say the dinosaurs died about sixty-some million years ago," Josh said quietly. "And they say man didn't appear until six million years ago—or maybe just twenty-five thousand years ago. It depends on which so-called 'early man' they're talking about. But I think Toby's on to something, Trace."

"You can't put dinosaurs with Noah!" Tracy scoffed. "Hmm, wasn't Noah about..."

"Twenty-five hundred years before Christ," Nate filled in. "Maybe 2500 or 2400 B.C."

"Okay, so see? That's way long after the dinosaurs disappeared. You're off by about sixty million years, Tobe," Tracy said with mock exaggerated sweetness.

166

"Back up a minute," Josh said calmly. "You're saying dinosaurs disappeared sixty million years ago as if that date was carved in stone. But it's not."

"Sure it is. *Exactly* in stone," Tracy insisted. "Like when they find dinosaur fossils in rocks from two hundred million to sixty million years ago, or in layers of sediment that are that old, then—"

"Who says the rocks or layers of sediment are that old?" Josh persisted in that ever-so-annoying logical voice.

"Well, the scientists—" Tracy spurted defensively.

"Not all the scientists," Nate contradicted her.

At a loss for words, Tracy glared at the three boys defensively. "So? Explain!" she challenged.

"A lot of scientists—"

"You mean like Christian school teachers, or professors at Christian colleges," Tracy scoffed. "Not real scientists, like research scientists."

"There are thousands of scientists, Christian *and* secular, who point out discrepancies with the so-called *deep time* dates of evolution," Nate answered. "It's not just the geologic evidence that doesn't fit. They can't explain problems with deep space background radiation, glacial ice cores and biological adaptation mechanisms, to name a few."

Tracy stared at her brother in amazement. She had no idea what he was talking about or where he had gotten those ideas.

"Think about the rock layers, Tracy," Josh added. "Say certain rock layers are dated two hundred million years old, so fossil dinosaur bones found in those rocks would prove that those dinosaurs lived two hundred million years ago. But those two hundred million year old fossils prove that the rock layer is two hundred million years old, right?"

"No, that's circular reasoning," Tracy snapped, spotting the trap.

"Exactly. But that's often how evolutionists date the layers—and the bones—and turn around and date other layers or rocks in relation to their first assigned dates," Josh finished.

"Yeah but—" Tracy began.

"Oh, *Little Peter Yeah-but*," Toby teased in a sing-song voice. When he was younger, the McKenzie family had used this twist on

Little Peter Rabbit to break him of the habit of starting all his sentences with *'yeah but.'* Now he was turning it back on his big sister.

"Ahem," she cleared her throat to signal her annoyance. *"As I was saying,"* she glared at her little brother, "all around the world there are rock layers, and they can be matched up, and the dating correlates with evolutionary ages dates that—"

"That's just evidence of a world-wide event," Nate cut in. "Maybe a global flood—like Noah's flood, right? But the evolution dates put on global rock layers are speculation."

"Top scientists," Josh stated unperturbably, "like research scientists and university professors know that old ideas of Darwinian evolution don't work. Most secular scientists have scrapped even Neo-Darwinism as being totally unrealistic, but more recent theories of evolution still depend on so-called deep time."

"Wait—we had to memorize all those evolutionary timelines," Tracy protested, irritated by Josh's didactic manner. "The Paleozoic Era starts with the Cambrian Period, the Mesozoic has the Triassic, Jurassic, and Cretaceous Periods, et cetera. Why would they keep teaching all that if they know it's wrong?"

"Top research scientists," Josh pointed out, "openly discuss the problems of various evolutionary assumptions in biology, geology, astronomy and so on. They write critical articles in their professional journals—"

"One evolutionary scientist criticizing or debunking the theory of another evolutionary scientist," Nate interjected.

"—but it doesn't trickle down to popular teaching," Josh continued, ignoring Nate's interruption.

"Why not?" Tracy asked, puzzled.

"The majority of research scientists are secular," Nate answered. "So they keep working to come up with a provable theory of evolution that does not include God."

"Oka-ay." Tracy didn't want to get into a Sunday school lesson, so she switched back to dinosaurs. "You're criticizing mainstream scientists, saying they don't have proof of evolution, but where's your proof that dinosaurs lived at the same time as man?"

Nate and Josh exchanged grins. Tracy didn't think that was a good sign. But Toby jumped in first.

"Remember the *behemoth* in Job?" he piped up. "The description sounds just like a *Brachiosaurus.*"

"Well, that doesn't prove anything. That could just be—" Tracy started to object.

"Wait, there's more," Toby interrupted. "Tell her about the paintings, Nate."

"The old bushmen in Africa did a lot of cave paintings, and they painted from real life, making realistic drawings of the animals they saw. In Zimbabwe—that's a country north of South Africa—explorers discovered cave paintings made by bushman who ruled the area from about 1500 B.C. until a few hundred years ago. The paintings show a realistic elephant and giraffe, and then they show an *Apatosaurus*—what we used to call a *Brontosaurus*—plain as day!"

"So you're saying these ancient bushmen actually saw an *Apatosaurus* as recently as 1500 B.C.? Or maybe even just a few centuries ago?" Tracy scoffed.

"Maybe they weren't the only ones to see dinosaurs in fairly recent times," Josh said quietly. "Do you know about the Ta Prohm temple in Cambodia?"

"The Ta-what?" Tracy replied irritably.

"The Ta Prohm temple in Cambodia. It's a Buddhist temple from the Middle Ages, about the twelfth century—

"So, like only 800 years or so ago, Trace," Toby interjected.

"Right," Josh continued. "Anyway, there are a lot of carvings on the stone walls of the temple—realistic carvings of birds and animals found in the area, like parrots, swans, monkeys, and water buffalo. But there's also a very clear carving of a *Stegosaurus*. And again, you have to ask the question, how did the Khmer—the people who live there in Cambodia—how did they know how to carve that realistic representation of a *Stegosaurus* if they hadn't seen one?"

"Well, how do we think we know what a Stegosaurus looked like?" Tracy objected.

"Paleontologists have reconstructed—" Josh began.

"Paleo-what?" Tracy interrupted.

"Paleontologists, sis," Nate filled in. "They're scientists that study fossils and try to figure out from the bone structure what the animals looked like."

169

"A lot of dinosaur bones started getting discovered in the 1800s," Josh added. "And paleontologists, with the help of people like biologists and forensic artists, came up with representations of what they think various dinosaurs looked like alive."

"Yeah, so?" Tracy challenged.

"So that's how we figured out what a *Stegosaurus* looked like," Nate said.

"But the people in Cambodia knew what a *Stegosaurus* looked like hundreds of years before that—because they saw 'em for real," Toby gloated.

"You only *think* they saw them," Tracy objected.

"How else could they have carved them?" Josh took it up. "The fossils hadn't even been found yet."

"But if the *Stegosaurus* lived only 800 years ago," Tracy said, rolling her eyes to emphasize her scepticism, "how come there aren't any around today?"

Josh shrugged. "Maybe disease wiped them out, or they were hunted to extinction, like the last Cambodian Javan rhino was in Vietnam in 2010. There are still Javan rhinos in Indonesia, but they are extinct now in Vietnam."

"A lot of species go extinct every year because of poachers or trophy hunters," Nate added.

"Whatever," Tracy yawned. She acted bored to cover up her irritation. "You guys can put Superman in the Ark for all I care. I have homework to do."

Tracy retreated to the hall and closed the door to Toby's room behind her. Geesh, it felt like her brothers had ganged up on her to make her look stupid in front of Josh. And she was thoroughly irritated by Josh's superior attitude. Really, he could be such a pain.

Why did she ever think Josh was special? He was just such a—such a—well, he was just a conceited nerd.

37

Tracy had left her cell on her desk. It was ringing as she walked into her room. Now she was surprised to see Charlie's number on the screen.

"Charlie, you found your phone," she said, picking up.

"Hi, Trace. No, I didn't find it," Charlie answered. "Sharon brought it by. She saw I'd left it at Deke's house so she took it with her when she left the party."

"Oh. Why didn't she bring it to you on Saturday?" Tracy asked.

"She couldn't. She was busy at the hospital and talking to the police," Charlie responded.

"The hospital and the police!" Tracy exclaimed. "What are you talking about?"

"Oh Trace, it's a long story. I've just now found it all out."

"Tell me what happened," Tracy urged. "Who ended up in the hospital?"

"Wendy did, for one." Charlie sounded very subdued. "Sharon said she was vomiting—just like we were reading about—and she had to be on IV's and everything. Wendy's parents were furious with Sharon so she didn't get to see her until late Saturday afternoon. But she's okay now, I guess. She went home on Sunday."

"Wow, that's awful," Tracy said. "Was Sharon sick?"

"No, she said she didn't eat anything. She got a little drunk, I guess, but she didn't eat. But three other kids ended up in the hospital, too—including Sondra."

171

"Oh my goodness, are they all right?" Tracy asked.

"I dunno. Sharon couldn't find out much about them. But she saw Sondra at the police station."

"The police station! What was Sharon doing at the police station?" Tracy had a sick feeling in the pit of her stomach.

"The police questioned a lot of the kids that were at the party," Charlie answered almost in a whisper. "I don't think any of the kids that were there were in school today. Well, I was for first period but then I went home."

"Did the police question you, Char?" Tracy whispered back, her eyes wide.

"No, don't even think that!" Charlie shot back. "I hope they miss my name. A lot of the kids didn't know me—only about a dozen of the kids were from our school. Sharon and Wendy didn't mention me. I think the M's were too drunk. And Sondra never pays any attention to me."

"What about Deke and Alex and Pete?" Tracy asked.

"Alex walked out early. He tried to get Wendy to leave with him but she refused. Anyway, he's clammed up. Deke and Pete are the ones in real trouble, Sharon says, because they're the ones who got the *edibles* and the beer. They're in trouble with the police. Their parents have hired lawyers. They've got bigger problems than ratting on anyone. And Sharon said that after I left Pete picked another girl out of the crowd and spent the rest of the party with her. I don't think he even remembers I exist," Charlie groused. "I don't know whether to hate him or be really glad about that."

"I'm voting for glad," Tracy said. "It's sure good you left that party early, Charlie."

"Yeah—uh, it's not just the beer and drugs, either," Charlie added hesitantly.

"What do you mean?" Tracy asked.

"A couple of the girls told the police how the boys acted. They're calling it sexual harassment. The police asked Sharon about it. That's how she found out."

"Oh, that's awful!" Tracy sighed.

"Trace, I don't want anything to do with any of those kids anymore. Honest, I'm just going to study and practice my clarinet and—and—"

"And hang out with me and Zoe," Tracy ended her sentence sympathetically.

"What?" Charlie exclaimed. "Zoe! What on earth are you talking about?"

Tracy sank down on the floor by her bed and rolled her eyes. Why did she have to go and let that slip out, and *now* of all times?

"Uh, well—it's a long story, Char," Tracy stalled.

But there was no putting Charlie off. Briefly she filled Charlie in on Zoe's conversation with her mom, conveniently omitting when they'd talked. Fortunately, Charlie was too focused on the disaster of the party to realize that the talk had been last Thursday, the exact time Tracy had said she couldn't go shopping with Charlie because she had company. Even more fortunate, Charlie didn't seem to remember Tracy's name-dropping the next morning—last Friday morning—at the locker before first period, when she said *Brett Hudson's sister* had been at her house the night before. Or if Charlie did remember, she probably thought Tracy had just made that up to razz her. Tracy completely omitted the part about the shopping trip with Zoe on Saturday. But she did refer to Zoe as a new friend. Then she waited for the explosion.

But Charlie just said "huh" and yawned. Tracy could hear her typing on her computer in the ensuing silence.

"Char?" Tracy asked tentatively. "What are you doing?"

"Internet search," Charlie answered enigmatically.

"On what?"

"What you were talking about. You know, that transgender stuff."

"Oh, I'm surprised you're interested in researching that, especially right now," Tracy said.

"Well, I am. Because now Sharon says that Wendy says— Oh, it's complicated. I'm really tired. Let's just talk tomorrow."

"Will you be at school?"

"Yes. Can I go to your house after school? We can't really talk in the lunch room about this stuff."

"Yes, of course," Tracy answered. "Just go to sleep and don't think about anything more tonight."

As she hung up, her mind was racing. The things Charlie had told her were so out of kilter from her own quiet uncomplicated life.

Or not so uncomplicated. Now Zoe expected to eat lunch with Tracy, and how was Charlie going to feel about that? And Tuesday night was when Josh came over to tutor her, although lately they'd spent most of the time just talking about whatever. And now here he was down the hall in her little brother's room on a Monday night. She seemed to be bumping into him a lot lately, but half of the time with Zoe or Charlie or her brothers in the middle of it.

Tracy sighed and put down her cell, her head spinning with a kaleidoscope of thoughts. A knock on the door brought her back to the present.

"Come in," she called softly.

Mrs. McKenzie opened the door and leaned against the door jamb. "I just wanted to let you know that Dad and I were talking about Josh."

"Josh?" Tracy echoed in surprise.

"Yes, hon. He's been a great help to you in math," her mother continued. "But you really don't need a tutor anymore. And Josh obviously doesn't need an excuse to come over," she laughed, as odd roars emanated from down the hall. "So we talked to him and he won't be tutoring you on Tuesday nights anymore."

Tracy was still absorbing that news when her mother continued.

"We're probably going to homeschool Toby for a while, so we need to cut back on expenses. I won't be able to work as many hours."

Tracy nodded, but her mind was racing. How many parts of her life were going to be upended by the crazy idea that boys were really girls or girls were really boys?

38

Tuesday morning the high school halls were a-swirl with rumors. Deke had been arrested. Deke had not been arrested. A girl had died. No one was seriously hurt. Someone had cocaine at the party. There were no drugs at the party. But all the rumors majored on hints of *conduct unbecoming* at the ill-fated party.

Tracy tried to tune it all out and concentrate on her classes. At noon she met Zoe and Charlie in the lunchroom. Zoe gave Charlie an encouraging smile. Charlie responded with a cautious half-smile. The three girls stayed on safe subjects, stilted chatter about homework and the weather. But all in all, Tracy breathed a sigh of relief. She thought it had gone fairly well.

But she hadn't thought ahead to after school. How was she going to work it when Josh and Zoe expected to give her a ride home but she had Charlie in tow? She figured it would be okay with Josh and Zoe, but how was Charlie going to feel about riding with them? Plus she felt bad to have invited *Charlie* over after school and not Zoe. That felt rude.

But the thing was, she couldn't talk with Charlie about the whole transgender thing with Zoe there. That would be impossibly awkward. It was all too tangled up for her to figure. Tracy kept pushing it out of her mind because that was easier than trying to figure out a way to handle all the sticky relationships. She'd never been good at that. She even hated having to be on committees. Politics was definitely not in her future.

But she got a reprieve, sort of. At least as far as the ride home went. She breathed a sigh of relief sixth period when she saw Charlie's text: *not after sch—see u tonite*. She didn't care what the explanation for the delay was. She felt like she'd dodged a bullet.

175

Neither Josh nor Zoe wanted to talk about the party in the car, which was fine with her. They spent the whole ride home from school talking about the rescued kittens. Zoe's younger brothers had chosen the kitten they wanted to keep as well as the mother cat.

Which reminded her, she didn't think Charlie had made the connection between Zoe and Brett yet. So much had happened that it just hadn't come up. Which was good, Tracy figured, because she would rather Charlie actually got to know Zoe a bit before she started trying to use her as a way to get to Brett.

Now that wasn't fair or kind, Tracy scolded herself. But on the other hand, based on Charlie's behavior this past year, it wasn't an unreasonable suspicion either. Still, Tracy was ashamed of herself for her cynical reaction. It seemed that lately she could think nothing but the worst of Charlie. Some friend she was turning out to be!

And what about Josh? Didn't he ever stay home? It seemed as if he was always either at Zoe's house or her house, but he hadn't come to the McKenzie house to see her, Tracy grumped. No, it was Josh-and-Zoe or Josh-and-Nate or Josh-and-Toby! Geesh, what a gadabout. She had thought he was a stick-in-the-mud nerd. She had sort of admired him for that. But maybe he was just as much a time waster as all the rest of the kids.

Tracy didn't know why she had thought Josh was so special. Why did he act nerdy at school when it turned out he wasn't much of a geek after all? It was irritating. But she really didn't care what he was like anyway.

It made Tracy feel foolish to think she had mooned over Josh as a possible boyfriend, and that made her resentful of her two friends, the very people who had given her a ride and who sat in the front seat cheerfully chatting about kittens.

Faking a carefree friendly smile, she climbed out of the car with the usual "thanks for the ride" and "see you guys soon." As she trudged up the walk, she saw her mom's car pull into the driveway. The garage door opened automatically and the car disappeared into the garage but not before Tracy caught a glimpse of Toby in the front seat, grinning from ear to ear.

"Now what's he all happy about," Tracy groused to herself as she unlocked the front door.

176

"Beat ya!" Toby called from the kitchen as she stepped inside the front door.

Big deal, Tracy sniffed to herself. After all, the side door from the garage opened directly into the kitchen.

As she walked down the hall to the kitchen she could hear her mother telling Toby to take his books to his room. Stepping aside to let him pass her she saw his arms loaded with notebooks.

"Wow, they must be giving second graders a lot of homework these days," she said to her mother as she walked on over to the refrigerator.

"Oh, those aren't from his school," her mother answered as she set a grocery bag on the table. "Those are his new homeschool books."

"You're really going to homeschool him?" Tracy balked.

"Yes, the situation at his school is just untenable now. It wasn't fair to Toby to be punished for the false beliefs of a group of parents and teachers, and Mr. Pullman has just caved to the pressure, although I don't think he actually believes the stories of all the kids who are transitioning."

"All the kids?" Tracy echoed.

"Oh yes, there are two boys now who say they are girls, and three girls who say they are boys," Mrs. McKenzie said, shaking her head in disbelief.

"Yuck, it's like it's catching," Tracy snorted.

"Exactly, it's almost like a fad. But it can have devastating consequences," Mrs. McKenzie replied. Her eyes welled with tears of concern as she continued, "Remember, you and I talked about the psychological and physical damage that is being done to these young kids. Two of the girls are in the fifth grade, which means they are at the age when soon their parents will be pressured to give them puberty blockers."

Subdued by the seriousness of her mother's tone, Tracy got a glass of juice and sat at the table in silence.

"Fortunately, Toby thinks homeschooling will be fun." Mrs. McKenzie tweaked her mouth in a lopsided grin. "Just wait til he finds out I'm a tough old school marm. But enough of that. Tell me what's happening with you, Trace."

177

This was the first chance Tracy had had to fill her mother in on the ill-fated party at Deke's house the previous Friday night.

"I heard something about that from a comment Nate made this morning," Mrs. McKenzie said, biting her lip. "But I had no idea it was this bad. Poor Charlie!"

"Well, hopefully she left soon enough to escape notice," Tracy answered. "By the way, she wants to come over this evening to talk."

"Good," her mother replied. "She's going to need a good friend like you right now."

If only you knew what a good friend I am not, Tracy thought. But she smiled dutifully.

"Well, scat girl!" her mother teased her. "If you are going to spend the after-supper hours gossiping with Charlie, you'd better go do your homework now!"

"Okay, Mom," Tracy grinned, taking her juice glass in one hand and a handful of nuts from a bowl on the counter in the other. "Brain food," she gestured, ducking out the kitchen door.

39

Charlie knew the McKenzie household schedule, so she was right on time after supper. Mrs. McKenzie gave her a hug and sent the girls off to Tracy's room with glasses of milk and a plate of gingersnap cookies.

"It's a good thing you told me some websites to check, Trace," Charlie whispered as she closed the door to the bedroom. "Have you seen the other websites out there? I mean if you just do a search for transgender?"

"Um-hmm," Tracy murmured, her mouth already full of gingersnap cookie. "Kind of scary, isn't it?"

"It's terrifying, actually," Charlie came back, her eyes wide. "And there are so many of them. Some of the things people post are really sick."

"Yep, I agree," Tracy said, swallowing. "But what can we do? People can put any kind of nonsense and lies on the net. I just stay off the LGBT sites. They can get really weird."

"I saw that," Charlie nodded. "I exited out right away."

The two girls sat on the rug in front of Tracy's bed and munched cookies silently for a minute. Then Charlie cleared her throat.

"Okay, now let me see if I've got this straight. We all have thirty trillion cells in our bodies—*thirty trillion*—and each one with a nucleus is marked or coded by an XX chromosome pair for girls or an XY chromosome pair for boys. Right?"

"Yes, right from conception," Tracy said. "But of course at conception we didn't have thirty trillion cells because—well, because the egg and the sperm just make the first cell."

179

"Yeah, but that first cell has either XX or XY, so right from the start the baby is *coded* to be a girl or a boy," Charlie said.

"I remember from eighth grade health class," Tracy added, "that the development of external male and female sex organs doesn't happen until seven weeks into the pregnancy."

"Right. But you can't see it on an ultrasound until about the twelfth week, sometimes not for sure until six weeks later," Charlie countered. "The point is, sex is set at conception."

"Um-hmm. Did you read the articles I forwarded to you?" Tracy asked, changing direction. "About hormones being able to change someone's outward appearance to look more like the opposite sex—like a woman taking testosterone and growing a beard—but it can't change the XX in a single one of her cell nuclei."

"Yeah, I read those. And I get the gender thing—that your gender is your biological sex."

"Mom told me the word *gender* historically—like even way back in the 1400s and up until recently—was used as synonymous with biological sex," Tracy said. "But Dr. Money, a psychologist colleague of Alfred Kinsey, was the first one to use the term in a medical journal in 1955. He popularized the use of the word gender as if it were something separate from your biological sex."

"Dr. Money! What a name! I've never heard of him."

"Most people have heard of Kinsey, though. He was the guy who did the Kinsey Reports in the 1940s and 50s, *supposedly* describing the sexual behavior of American adults."

"Yeah, everyone thinks that Kinsey was a psychologist but I read that he was really just an entomologist—a guy who studies bugs," Charlie snorted. "He called himself a sexologist."

"He was sure twisted," Tracy frowned. "Did you read the stuff about Alfred Kinsey's personal life?"

Charlie grimaced. "Yeah—he was bisexual, a homosexual. And he interviewed incarcerated *pedophiles* about their sexual experiences with *babies* for his sicko so-called sex research."

"Makes me want to throw up," Tracy nodded. "But that's what he used to publish *Sexual Behavior in the Human Male* in 1947, as if those pedophiles set a standard. And he followed with the book purportedly analyzing female sexual behavior."

"Yeah, and even though Kinsey's research was unscientific, the media pushed it," Charlie interjected.

"But Kinsey's shoddy 'research' led to the start of what is called the sexual revolution," Tracy sniffed. "Which led to having sex ed classes in school."

"Geesh, they get so embarrassing," Charlie added. "I mean, the stuff they talk about with the boys sitting right there."

"Yeah. Back in the 1950s or '60s it was some of the doctors and psychologists like Dr. Money who supported Kinsey's research—and profited from it—and who coined the terms *gender identity* and *gender expression*. Now those terms have been mainstreamed by LGBT activists and the media."

"I was always confused about what they were talking about on the news," Charlie sighed, "but I think I've got it straight now. Gender identity is whatever sex you think you are, which logically would be your biological sex."

"And gender expression is how you show what you think your sex is," Charlie continued. "So if you are a guy, you cut your hair like a man and wear male clothes. Or if a man says he *feels* he is *really a female,* he starts wearing make-up and women's clothes."

"It's so subjective," Tracy snorted.

Charlie ignored her interruption and went on, "What is really ironic is how a woman who says she is a man says her biology does not matter because she knows—she *feels*—she is really a man. But that's crazy, because how can someone *know* what it feels like to be the opposite sex? That's totally guessing."

Jabbing her right index finger into the air, Charlie continued, "She says her female body parts do not define her sex!"

"But then," she added, pointing her left index finger in the opposite direction, "she insists on having a double mastectomy and taking testosterone so she'll grow facial hair. If her physical body does not define her sex, why is she using hormones and surgery to get rid of female body parts and to try to make her body *look like* the opposite sex? It's not logical."

"As Spock would say," Tracy deadpanned. "Did you read anything about intersex?"

"No, you didn't give me any web articles about intersex," Charlie said. "What is it?"

Tracy shook her head. "I'm not sure."

"Ask your Mom," Charlie shrugged. "I think I've done well just to get gender, gender identity, and gender expression straight at this point!"

"Huh," Tracy simply grunted. But she was impressed. Charlie seemed to have figured it out pretty quickly. If she ever put as much effort into her homework as she had obviously put into transgender research since yesterday, Charlie would be in AP classes and on a scholarship track, Tracy thought.

But there was something puzzling her. She still didn't know the reason Charlie had changed her mind about coming home with her after school. Maybe it was because she didn't want to ride with Josh, Tracy thought. Had she mentioned that Zoe rode home with him now too? Charlie had seemed okay with Zoe at lunch, but just okay—not really friendly. If Charlie didn't warm up to Zoe, it was going to add another complication to her life.

"Oh, I forgot to ask," Tracy said casually. "Why did you change your mind about coming over after school today?"

"It was the police," Charlie answered in a flat tone.

40

"What do you mean, *the police?*" Tracy asked, her eyes wide.

"The vice principal called me into his office fifth period and told me I had to call a Sergeant Drovan at the police station right after school. He gave me the sergeant's card. I thought about just 'losing' the number, but I figured it might not be a good idea to fool around with the police."

"So what did you do?" Tracy asked.

Charlie shrugged. "I called. Then this Sergeant Drovan insisted on coming to my house to talk to me. I didn't like it but I didn't see how I could get out of it."

"So what happened?"

"I went home. Fortunately my mom wasn't there, of course. So this policewoman came and asked me questions about the party. I played real dumb, told her I was just there a real short time and didn't like what I saw so I left."

"What did she say to that?"

"She said that was smart. But she pushed a little for details and names. As I said, I played real dumb. I'm pretty sure she knew I wasn't telling everything, but she seemed okay with that. I told her I wasn't going to have anything to do with any of those kids anymore. That seemed to satisfy her, and she left."

"Wow, that's pretty scary," Tracy sighed, rubbing Charlie's arm. "What did your mom say about that?"

"You don't think I'm gonna tell her, do you?" Charlie snorted. "She doesn't know anything about it, and my sister can't fink on me because she doesn't either. My mom would probably just laugh anyway, but she'd tell my dad, and he'd blow a gasket. But then he wouldn't do anything since he's always out of town on business and wouldn't care."

Tracy felt really bad for her friend. Her parents were so different from Charlie's. Sometimes it got on her nerves how involved her parents were in her and her brother's lives. She'd envied Charlie for her ability to do what she wanted without ever having to ask permission or give a report on her conduct. But now she thought it must be awfully lonely and sad to have parents who didn't even care enough to check up on their daughter or be involved enough to know who her friends were and what she was doing or where she was going.

"Geesh, I'm sorry, Char," she said softly.

"Oh, it's okay," Charlie shrugged. "The policewoman wasn't that bad. She actually seemed like she cared what happened to us kids."

Tracy couldn't think of anything to say to that. It made it all the worse, she thought, that Charlie was grateful a *police* person seemed to care about her when her own parents didn't seem that interested.

"Yuck, I just don't want to talk about it anymore," Charlie sighed. "Tell me something interesting, something weird, something funny. Just anything—as long as it has nothing to do with that party!"

"Oh, well—uh," Tracy began, searching her mind for something to say. "Oh wait—listen to this. Last night Josh came over to play with Toby."

"What?" Charlie shrieked, laughing.

"Yeah—well actually with Toby and Nate," Tracy replied. "They were telling me that dinosaurs and people lived at the same time."

"That's crazy," Charlie hooted. "Everyone knows that dinosaurs died millions of years ago."

"Well, that's what I told the boys, but they told me cave paintings in Zimbabwe showed dinosaurs. And the paintings were made by humans, obviously."

"So they're making up stories to trick you again," Charlie sniffed.

"Actually, I was curious so I did a search on my computer," Tracy grimaced. "I found some really weird stuff."

"Yeah right. Show me," Charlie said, rolling her eyes.

Tracy clicked a few keys. "Okay, look here. This article talks about a canyon in Arizona, the Havasupai Canyon. It says that a man named Dr. Samuel Hubbard—he was an evolutionist and the curator of archaeology in the Oakland (California) Museum, so not some wacko creationist—anyway, he photographed and made castings of carvings on the canyon wall. The carvings showed dinosaurs that look like a *Diplodocus*. The canyon was red sandstone but it had a black stone crust or something, so the Indians—"

"You mean Native Americans," Charlie corrected her.

"Yeah, so they carved lines through the black stone, which made the red sandstone below show through. Dr. Hubbard was upset by his discovery because he was an evolutionist—he believed there was no way the Indians could have seen dinosaurs! The dinos should have been long dead before humans evolved. But he said the drawings showed the animals standing up in natural poses—they weren't dead—so the Indians had to have seen them alive. He couldn't make sense of the evidence."

"Weird," Charlie muttered. "Oh look, here's another article. It says, um—look, it says at Natural Bridges National Monument in southeastern Utah there are three or four petroglyphs—uh, pictographs—of dinosaurs. One looks like an *Apatosaurus* and another like a pterosaur."

"Whatever those are," Tracy laughed.

"Yeah, but the guys know," Charlie shot back.

"You're right about that. Here's another article," Tracy continued. "It says a Dr. Javier Cabrera Darquea collected over 11,000 ancient carved stones found in the Ica Province in Peru that native tribes used as burial stones. About a third of the carvings on them looked like specific dinosaurs, like a *Stegosaurus* or *Triceratops*—"

"Oh, I know that one, the *Triceratops*. That's the one with the fringe on his head and three horns," Charlie interjected.

"You know *Stegosaurus*, too," Tracy nudged her. "Remember how we used to sing in first grade, 'My name is *Stegosaurus*, I'm a funny looking dinosaur. For on my back are many bony plates and on my tail there's more."

"Oh yeah, I do remember that," Charlie grinned. "So the Incas carved burial stones to look like dinosaurs? When did the Incas live? I've forgotten."

"It says 500 to 1500 A.D. Geesh, that's only like 500 to a thousand years ago! But how could they know how to draw specific dinosaurs unless they actually saw them?"

Charlie shrugged and rolled her eyes again.

"What really gets me is, they don't tell us anything like this in school," Tracy frowned.

"Yeah, they just tell us dinosaurs became extinct millions of years ago," Charlie responded, her lips pursed. "Why?"

"The boys said it was because dinosaurs and man living at the same time sounds more like the creation story than the theory of evolution," Tracy replied.

"Well, the creation story is a Bible fable," Charlie snorted.

Then she noticed Tracy's face. "Uh, I guess you believe that though, don't you? Sorry."

"Well, how do you explain these drawings and carvings?" Tracy said, flushing. She was embarrassed, but she was angry at herself for feeling that way. After all, they'd just been reading evidence of man and dinosaur living at the same time.

"I think those Indians were smoking something hot," Charlie joked.

Tracy grimaced and tried to let it go gracefully, but it annoyed her that Charlie simply dismissed this evidence. The unspoken message was that anyone who believed the Bible account of creation was naive or stupid. That wasn't anything new—Tracy had felt ridiculed that way in school ever since grade school. Not by name, but with the implication that belief in a young earth (an oblique reference to the creation story) was unscientific and ignorant.

"But *evolution* is not scientific," Tracy retorted out of the blue. "The theory cannot be proven or reproduced, which is supposed to be the way science works."

Charlie looked at her in surprise. "Well, creation can't be proved either."

"Actually that's true," Tracy conceded. "But Nate and Josh keep talking about all kinds of evidences—scientific discoveries and experiments—that seem to support the creation narrative."

"Hmm, whatever," Charlie shrugged. "At least you got my mind off that stupid party!"

186

"You should have seen Nate and Josh down on the floor playing dino-land with Toby." Tracy forced a grin, grudgingly letting go of the disagreement.

"That would have made a great you-tube video," Charlie giggled. "Next time sneak your phone in there and record them."

"Are you kidding?" Tracy came back. "They'd skin me alive."

"Well, that would be okay, too," Charlie grinned.

"Oh, you!" Tracy growled, snatching a throw pillow off her bed.

Charlie grabbed another pillow and the two girls ducked and batted at each other until they collapsed on the rug laughing.

"Ay-yi-yi, look at the time," Charlie sighed. "I'd better scoot. See you tomorrow, Trace."

As Tracy locked the front door behind her best friend, she sighed. Why was life so complicated? Why did she have to be a Christian anyway? It often felt like she was swimming against the stream and the other kids at school were laughing at her—or they *would* laugh at her if she spoke up. Which she seldom did. Why should she stick her neck out?

But she felt a pang of guilt as she made excuses for herself. After all, if she really believed the whole Bible story, shouldn't she be confident to defend it?

41

For the rest of the school week all the talk in the halls continued to be about the party. Tracy stopped listening to the conversations around her as contradictory rumors gained traction. She knew as much as she wanted to know from Charlie.

Sondra resurfaced by Wednesday, looking tougher than ever and claiming the whole party was no big deal.

Sharon was also back in class on Wednesday. She proceeded to gather her sycophants around her and lead them off to the pizza place after school, gaily laughing off any questions about the party while oozing excitement about the game that coming Friday.

Wendy didn't reappear until Thursday. She seemed withdrawn and sullen but faithfully followed Sharon around like an unhappy shadow.

The M's also came back to school on Thursday but you would not have known they were the same girls. Neither one of them was wearing any make-up and their clothes were different. Even more shocking, their demeanor had changed. They slouched at their desks like sullen mimes.

Tracy shook her head in disbelief. What was up with the M's, the annoyingly effervescent Megan and Marline? They almost seemed frightened—but of what?

Meanwhile Charlie was also a changed girl. She studiously avoided Sharon and made a beeline at lunch for the table where Zoe and Tracy were sitting. After only two days of gradually warming up to Zoe, she seemed to treat her as an old friend, chatting and giggling with her.

Tracy missed what they were talking about when she turned to watch Josh as he met up with some guys on the other side of the lunchroom. When she turned back to Charlie and Zoe, she couldn't figure out what they were discussing. Intervals. Something about intervals. That had something to do with music theory, didn't it? Did Zoe play a musical instrument? Tracy had never taken any lessons and she felt distinctly left out.

It was still raining after school, which didn't help to lighten Tracy's slight depression as she trudged to the front of the courtyard. Through the gate to the sidewalk she could see the cars lined up at the curb to pick up students. She saw Josh pull up. But as she started toward the car, Zoe and Charlie cut in front of her from the side without seeing her. They walked arm in arm. They opened the car doors and got into the car without a backward glance.

Tracy stopped in her tracks in amazement. So now Charlie was not only tolerant of Zoe, the girl she had been completely dismissive of only days ago, now she was all chummy with her? Like a new best friend?

Tracy couldn't help but resent this sudden new chumminess between her old best friend and her new friend Zoe. After all, she had been the one to bring them together. And now it looked as if Josh and the two girls were ready to drive away, having totally forgotten her.

Swallowing her jealousy, Tracy marched forward and tapped on the window. After all, it was probably just an oversight, she told herself, and she certainly didn't want to walk home in the rain.

With four of them in the car it seemed that the talk jumped all over the map. First Josh and Charlie and then Josh and Zoe chatted about events that Tracy didn't know anything about so she had nothing to add to the conversation. Then Zoe and Charlie started talking about intervals again and Josh immediately joined in as it developed he played not only the guitar but also the keyboard. Huh, he'd never mentioned any of that to *her,* Tracy grumped to herself.

So Tracy just sat quietly in the back seat, feeling very left out. She couldn't join the conversation without revealing she was completely ignorant about music theory and had no idea what they were talking about. Oh well, no big deal, she shrugged to herself. It was just one conversation.

Since her house was the first one on the route home, Tracy was the first one out of the car. She waved gaily as Josh, Charlie, and

189

Zoe drove off together. No sense getting wetter than necessary in the drizzle, she told herself as she ran lightly up the sidewalk.

She tried to convince herself that her friends had not meant to ignore her in the car. It was just that they shared a common interest in music theory. But it hurt that they seemed to be quite comfortable leaving her out of the conversation. Worse, it bugged her they didn't even seem to be aware they were ignoring her.

"Oh, grow up," Tracy grumbled to herself. "It's just—it's just— well, it's raining and it's Thursday, which means I have to study for pop quizzes tomorrow. It's normal to feel a bit depressed. So quit feeling so sorry for yourself."

It was a good attempt, but it failed. Tracy was still depressed and still felt sorry for herself. Which meant that even though she had been trying to lose a pound or two, she took four cookies to her room with her tea.

No one else was home. Now that Toby was home schooled, he didn't arrive at the door shortly after Tracy. She never thought she'd miss her little brother slamming the door or bugging her about baking cookies as soon as she got home from school, but somehow his not being there made the house seem too empty and quiet.

With no public school schedule, Mrs. McKenzie now took Toby to the grocery store or the library or the bookstore at whatever time they happened to feel like it. They didn't have a rigid routine to worry about any more.

But it was Thursday. Her mom was supposed to be in nursing classes Thursday afternoon. Had that changed too?

Geesh, you'd think someone in the family would think to keep her informed of schedule changes, Tracy huffed. After all, what if she'd wanted to go home with Zoe because she didn't have to be home to babysit Toby today?

Well there you go, Tracy thought sullenly. Even her own family didn't bother to keep her in the loop. Her friends certainly hadn't bothered to include her in their conversation on the way home. Or even in the lunchroom, Tracy remembered.

She was working herself up to a real pity party when her cell rang. She recognized her mother's number as she picked up.

"Trace, listen hon," Mrs. McKenzie said softly. Tracy thought her voice sounded strained. "We've got a little problem. I took Toby with me because they scheduled an old cartoon movie for the nursing students' kids in the next-door classroom and class was supposed to be out early today anyway. They're trying to finish the painting here at school. I figured we'd be home about the same time as you."

The cell went quiet for a moment. "Mom?" Tracy prompted.

"Oh, sorry. The thing is, they started showing a zombie movie, which you know I don't approve of and Toby is terrified of. So Toby left and wandered down the hall," Mrs. McKenzie said. "It's a long story but—oh, they're calling me. Gotta go. We'll be late getting home."

"Uh, okay Mom," Tracy shrugged. Her mom hadn't said who was calling her. She was probably in line at a fast food place.

"So you'll be okay, right?" her mom added.

"Of course. Yeah," Tracy said, a little irritated. Her mom was acting like she was ten years old, she thought glumly. Of course she'd be okay. *She* didn't need a babysitter.

"Okay. Bye, hon."

Tracy sniffed sullenly and plopped down on her bed. She didn't feel like studying. She wasn't tired enough to nap and the book she was reading for English had hit a really boring section.

She lay on her back and stared at the ceiling, wondering if Toby had gotten into trouble at the community college. He probably blew up some test tubes in an empty classroom, she thought with dark humor.

Despite being sure she wasn't sleepy, Tracy dozed off. With a light rain striking the window, she snuggled into her comforter. But her dreams were not comforting.

She dreamed she was in a small row boat on a lake when a terrible storm arose. As she struggled with the oars, trying to reach the shore and safety, she saw a larger boat—a sleek motor boat with a powerful-sounding engine—close by. It slowly circled her tiny boat as she valiantly rowed against the waves. If the people in the motor boat would simply throw her a line, she would be saved from the storm. But the motor boat suddenly zoomed away into the distance. As it disappeared over the horizon, she clearly saw the faces of the three people laughing gaily at the boat rails. The faces of her friends—Charlie, Zoe, and Josh.

191

42

Tracy had been right about Friday being pop quiz day. But she hadn't studied when she got home after school and later things had gotten too crazy to even think about studying.

What had happened was that Toby had left the zombie cartoon for the nursing students' kids and walked down the hall toward the lab where his mom was in class. A painter had set up a scaffold he was using to paint the ceiling of the hallway. He left an open paint bucket on the scaffolding while he went to get some extra paint tarps out of his truck.

Just as Toby was passing the scaffold, two male college students came out of another classroom. They were jostling each other and pushing a bit—just a friendly teasing shove or two. But they bumped a corner of the scaffold just hard enough to jiggle the paint bucket off its platform. As it fell, it splashed in a wide arc, thoroughly drenching a very surprised little boy.

The angry voice of the painter was the first sound to reach the nursing lab, Mrs. McKenzie told Nate and Tracy when they finally got home. When the nursing students looked out to see what the commotion was about, they saw a frozen little statue in white. Toby, his mother reported, had not made a sound. But his face and clothes were covered in paint.

Someone called the paramedics, which turned out to be the right thing to do because getting all that paint off a little boy—off his eyelids and nose and arms and peeling him out of his clothes—was indeed a medical emergency. The paramedics took Toby and Mrs. McKenzie to the local hospital, where treatment involved all kinds of chemicals and solutions and washings and lubricants, administered by many patient gentle nurses. In the end Toby had raw skin and a terrible headache, both from the paint and from the fumes of the various solutions used to remove the paint. Mrs. McKenzie was told to watch for complications and report back to the hospital on Friday.

No one was quite sure where the blame for the accident lay, but everyone was taking steps to point the finger away from themselves. The two college boys blamed the shaky scaffold, the painter blamed the college boys, and the school blamed the painter.

Except no one blamed Toby. He was just a little boy walking down a hall. That was one point they all agreed on.

But with all the upheaval at her house that night, with the whole family concerned about Toby having medical complications from this bizarre accident, Tracy never did study for her Friday quizzes. Unfortunately, she didn't think her teachers would be too sympathetic to the excuse, "I'm not prepared for this quiz because my little brother got covered in paint last night."

So between her hold-over funk from her friends ignoring her in the car, her concern over her little brother, and her anxiety about being unprepared for her quizzes, Tracy harbored little patience for Charlie's usual gossipy chatter Friday morning at the lockers before first period.

But what Charlie actually said was enough to choke Tracy's irritated reply right back into her throat. Because what Charlie said stung.

It wasn't anything stupendous or shocking, not even a juicy gossip tidbit. Nothing out of the ordinary. Just a few simple words.

But they stung, and stung deeply.

Because what Charlie said was, "I spent the afternoon at Zoe's yesterday."

43

"What?" Tracy gasped.

"I spent the afternoon at Zoe's yesterday," Charlie repeated nonchalantly. "We spent hours talking. She's really nice, you know? She invited me to go over there again after school today."

Tracy stood frozen, staring at her old chum.

"Oh, there's the warning bell—I've got to scoot. See ya, Trace!"

So after they dumped her on her doorstep, Tracy thought, her three erstwhile friends rode off merrily together. Josh then dropped the two girls together at Zoe's house, where they spent *hours,* as Charlie said, talking. Talking about what, Tracy wondered? Were they talking about her? They hadn't bothered to include her, obviously.

Tracy trudged through her classes on automatic. She guessed she hadn't flubbed her quizzes too badly, but still she expected a few raised eyebrows from her teachers come Monday. That was something lovely to look forward to, Tracy thought sarcastically.

Well, she sighed, what else was new? Her friends ignored her, her mom acted like she needed a babysitter, and her teachers were going to be disappointed in her. Geesh, everything was going just great.

Besides all that, Tracy's stomach was tight all day wondering how her little brother was doing. She shuddered to imagine how he felt when all that paint dropped on him and covered him from head to foot. She herself would have been totally terrified. She was claustrophobic. Being covered with a thick skin of drying paint was the thing that nightmares were made of, Tracy thought.

194

But Toby really hadn't said anything at all about it. He had been unusually quiet, kind of resigned. That, Tracy knew, worried her mom and dad as much as the physical ramifications of the accident. It was like mini post-traumatic-stress. Her mom said the hospital wanted a staff psychologist to talk with Toby on Friday, to sort of debrief him about the whole incident. Just like people who had been victims of a crime.

The whole thing was bizarre. The only positive aspect to the whole situation, as far as Tracy was concerned, was that her worry over her little brother took her mind off the way her friends were treating her.

But thinking of her friends brought her back to Charlie's comment that morning about going to Zoe's after school. By fourth period Tracy was dreading going to the lunch room. It was going to be awkward if neither Zoe or Charlie mentioned anything about their after-school plans. But it would be even more strained, from her point of view, if they did. Like, "Oh, Charlie's coming over to my house after school, Tracy. We're going to blah blah blah together." And then they didn't invite her. Yep, that would be a very uncomfortable situation.

Unless she had something she could announce she was doing and didn't offer to include *them,* Tracy thought. Sort of a pre-emptive one-up-manship. Like—like—what? Great, like going home to finish her book report? Or check on her little brother? Not exactly exciting activities to make her friends jealous.

That was the crux of it, Tracy realized. She was jealous of her friends suddenly being all chummy together and leaving her out. And her reaction had been to try to make her friends jealous of her for some reason. She felt ashamed of herself for such a petty reaction and tried to reorient her feelings. She should be happy for her two friends, that they were enjoying getting to know each other. It could be a good relationship for both of them.

Unless, of course, it was just because Charlie had figured out that Zoe was Brett's younger sister—yep, Zoe *Hudson,* younger sister of Brett Hudson the high school's football star. And she was just using Zoe to wiggle her way into getting an acquaintance with Brett.

Oh come on, Tracy said to herself. Now that was a real low. Here she was mentally trashing her best friend again, and at the same time implying that Zoe was not in herself interesting enough to be sought after as a friend. Sometimes she astounded herself with how immature she could be, Tracy scolded herself.

Still, lunch was going to be awkward. Well, she told herself, she would just have to face that when the time came. Which was in fifteen more minutes.

Except that just then the classroom phone rang. The teacher spoke briefly with the office—only the school secretaries ever called the classroom phone—and then beckoned Tracy up to the front of the room.

"Gather your things, Tracy, and go down to the office," the teacher said. "The secretary needs to speak with you."

44

Puzzled, Tracy stuffed her notebook and textbook into her backpack and headed toward the office. What now, she wondered? She hoped it wasn't some new emergency with Toby.

She was even more alarmed when the secretary ushered her into the vice principal's office and she saw that the school nurse was there. Now she was really frightened that something had gone wrong with Toby. Some reaction to all those chemicals. Had he been rushed back to the hospital?

She was about to open her mouth and ask if Toby was all right when the vice principal spoke.

"We've heard some things about your conduct that need to be discussed," he said rather severely.

My conduct, Tracy thought in astonishment? I'm practically a model student. Well okay, I'm tardy once in a while, but I do my homework and my grades are decent and I don't have any trouble with other students. I'm not the most popular student—it's more like I'm a fairly anonymous student—but I don't think anyone has a bone to pick with me. They may ignore me but—*what is he talking about?*

"It's your attitude, Tracy," the school nurse chimed in.

Tracy looked at her in consternation. She had no idea what the nurse was getting at.

"We know about what you did with Zoe," she continued in a harsh, almost angry, tone.

"What I did with Zoe?" Tracy repeated in bewilderment.

"There are other students in this school," the nurse went on, "who have more serious concerns than Zoe did. I suppose she was just experimenting with lifestyles, a trial run charade. But other students are not playing games. We do not want you interfering with them as they discover their sexual orientation and gender identity."

197

Tracy was trying to decode the part about students discovering their "sexual orientation and gender identity" when she backtracked and zeroed in on what the nurse had said about Zoe. That was so unfair!

"There was no charade!" she burst out angrily in Zoe's defense. "She wasn't pretending anything."

"That's enough, Tracy," the vice principal interrupted. He scowled at her as he added, "What Ms. Kruger is saying is, don't interfere with her counseling other students in SOGI."

"SOGI? But I wasn't—"

"This is a warning," he continued. "Ms. Kruger is a highly trained professional and she knows what is the correct way to handle students who are exploring their *sexual orientation* and *gender identity*. Your interference is not only completely out of line but also may cause irreparable harm to students who are vulnerable because they are in the process of discovering their true selves."

Tracy was so astounded at his words that she simply stared dumbly at the scowling vice principle, while the school nurse glared at her with a mixture of disdain and gloating as if dismissing a silly but nonetheless properly eviscerated foe.

"That's all," the vice principal concluded, abruptly dismissing her.

Tracy left the office and picked up her lunch from her locker. But she didn't go to the lunchroom. In a disbelieving daze she took her sack lunch to the band room. Mr. Jamulka sat at his desk as before, working with a CD player, trying to find the exact spot in the score of some musical piece that he wanted to record on another machine behind the desk. He smiled and waved at her when she entered the room and then seemed to forget her existence as he concentrated on his task.

That was exactly what Tracy wanted. She walked to the back of the room and sank down on the same low riser she'd sat on the last time. She sank down on it wanting to disappear, to be alone and try to figure out what had just happened in the vice principal's office. Geesh, what were he and the school nurse talking about? Students discovering their sexual orientation and gender identity? That was SOGI? And she was not supposed to interfere?

It was the gender thing again, she realized with dread. But what did that have to do with her? And what did that mean as far as the student body was concerned? She didn't know anyone who was exploring their gender identity. Or did she?

45

"We missed you at lunch," Zoe greeted her at their gym lockers. "Where were you?"

"Uh, I got a message I have to go straight home after school to help my mom," Tracy fibbed. She didn't want Zoe to think she was hurt by being left out.

"Oh, that's too bad," Zoe answered guilelessly.

As if you didn't purposely leave me out of the after-school invite, Tracy thought sourly. She turned her back and started changing into her gym clothes, hoping to forestall any further conversation.

"Josh said something about intersex in the car yesterday after you left," Zoe continued, oblivious to Tracy's silent withdrawal. "Charlie and I didn't know exactly what that was but we sure didn't want to discuss it with Josh! You know how he is, everything is just academic to him and he can discuss anything without getting embarrassed, but Charlie and I were absolutely dying, trying to shrink under the seats. So we interrupted him and got onto a different subject. Then I whispered to Charlie to get out with me at my house. We spent a few hours on the internet and found out all kinds of weird information."

Tracy was trying to tune Zoe out as she rattled on. My word, she thought irritably, did the girl ever stop her mouth? And to think it used to seem to her that Zoe never talked at all!

"So anyway, we're going to get together after school again and we were hoping you could come, too," Zoe sighed. "But then you weren't at lunch and I was afraid that meant something was wrong. Are you sure you can't come? Is Toby okay?"

Geesh, just when she thought her friends were dismissing her, it turned out their get-together yesterday was a spur-of-the-moment deal after she was already not with them. But then again, they could have called and asked her to join them, Tracy thought. Still, they hadn't *planned* to exclude her. It just sort of happened because of the subject Josh had brought up after she was out of the car.

Josh again. He was the source of a lot of trouble these days, she thought. Not only did he take her friends off together in his car, leaving her alone on her doorstep, but now he was the one responsible for their having spent *hours* together yesterday talking and talking (researching, Zoe claimed) without her. His role in her girlfriends' actions, even if he hadn't consciously perpetrated her exclusion, did nothing to engender kindly feelings for him.

So now Zoe was inviting her to join Charlie and her after school, but she had just said she couldn't go because she had to help her mom. Well, she could probably weasel out of that little fib by twisting it somehow—if she *wanted* to join her girlfriends, that is.

Her emotions were so mixed up at the moment that she didn't know what she wanted. She still felt neglected or worse by her friends, abashed and stung by the vice principal's attitude, and resentful of the nurse's accusation that she was interfering with students exploring their gender identity.

Obviously the school nurse had heard about her bringing Zoe home to her house, with the result that Zoe had returned to school the next Monday as a completely different person—a happy and confident girl, not an awkward girl trying to act and look like a boy. Tracy guessed that after Ms. Kruger had been grooming Zoe to adopt a male persona for some months, she had taken offense to see her efforts thwarted.

But what was really bugging her was the vice principal's implication that there were other students—kids that she must know—who were exploring SOGI, as he put it. Trying to figure out their gender? Gee willikers, she thought, in her consternation borrowing another expression from her grandpa. Didn't they know which sex they were? They were supposed to have that figured out by the time they were two years old!

"So if your mom says it okay, could you come over too?"

201

Tracy came out of her reverie to hear Zoe's last words just as the whistle rang to get out on the gym floor.

"Uh, yeah—maybe," she grunted. "I'll call her and ask."

Zoe pulled on her arm as they started for the gym floor. "Do try to come—it'd be more fun with you there, too!"

There it was again, Tracy thought as they trotted together to the girls lining up for their class. Her friend had the high ground with what sounded like a sincere invitation, and she had been having all kinds of nasty thoughts about the two girls who were supposed to be her new friend and her old forever friend.

She was getting really tired of being disappointed in herself, Tracy thought. When would she ever grow up and stop being such a self-centered little snit?

46

Tracy texted her mom's cell several times during the day but she always got the same answer: *Tob ok. Tell u more tonight.*

Charlie and Zoe caught up with Tracy as she crossed the courtyard after school. Zoe started to repeat the invitation to come to her house, but Tracy cut her short. "I can't. Not until I find out what's happening with Toby."

Her friends nodded with sympathetic understanding.

"What a horrible accident!" Charlie exclaimed as the three girls climbed into Josh's car. "That painter was totally negligent."

"And what about those college boys?" Zoe chimed in. "They should have watched where they were going."

"There's a story—an urban legend—that James Bond's girlfriend in the old movie Goldfinger died because she was covered with gold paint, and she suffocated," Josh said. "But that's medically improbable. She could breathe through her mouth and nose."

"But Toby's lips and nose were covered with paint," Tracy sputtered.

"Were they totally obstructed? How long before they got his respiratory passages clear?" Josh questioned.

"I don't know!" Tracy snapped. *Gimme* a break, she thought. She was already frustrated by her lack of information all day and now Josh was pestering her with questions she couldn't answer.

"*I wasn't there,*" she added irritably. "The paramedics came and—and did whatever they do."

"The first thing they do is make sure the airways are clear," Josh responded unemotionally.

His calm response was exactly the kind of thing that bugged Tracy about Josh. He could be so infuriating! He acted as if her little brother being doused in paint was merely an incident of academic interest, not a terrifying episode of danger to someone she loved.

"Since this was a commercial building, the painter was probably using an oil-based paint," Josh continued. "Oil paint wouldn't drip off as fast as water-based paint. So the paint coating could dry thick enough to prevent respiration through the skin."

"What would that mean?" Zoe asked.

"If the paint was left on too long, a person could get heat stroke. But the higher danger comes from the removal."

A person, Tracy railed inwardly. *This is not "a person," Mr. Know-It-All. This is my little brother!*

"What do you mean, Josh?" Charlie prodded. "How is the paint removed?"

"You have to use strong solvents to dissolve oil paint. Those solvents can dissolve natural skin oils and erode the epidermis, which is the body's main protection against contact toxicity. So the toxins in the solvents—and paint solvents are extremely toxic to the human body—can penetrate to the internal organs. The liver and kidneys are especially vulnerable," Josh shrugged.

Sitting in the back seat, Tracy was seething. How could Josh talk so casually, driving along blabbing away. This was about *Toby,* the little boy he had been playing dinosaurs with a few days ago.

"Of course, the most immediate effect usually observed is depression of the central nervous system. Like unresponsiveness or sleepiness," he added.

Exactly what they had seen last night, Tracy thought morbidly.

Suddenly Josh—normally a very smooth driver, swerved into the curb in front of her house and stopped with a jolt. In a flash he was out of the car and around to her door on the curbside. He opened her door—*that* was a first—and waited for her to step out of the car. She was shocked to see he had tears in his eyes.

"Trace, tell Tobe I'm praying for him. And your parents. If there's anything I can do..."

He put his arm around her and gave her a quick squeeze.

Stunned, Tracy had barely absorbed her shock over Josh's show of emotion when the girls, who had jumped out of the car right after him, were both hugging her. They mumbled their sympathy into her hair, echoing Josh's offer to help. Tracy was teary-eyed as she thanked her friends and started awkwardly up the walk to the front step.

As the car started up, Zoe rolled down the window and yelled, "Call us to let us know how Toby is, Trace. And if you can, come over this afternoon! Charlie and I will be waiting for you!"

47

Toby was sitting in the living room watching cartoons when Tracy walked in. He looked like he was in a trance, staring at the screen but not really seeing it. When Tracy tousled his hair, he smiled weakly and sighed, but that was all. Normally he would have ducked and said something about not being a little kid anymore. Today his reaction to her messing his hair was muted.

Tracy left her little brother staring at the TV and walked across the hall to the kitchen. Her mother hung up her cell as she came into the room.

"What's happening with Toby?" Tracy asked, her eyes clouded with concern.

"I was just talking to the hospital," Mrs. McKenzie replied. "They have the blood tests back. Bottom line, Toby is going to be okay, but we'll do some treatments to help cleanse his liver and kidneys."

"Oh-oh, like what?" Tracy asked. "Will they hurt? And what about the psychologist? Didn't he have sort of a *de-briefing* today?"

"No and yes," her mom smiled. "The second one first. Yes, he had a session with the psychologist. I was in there with them. The man was very nice. He gently asked questions and got Toby talking about the whole experience. That was the point, the psychologist had told me privately beforehand—to get Toby talking about how he felt when he was suddenly covered with paint head to toe."

"What did Toby say?" Tracy asked.

"Mostly he said he was surprised and confused. He said he didn't get scared until later when all the adults were freaking out, to use his words. Although he did say he was a little scared of the paramedics and the ambulance," her mom began.

"But he said he didn't mind the nurses at the hospital because after all his mom was a nurse, or going to be one," she added parenthetically. "So he said he wasn't scared of the nurses."

Mrs. McKenzie smiled when repeating that, looking pleased and a little proud. Tracy gave her mom a quick squeeze and sat down at the kitchen table.

"What did the nurses do?" she asked.

"First they peeled off his clothes and taped on protective non-porous underwear. Then they had to wash his skin with various solvents while he stood in a shower. But they didn't use soap and water until they had done multiple washings with various kinds of solvents."

"Did that hurt?" Tracy asked.

"Yes, Toby said the washings hurt a bit because even though the nurses tried to be gentle, they really had to scrub his face, neck and arms. They had to be especially careful around his eyes. His clothes protected his chest, abdomen, and legs from the worst of it. His skin got rubbed raw in some places, so he is pretty sore. Plus he has a headache and stomachache. He says he just doesn't feel good."

"Poor kid," Tracy said. She was thinking first of the whole Jason/Jessica affair, and now this. It wasn't fair.

"Actually, once the psychologist got him talking, you couldn't get him stopped," her mom continued. "The psychologist was pleased with that, said that was a good response. He told me Toby would be fine. He said we should keep him talking about it until all the emotions associated with the incident were dulled and became boring, like old news."

"Huh," Tracy grunted. She stood up and walked over to the cupboard for a glass. But as she opened the refrigerator door, she paused and turned to her mother. "Wait—you said Toby will have to have some treatments? What kind of treatments?"

"It's a special kind of massage that will help his lymph system clean toxins out of his organs—his liver especially, and also the kidneys," Mrs. McKenzie replied. "We're fortunate because the hospital referred us to an excellent lymphatic massage therapist. It's hard to find one of those, and the doctor said this one is particularly skilled."

"Massage?" Tracy frowned. "A little boy getting a *massage?* That's kind of weird."

"Well, that shows how little you know about anatomy and physiology, my girl," her mom shot back, smiling. "Actually, the lymph system is critical to your overall health."

"Really? Geesh, I never heard that before," Tracy shrugged. "Anyway, if it helps Toby, that's great. So when's he going to his first massage?"

"The appointment is in thirty-five minutes," Mrs. McKenzie replied. "So we'll be leaving in ten minutes."

Tracy stopped pouring orange juice into her glass and turned around. "Oh, Mom—in that case, can you drop me at Zoe's house? She invited me over for the afternoon but I wanted to check on Toby first."

"Of course, dear. Just drink up and be ready," her mom answered. "I'm going to freshen up. Don't forget to rinse your glass because—"

"Yeah, I know," Tracy rolled her eyes. "Because the orange juice pulp really sticks to the insides of the glass if you don't rinse it right away."

I always rinse my glass, Tracy snorted to herself. Nate and Toby were the ones who left their glasses on the counter without rinsing, so all the crud dried and stuck to the inside. But Tracy was instantly repentant for carping inwardly about her brothers today. After all, poor Tobe was having a rough time of it right now, and Nate was okay. He could be an annoying big brother sometimes, but basically he was okay. Especially as he'd gotten a little older and seemed to have better things to do than think up ways to tease his sister.

Well, no matter. What she needed to do now, Tracy thought as she picked up her cell, was to let Zoe know that she was coming over. Intersex was the topic of the day? That sounded like a dangerous subject to research on the web.

Her mom had never gotten around to explaining what intersex was. In fact, she remembered that when she asked about it, her mom had kind of put her off. Maybe it was too gross to talk about, or her mom didn't think she was old enough to know about it. Or maybe it was scary.

What was intersex anyway? Was it something she should be talking with girlfriends about, or not?

48

When Tracy got to Zoe's house, it was Josh who answered the door. She was taken aback by that. She didn't want to see him right then. It was embarrassing. She knew the quick hug he had given her when he dropped her off at her house twenty minutes earlier had just been a sympathetic brotherly squeeze, but still— well, it was still disconcerting to see his face when the door opened.

But Josh wasn't paying any attention to her. In fact, she didn't really see his face. More like his right ear. Because he had his face turned away from her calling to someone in a far room.

"Montana," he yelled. "Not Wyoming."

"Montana?" Tracy sighed.

"Oh, sorry, Trace," Josh said, as if he had just noticed her. He stepped to the side and closed the door after her. "We're all in the den. Come on, I'll show you."

Tracy didn't see the girls as they passed what looked like the living room and she didn't know where Zoe's bedroom was, so she simply followed Josh down the hall toward the back of the house. Halfway there she heard a sudden eruption of boys' voices. She recognized one of the voices—her brother Nate.

"You sure it was Montana?" Zoe's brother Brett challenged Josh as they entered the room. He was staring at his phone, scrolling with his thumb.

"Yep, positive," Josh nodded. "Right, Nate?"

Nate was sprawled on the floor staring at a laptop.

"Hah, you think Nate will side with you, Josh?" Brett teased.

"I'm not siding with either of you two bozos," Nate scoffed with a chuckle. "I'm doing my own search."

"Hey Josh, who's this?" Brett asked, looking up for the first time.

"Oh, this is Nate's little sister, Tracy," Josh said distractedly.

So that's all I am? Just Nate's little sister? Tracy thought. Josh already had his nose glued to his phone, ignoring her. He was back to being his usual annoying self, she sniffed peevishly.

"Nice to meet you, Tracy," Brett nodded politely. "You came to see Zoe and Charlie, I'll bet. They went next door for a few minutes. Have a seat. They'll be back in a jiff."

Nate glanced up briefly. "Hi, Trace." With that typically off-hand brotherly interchange, he turned back to the laptop.

Tracy sat on the edge of an old leather sofa that looked as though it had seen better days. When Brett plopped down on the center cushion, the whole couch bounced. Brett didn't seem to notice, though, as he was focused on his phone.

"Ah, you're right, Josh. Montana!" he burst out, leaning forward suddenly.

Tracy didn't have a clue what they were talking about. The boys seemed oblivious to her continued existence, which was fine with her. She was intrigued, watching the dynamics between them. Josh was a sophomore, Nate a junior, and Brett a senior, but that didn't seem to bother the boys at all. They didn't seem to care.

Most of the girls at school seemed to stick to cliques within their own class year, and the girls were definitely more fashion conscious than the boys.

But the three boys seemed totally at ease with each other, even though Josh looked sort of preppy, Nate was wearing a casual tee shirt and old jeans, and Brett looked like he'd slept in his shorts and tank top for a week. And being boys, even in what was obviously a friendly argument, their boisterous kidding was conducted at full volume.

"And Mongolia. Montana and Mongolia," Nate exclaimed, jumping up and waving the laptop around with one hand. "Look, it's right here."

"Watch out, man—you're gonna drop my laptop!" Brett yelped, scolding. But he was grinning.

"Let me see," Josh demanded.

Nate set the computer down none too gently on the coffee table in front of the couch. The three boys dropped down on their knees and crowded around the laptop.

"Look, it says it right here," Nate pointed to the screen. "Dinosaur fossils in China—that's the Mongolia part. That's the far northwest part of China. They found marine fossils and dinosaur fossils together in the same layers of Cretaceous sediments."

"Wait," Brett objected. "Marine fossils *with* dinosaur fossils? Marine—that's sea creatures—"

"Yep, and dinosaurs are land creatures," Josh chimed in.

"So how did that happen?" Brett objected.

"A monster Mongolian flood?" Nate drawled mischievously.

"But it gets even better," Josh added. "Because the scientists found the same thing in Montana."

"Aw, come on. Another flood?" Brett scoffed.

"How about one big gigantic flood?" Josh grinned.

"You've got to be kidding," Brett came back. "I know my maps, Josh. Mongolia and Montana are basically on the other side of the world from each other. So you're talking about a global flood if you're talking about the same time period."

"That's right," Nate put in. "A global flood. These are sedimentary layers with a mixture of sand, silt, and mud that show fast flow patterns. The layers match up age-wise and composition-wise in both places."

"The Erlian Basin in Mongolia and Hell Creek Formation in Montana," Josh mumbled.

"Yeah but a global flood—that's mind-boggling," Brett mused. "A flood like that would wipe out everything—and everybody."

"Unless they were in a big boat—like Noah's ark," Josh added.

"Oh, now I get it," Brett laughed. "You're trying that Bible stuff on me again."

"Well, look at the evidence," Nate urged. "Look, here it says that in China they found dinosaur fossils like *Gigantoraptoer, Erlianosaurus,* and *Sonidosaurus* in the same place as crocodile fossils, plesiosaurs—those are long-necked marine creatures, extinct now—turtles, sharks, other fish, rays and clams. Land dinosaurs with marine creatures."

"And in Montana," Josh cut in, "secular scientists found fossils like *T. rex* and *Triceratops,* both land dinosaurs, in the Hell Creek Cretaceous sedimentary layer—"

"The *T.rex* Sue was found in South Dakota," Nate corrected.

"True," Josh conceded, "but it's the same Hell Creek layer that stretches from Montana into South Dakota. And it has similar characteristics to the Erlian Formation in Mongolia. The scientists clearly label this Hell Creek layer as a marine formation. They found tooth fossils from an extinct marine animal that links to today's carpet sharks. And five other kinds of sharks mixed in, too."

"Okay, okay," Brett chuckled, holding up his hands in mock surrender. "But," he suddenly challenged, "you claim Noah in your Bible was—what, four or five thousand years ago or something? But everyone knows the dinosaurs went extinct millions of years ago."

"Not so fast," Nate came back. He did a quick search and brought up another article. "See here? Soft tissues like blood vessels and white connective tissue, which under certain conditions *may* last for a few thousand years but absolutely *cannot* last for millions of years, have been found in dinosaur fossils."

"What? No!" Brett laughed. "Let me see that. *Triceratops* blood vessels and transparent *T.rex* bone cells? An article published in Proceedings of the Royal Society in 2007... Hmm, that doesn't sound like a religious journal."

"The Royal Society is the leading national organization for the promotion of scientific research in Britain."

Vintage Josh, Tracy thought. Just spout some obscure factoid as if everyone knew what the Royal Society was. She would have guessed it had something to do with the queen's social engagements. She never knew whether to be impressed or just really annoyed when Josh did that.

"What was that other article?" Nate asked. "Do you remember, Josh?"

"Yeah, here it is." Josh turned his cell phone so Brett could see. "*T. rex* white connective bone tissue. That finding was published in *Science* in 2005. That's a top academic journal, the peer-reviewed academic journal of the American Association for the Advancement of Science."

"Incredible," Brett sighed. "I admit you've got me stumped on this one. I'll have to think—"

At that moment Zoe and Charlie came bursting into the room.

"Tracy, when did you get here?" Charlie exclaimed. "So sorry—we were next door looking at German shepherd puppies. They are so cute!"

"Hey, come on, girls," Zoe urged. "We don't want to be stuck with these guys. Let's go to my room."

As Zoe and Charlie led her out of the room, Tracy felt a sense of foreboding. The boys' conversation had been fascinating, and besides, she was trying to remember it to tell Toby. She knew he'd be interested in anything about dinosaurs. Maybe the information about a mix up of land and marine fossils would perk him up. And the blood thing. Anything about blood and gore seemed to interest boys.

The girls had a different agenda. They wanted to catch her up on what they'd learned about intersex yesterday, maybe do more research together. But researching intersex on the internet sounded a bit dicey.

Maybe she should have mentioned to her mom what the plan for the afternoon was. But it was too late now.

Whatever they were going to find out, she hoped it wasn't gross.

49

The girls went to the kitchen first. Zoe took a half-empty package of cookies off the counter.

"Coffee, tea, juice, or milk?" she asked, gesturing to cups and glasses in the cupboard.

"Coffee?" Tracy asked. "You drink coffee?"

"Yeah, don't you?" Zoe seemed puzzled.

"My mom doesn't want me to drink coffee yet," Tracy said, shrugging. She immediately worried she had sounded judgmental. Fortunately, Zoe didn't seem to take it that way.

"Huh, my dad and I like to drink coffee together in the morning," Zoe answered simply. "My little brothers are too young, he says, and Brett is always gone before the four of us have breakfast, but Dad likes to have a cup of coffee with me. It's companionable, he says."

"That does sound nice," Tracy said apologetically. "What about you, Charlie?"

"Breakfast *together?*" she snorted. "I never see my parents in the morning. I just grab something to eat. I can have beer and pizza if I want. Of course, then I have to use mouth wash before I go to school so I usually skip the beer. But cold pizza is great for breakfast."

Zoe sighed. "The boys just have cold cereal. Sometimes I make them toast but my dad usually just has coffee."

Tracy was mulling over how different their families were as Zoe put the kettle on for tea. The girls each picked an herbal flavor while Zoe put three mugs on a tray.

"So tell us," Charlie said, "what's happening with Toby?"

"He's not feeling super but he's going to be okay," Tracy answered. "He had an interview with a psychologist today. Apparently we're supposed to keep him talking about the accident—like how he felt and all—until he gets tired of the whole thing."

"Yeah, I read that's what they do for crime victims and for soldiers with post-traumatic stress," Charlie said.

"I guess," Tracy shrugged. "But he has to get his liver cleaned out, too."

"What?" the girls hooted. "How do you clean your liver? Does he have to drink some nasty stuff?"

"No, he's going for a massage."

"You're kidding!" The girls howled with amusement. "A seven-year-old boy having a massage? That's crazy!"

"Ma mere sayz you only say zat because you do not know ze physiology," Tracy laughed, putting on a fake French accent and pulling her neck up to look down her nose like a *professeur.* "My mom says," she continued in a normal tone, "that much of your health is related to your lymph, or in your abdomen, or to the lymph in your abdomen, or something like that."

"What does lymph have to do with your liver?" Charlie asked, puzzled.

"It's the massage. Toby is getting lymphatic massage to clean the lymph in his liver," Tracy explained.

The girls looked at each other and shrugged.

"Whatever," Charlie said. "Still sounds weird—I mean, a little kid?"

"Yeah, but a little kid who had a whole bucket of paint dumped on him," Zoe murmured sympathetically, pouring boiling water into the three mugs.

Zoe carried the tray to her bedroom, the girls trailing behind. Closing the door, she said, "Welcome to my *sanctum sanctorum.* It's not much, but it's the one place I'm guaranteed privacy. Well, here and the bathroom, that is. Absolutely no boys allowed!"

Charlie and Tracy grinned in sympathy and sat on the floor beside her bed. Zoe placed the tray on the floor between them and sat facing them.

"Not to change the subject," Tracy said a little apprehensively, "but what did you two find out about intersex yesterday? What is it, anyway?"

"First off, there's a lot of controversy about that," Zoe began.

"And we found some pretty lurid websites, didn't we, Zoe?" Charlie added.

"Yes, we did," Zoe frowned. "But we got off those pretty fast."

"Some of it was disgusting," Charlie interjected.

"Or just plain ridiculous," Zoe added. "And some of it seems to be political."

"That's true," Charlie rejoined, becoming serious. "There's a biologist who wrote a book called *Gender Politics*. It definitely seems political for her. And some say she inflated her numbers to support her political ideology."

"What do you mean?" Tracy asked.

Zoe pulled her laptop over. "Here's an article we saved from yesterday," she gestured. "See, in *Gender Politics* the writer claimed that as many as 1.7% of the population—or 17 babies out of 1000—are intersex. But a psychologist named Leonard Sax wrote a rebuttal to her claims."

"What did the Sax guy say?" Tracy asked.

"*Sax on sex*. It sounds like a Dr. Seuss book," Charlie giggled.

"Yeah, but what did he say?" Tracy prodded, grinning.

"He gets pretty technical," Charlie groaned. "Basically, he says the writer, Fausto-Sterling, was loose with her terminology. So she inflated the numbers to include a lot of people who are *not* intersex. Wait—look, here's the article."

Charlie angled the computer screen toward Tracy. "See, right here is the definition of intersex by Dr. Sax," she paraphrased. "It's when a person's phenotype can't be classified as male or female, or chromosomal sex doesn't match phenotype."

"What's phenotype?" Tracy asked.

"What you look like. I mean, if a newborn baby looks like a boy—like *duh,* he has a penis—then you say his phenotype is male," Charlie answered.

"Yep, and Sax says that 99.98% of all babies born are easily classified as male or female right off the bat—just by looking at their bottoms," Zoe added.

"So what was the chromosome part?" Tracy asked.

"If a baby's DNA shows XY chromosomes, we say he's a boy—a male," Zoe clarified.

"Okay, what's genotype?" Tracy groaned.

"What Zoe just said. Your chromosomes. Your DNA," Charlie shot back.

"Okay," Tracy mulled, "so what's intersex?"

"What Dr. Sax is saying is that if a baby has male external genitals, we say he's a boy, or if his DNA shows XY, we say he's a boy. That is, phenotype (what he looks like) matches genotype (his chromosomes)," Zoe explained.

"What did Fausto-Sterling mean by intersex?" Tracy asked.

"She claimed that some people can actually be part male and part female, and she said that included for example a baby who had a penis but ovaries, or the reverse—a vagina but testes," Zoe answered.

"Can that happen?" Tracy asked sceptically.

"Yep, apparently," Charlie snorted.

"But Dr. Sax says that by itself is not intersex," Zoe said. "You see, a person can have a penis and all his male equipment, and his DNA is XY, but he also happens to have an ovary. An extra part. He's still all male—just has a stray female part. But he is still completely a male."

"Huh," Tracy grunted, feeling overloaded and confused.

"See, if a person looks like a male, functions physically like a male, and has XY chromosomes but also happens to have an ovary which is probably discovered later in life on an ultrasound, he is not intersex," Zoe elaborated. "Because despite the extra part, he is phenotypically and genotypically male."

"Okay..." Tracy nodded.

"The point is, genetic mistakes happen," Charlie said, "but 99.98% of the time phenotype and genotype match, and a baby is easily classified as male or female at birth."

"But that's—wait, 99.98%... That would mean that only 0.02% of babies are not easily classified as male or female at birth. That's .0002, which would be only *2 out of 10,000* babies that are intersex," Tracy figured. "Not seventeen out of 1,000 like the *Gender Politics* writer said."

"Right. Sax said intersex is only half as common as spina bifida," Charlie emphasized. "And spina bifida is a rare genetic defect."

"Sax points out how rare intersex is by explaining why the five most common conditions Fausto-Sterling claims are intersex are *not* in fact intersex at all," Zoe explained. "For example, the two that account for the majority of Fausto's inflated percentage are Klinefelters and Turner Syndrome."

"Have you ever heard of those before?" Charlie asked.

"No, but it looks like it gets awfully technical," Tracy said, scanning the Sax article. "Geesh, you practically have to be a doctor to understand all this."

"Yeah, I think that's why Sax keeps talking about clinical distinctions," Charlie said.

"He says if the term intersex is to mean anything, it has to be used in the clinical sense—that is, the way a doctor says whether a person is male or female," Zoe added.

"Klinefelters is not intersex because the baby is obviously a male—"

"From his phenotype or appearance," Charlie interjected.

"—because you can see his penis when he's born," Zoe continued, "and he has all his male parts. But his genotype is 47,XXY. That XY means he's a male, his genotype is male."

"So phenotype and genotype match. Clinically he's a male," Charlie summed up.

"What's with the extra X?" Tracy asked.

"It means he has the usual 23 chromosome pairs, including one XY chromosome pair which is normal for a male. Plus, he's got an extra X chromosome," Zoe said. "But despite the extra X, his genotype is still male."

"With Klinefelters some of the males grow up to be infertile, but not all of them," Zoe pointed out. "They are definitely males."

"And here's the other big category, the Turner one," Tracy muttered, skimming on down. "It says these are girl babies who look like girls—no phenotype problem—but later it may be discovered that their genotype is 45,X. They are missing one X in their twenty-three pairs of chromosomes—or twenty-two pairs and a half. They're unambiguously female, but they may be shorter or have trouble getting pregnant."

"So despite what the *Gender Politics* writer claims, Dr. Sax says that Klinefelters and Turner Syndrome, which clearly show the individuals are male or female, should not be grouped with intersex cases," Zoe summed up.

"And since Fausto-Sterling used these two major categories that are not intersex to inflate her numbers, her percentage is completely inaccurate," Charlie emphasized.

"To avoid this kind of bias, doctors *clinically* define intersex as only when phenotype (appearance) and genotype (chromosomes) don't match," Zoe repeated.

"And you said intersex is only half as common as spina bifida," Tracy said. "That means intersex is an *extremely* rare medical condition."

"Yes," Zoe nodded. "But it seems it is hyped as more common than it actually is for political reasons."

"Why do you think that is?" Tracy asked.

But at that moment there was pounding on the bedroom door accompanied by boisterous male voices. Zoe jumped up and opened the door. Nate and Josh leaned in on opposite sides of the door frame.

"Time to go, girls," Nate announced. "Come on, Charlie. Josh will drop you first."

50

In the car, Nate sat in the front seat with Josh. The two boys continued a conversation they had been having with Brett about some kind of bicycle gear, completely ignoring the girls. In the back seat, Charlie and Tracy looked at each other and shrugged. Tracy didn't feel like talking with the boys anyway after the heavy subject the girls had been discussing.

At her house, Charlie hopped out quickly. "Thanks for the ride, Josh," she called back as she started up the walk to her door.

Nate and Josh had resumed their discussion of the merits of differing types of bicycle gears before the car even pulled away from the curb. But at the McKenzie house, Josh made a point of saying a separate good-bye to Tracy. "And tell Toby I'll come over after school tomorrow," he added.

It was quiet at the McKenzie dinner table that night. Toby didn't want to eat anything. He said he just wanted to go to bed, so Mrs. McKenzie excused herself and tucked him in the way she used to when he was younger.

"Is Toby going to be okay?" Nate asked when she returned to the dinner table.

"Yes, I'm sure he will be," Mrs. McKenzie said. "The massage therapist warned me that Toby would be very tired tonight."

"What is this massage guy like?" Nate persisted. 'Is he really strong or what?"

"*She*. Cassandra. She's very nice. Young, very gentle—"

"Um, is she pretty?" Nate interrupted with a twinkle in his eye. "I think I might need my spleen cleaned."

"I've heard that the best thing for cleaning your spleen is to wash the dishes," his mom shot back with a deadpan expression.

"Gotcha, Nate," his dad chuckled. Turning to his wife, he continued, "Did she say how long Toby would need these treatments?"

"Only once more this week, and then once or twice next week," Mrs. McKenzie answered. "She said that since he's so young, his body is responding quickly."

The family lapsed into silence, each with private thoughts. Tracy was mulling over the information the girls had shared on intersex when she picked up an exchange between her parents.

"I was able to schedule it, and since Toby should be done with the treatments by then, I don't see any reason to change our plans," her dad said.

Tracy had forgotten all about the trip the family had planned for spring vacation.

"Good," her mom nodded. "I've made arrangements for Reuben Salazar down the block to take Flounders while we're gone. He says now that he's retired, he'll enjoy having a dog for the week."

It would be great to see her grandparents, Tracy thought, but twelve hours in the car with two brothers had its downsides. Besides, she was just starting to get really acquainted with Zoe.

Zoe had said she wanted to be a physical therapist. Tracy wondered if now she would be interested in this new thing, this lymphatic massage therapy. She sighed in exasperation. Here was Zoe—in Tracy's mind—already deciding what *kind* of therapist she wanted to be and she herself didn't have a clue what she was interested in studying after high school.

"Well, that's settled then," her dad said. "We can leave Saturday after next."

I guess I won't miss too much while we're gone, Tracy thought, since school will be out. On the other hand, if Charlie and Zoe spent all their time together spring vacation week, Tracy figured she'd be odd-man-out, so to speak, by the time she got back. And if Josh hung out with Brett that week, he'd probably see a lot of both girls—both of her smart, attractive, fun girlfriends.

Tracy was working herself up to another pity party when Nate blew her mind with a simple question.

"Do you know a girl named Sondra? I heard she changed her name to Dran."

221

51

"Dran? What kind of name is that?" Tracy huffed. "That's not a name I've ever heard."

"Hmm, that is different, isn't it?" Mrs. McKenzie sounded puzzled. "I wonder why she changed her name."

"She's doing the *trans* thing," Nate said nonchalantly, as if discussing the price of eggs. "At least, that's what Josh said."

Josh again, Tracy thought peevishly. Why was it always Josh who was the first one to know something juicy? He didn't seem like the gossiping type, but wasn't he the one who knew all about Charlie at the party? And the deal with Deke—his family and the drugs and all. Plus, there were other times it seemed like he had the inside corner on some school gossip.

So now Josh was reporting that Sondra was *going trans* and calling herself *Dran?* Did that mean she was claiming to be a boy?

Well, with Sondra, that wasn't such a stretch, Tracy thought. Sondra's hair had been cut like a boy since sixth grade. She did look kind of cute that way, in a tough street look way. And Sondra had always pushed the limit on clothes, wearing boy's tank tops and cut-offs to school. Her tattoos also pushed the limit. It never failed to shock Tracy what the vice principal allowed these days. So if any girl at school was going to pretend to be a male, Sondra was not a total surprise.

But what was with the name *Dran?* That wasn't any boy's name that Tracy knew. It didn't seem like either a male or female name. Maybe that was the point, Tracy thought, since Sondra couldn't be a real boy but she apparently didn't want to identify as a girl either.

"How sad," Mrs. McKenzie murmured. "She must be a very unhappy little girl."

Little girl? Tracy scoffed silently. Sondra was a sophomore, like Josh—a year older than she herself was.

But surprisingly, the rumor mill at school seemed to have gone mute the next day. In fact, the entire rest of the week, Tracy didn't hear a thing. Charlie was uncharacteristically disinterested in the subject, while Zoe seemed oblivious to the whole topic. Zoe apparently did not have a gossip bone in her body.

To cap it off, there was no *news flash* in the car after school all week. Josh studiously turned any question about Sondra aside with a nonchalant shrug and a quick change of subject, and even though Tracy was seething with curiosity about why Sondra had decided she was actually "a male in the wrong body," she was too embarrassed to pump Josh for information.

Fortunately, the family trip to her grandparents' house succeeded in diverting her attention from the whole Sondra affair. Toby seemed a happy little boy again, away from the context of Jason/Jessica, leaving public school, starting homeschool, and falling paint buckets. Nate actually worked some crossword puzzles with her on the car trip since he didn't have any of his school pals around, and her grandparents were welcoming and loving as always. Her grandmother taught her how to bake perfect pie crusts, which she thought might be a useful skill in case of any future tutoring. And her grandpa took all three siblings fishing several early mornings at a private spot on the river. It was an idyllic vacation, the kind you realized you'd be telling your own children about someday as the *good old days*.

Tracy wasn't ready to return to school the next week, but the inevitable was unavoidable. She was opening her locker before first period when Charlie, sounding like her old cheery self, came up behind her quietly.

"Hi, Trace," she chirped in a muted voice. "Now it's Wendy, too."

"Now what's Wendy, too?" Tracy asked, instantly annoyed by her friend's habitual pattern of talking in riddles.

"Like Sondra," Charlie responded breezily, taking a bite of her power bar.

"What do you mean, like Sondra?" Tracy sighed.

"She's gone *trans*," Charlie shrugged.

"What!" Tracy exclaimed. "What are you talking about?"

"I told you," Charlie answered. "She's gone trans like Sondra—or Dran, as she wants to be called now. Oh, there's the warning bell. Gotta run!"

With that Charlie sped down the hall, leaving Tracy standing with her mouth open, frowning.

All morning Tracy tried to overhear conversations in the hall or classroom, but she picked up no clue about what was going on. At lunch Charlie said she hadn't heard any additional tidbits at all, and Zoe looked at them with puzzlement. When they told her the rumors about Sondra and Wendy, she looked very sad and shook her head. "Poor girls," she said gently, "they must be so unhappy."

When the girls met in the courtyard after school, Zoe said Josh had texted her during last period. "He said he's staying after school today so he can't drive us home."

"Why is he staying?" Charlie asked.

"He didn't say," Zoe shrugged.

The girls fell in step as they crossed the courtyard.

"Sharon told me something seventh period," Charlie said. "About Wendy."

"What was it?" Tracy asked.

"Not here," Charlie answered, glancing around nervously to be sure no one had overheard.

"Why don't you both come to my house?" Tracy suggested. "We can talk in private there."

It was a nice day to walk together. The long rainy spell that had made for a dreary wet spring had finally passed. The bushes were blooming and the lawns were lush with tender green grass.

As they walked along the girls talked about what they had done over spring vacation. Charlie and Zoe, who had not gone anywhere, listened raptly to Tracy's tales of pie making and river fishing.

"I wish I knew my grandparents," Charlie said wistfully.

"We see my dad's parents once in a while," Zoe said, "but they live pretty far away. I guess mom's parents lost interest in us after she died. I don't really remember them."

"My sister went on a car trip with a girlfriend, my dad was out of town as usual, and my mom booked a spa special for four days. For herself, that is," Charlie huffed. "So I was alone, which wasn't all bad. I could do whatever I wanted. But it was boring. No car so I couldn't go anywhere. And Sharon was *incommunicado*. No big deal. I don't really want to hang out with her anymore anyway. But I helped Zoe paint the shed in her backyard," she ended more brightly.

"Yeah, that was great," Zoe smiled. "Brett was gone at a sports camp all week. We got my two little brothers to help clean out the junk in the shed, but they started fooling around with the paint brushes so Charlie and I finished painting the shed ourselves."

"That was actually kind of fun," Charlie added. "I've never done anything like that before."

Again Tracy thought how lucky she was to have the family she had. She felt guilty for all the times she'd complained about her brothers messing with her stuff or her parents keeping a close check on her. She also felt a little jealous about the closeness that seemed to have developed between Charlie and Zoe over the week she had been gone. And neither reaction made her feel very good about herself.

"Does your mom have classes today?" Charlie suddenly asked.

"No, she's home with Toby," Tracy answered.

"So do you think we could talk to her?" Charlie continued. "You know, about this trans stuff?"

"Uh, sure." Tracy responded with surprise. "I'm sure she'd be glad to talk with us."

In all the years the two had been best friends, Charlie had never asked to talk to her mom about anything. Tracy told herself she should be glad to see this new side to Charlie, a pleasant switch from the hip flip girl her old chum had become over the last two years. But the change in Charlie had happened too fast, like a molting caterpillar emerging as a butterfly. Only in this case, Tracy thought, it was more like a butterfly transforming into a—a— Well, it just wasn't like the Charlie she had gradually learned to tolerate over the last two years at all.

Wow, Tracy thought. Had she just been *tolerating* the girl who was supposed to be her closest friend? Was that because Tracy had been too much of a coward to call Charlie out for her dismissive behavior as she ran after the Sharon group and ignored Tracy most of the time? Or was it because she was a faithful friend who had waited out Charlie's hip chick period so that she could now enjoy a renewed and deepened friendship with her?

Yeah, right, Tracy told herself sarcastically. Was she a rat or could she pretend to be a saint, at least to herself? She suspected that most of the time over the last few months, a jury would have voted for the former. And in some odd psychological turn-around, that unflattering conclusion made her slightly resent Charlie's reformation.

Tracy sighed. These days it seemed that Zoe and Charlie, the two girls who a few short weeks ago she had secretly criticized as odd or silly, were the ones showing more maturity than she was.

52

"So what's the deal with Wendy?" Tracy demanded when the girls were seated at the kitchen table with a plate of cookies.

Charlie leaned forward and dropped her voice, even though it was only the three girls in the room. "Sharon says that Wendy was so traumatized by the party that she just doesn't want to be a girl anymore."

Tracy and Zoe looked at each other in astonishment.

"Uh, Char," Tracy began hesitantly, "what exactly happened to Wendy at that party?"

"Sharon didn't say," Charlie answered. "She said Alex was so disgusted by the way kids were behaving that he tried to get Wendy to leave with him. But she was a little drunk and refused to go. So he left. But some of the boys at that party were real pushy."

"And?" Tracy asked.

"Again, Sharon didn't say. But Wendy had to go to the hospital the next day. Maybe it was the drugs. Remember she didn't come back to school for a week. And Sharon said she's been wonky ever since."

"Wonky?"

"Depressed, withdrawn, wouldn't go anywhere after school, grades dropping. Sharon said she got tired of Wendy's negative attitude and just stopped calling her."

Just then Mrs. McKenzie came into the kitchen abruptly. "Hello, girls," she said cheerily. "I had to submit an on-line assignment I'd been working on before four o'clock. But that's done now. So, how are you girls?"

The three girls glanced at each other before mumbling banal replies.

Mrs. McKenzie sensed something was up. She looked at the girls expectantly.

"The thing is, Mom, Charlie told us something more about Wendy, and we wanted to ask you about it," Tracy explained.

"But before we go into that, may I ask a question about intersex?" Charlie asked. "I mean, can a person really be part male and part female? So if a guy has an ovary, is he part female?"

Mrs. McKenzie smiled wryly. "You girls really come up with some zingers, don't you?"

The trio grinned back at her.

"Okay, here's the deal. To begin with, the term 'intersex' is a somewhat confusing expression because what is really being discussed is Disorders of Sexual Development—DSDs for short. Maybe one in every 5,000 babies has some kind of DSD—a mistake in the unfolding of his or her sexual development in the womb. This may stem from a genetic mutation of the sperm or egg, from chromosomal abnormalities at the time of fertilization, from hormonal influences, and so on."

"Did you know," Mrs. McKenzie continued, "that for the first six weeks of a baby's development there really is not much observable difference between the developing male or female baby? They look the same, but are already genetically male and female."

The girls nodded sagely.

"You see, the Y chromosome has a special gene called an SRY gene. About week seven, the SRY gene stimulates the development of testes, and from the testes come all further male characteristics. In the female baby, the XX chromosomes, lacking the SRY gene that is only on the Y chromosome, develop the ovaries, which are the gonads governing further female development."

"So what's the deal with the *two hundredths of one percent* of babies that are not easily identified as male or female at birth?" Charlie pushed. "What's the problem with them?"

"If a genetic mutation affects the SRY gene or there is a chromosomal abnormality at fertilization, those are some ways that developmental mistakes—called Disorders of Sexual Development—can occur," Mrs. McKenzie nodded. "As I said before, there are various causes of DSDs. But stop and think—what are the gonads? Do you know?"

"Uh, you mean the testes and the ovaries?" Zoe asked hesitantly.

"Exactly. Any other?" Mrs. McKenzie pressed.

The girls looked at each other and shook their heads side to side in unison.

"Okay, no third type of gonad, no third sex," Mrs. McKenzie concluded. "And the same is true of the gametes, the sex cells. There are only two kinds—sperm and ova."

"So we all start from only two kinds of cells—sperm and ova," Charlie repeated.

"Exactly. And even in the classically *claimed* 'intersex' situation where a chromosomal mix-up at fertilization results in a one in 100,000 chance of a case, for example, where an XY male could have a useless extra part like a nonfunctional ovary—a male with a (usually failed) spare female part—that baby is still not a third sex. He is a boy," Mrs. McKenzie said firmly.

"Yeah well, none of us is perfect. We all have imperfections or, um—*disorders*—in our bodies. But there's no *in between* being male or female. So *'intersex'* is a misleading word," Zoe wrapped up.

"That's correct, Zoe," Mrs. McKenzie nodded.

"Oh, this all makes my head hurt," Charlie groaned. "Let's get back to the question about Wendy."

"Let's see, Wendy is...?" Mrs. McKenzie asked, smiling.

"She's Sharon's sidekick," Charlie replied. "Or she was."

"And Sharon is your friend at school," Mrs. McKenzie said. "Was."

Mrs. McKenzie kept a pleasant expression on her face but raised one eyebrow as she looked at Charlie. "Was?"

"Well, I don't hang out with her anymore," Charlie responded, somewhat shamefaced. "Not after that party."

"Ah," Mrs. McKenzie nodded. "So what's going on with Wendy?"

"Sharon said she's going trans, like Sondra did," Charlie answered.

"Ummm," Mrs. McKenzie nodded. "Well, the research shows this does sometimes happen in waves."

"Waves?" Tracy puzzled.

"Not ocean waves," her mom chuckled. "In groups, or cliques. That is, especially with teenage girls, this phenomenon—

229

some people call it Rapid Onset Gender Dysphoria or ROGD—is almost like a social contagion. Like chickenpox is contagious physically, a sudden expression of gender dysphoria can be contagious socially. Sort of *psychologically* contagious."

"What do you mean?" Zoe asked softly.

"Well, girls who had never expressed any issue with their gender identity as children—that is, girls who happily self-identified as girls—suddenly decide as teens that they are not girls and they want to transition to being males." Mrs. McKenzie took a breath. "Which we know is impossible, right?"

"Yeah, but that sure describes Wendy," Charlie responded. "She was all boy-crazy and ga-ga about clothes and make-up, and then after the party she got weird. And now suddenly right after Sondra went trans, Sharon says that Wendy is doing it, too."

"But why?" Tracy interjected. "It makes no sense at all. Wendy wasn't like Sondra."

"I don't know much about Sondra—just what you've told me. There could be several reasons why she developed gender dysphoria. But for Wendy, whatever the underlying cause for her gender confusion, the sudden onset of it fits right in with what is being seen in many places across the country. Around the world actually. Especially among young girls—pre-teens or teenagers."

"But why?" Zoe asked. "Why would Wendy catch gender dysphoria from Sondra, while other girls at school haven't?"

"Good question, Zoe," Mrs. McKenzie answered thoughtfully. "First, let me forewarn you that Wendy may not be the last. I wouldn't be surprised if two or three or even a dozen more girls at your school develop gender confusion in the next few weeks."

The three girls exchanged astonished glances.

"But let me say a little more about Wendy," Mrs. McKenzie continued. "No, that's not a good idea," she grimaced. "I'll just tell you some general ideas. But we need to be careful about extending ideas about causes to specific individuals. Agreed?"

The girls all nodded solemnly.

"Now with Wendy, it sounds as if she had a sudden or rapid onset of gender discomfort and confusion, very soon after Sondra expressed her own gender dysphoria. That fits a pattern. ROGD can be passed around a group or a school in the same way as other social phenomena, for example like anorexia."

"Anorexia?" Charlie snorted. "Uh, Mrs. McKenzie, Wendy is what you would call—well, she's not exactly fat but she's sure not skinny."

"I see," Mrs. McKenzie smiled. "But I'm not talking about whether someone is actually skinny or not. When a girl has anorexia, she's convinced she's fat even if she is way underweight. She has a false body image. Teenage girls in social circles or friendship cliques may convince each other they are fat, when in fact they are not. Social or peer pressure reinforces their false body image. The girls then encourage each other to starve themselves to get rid of their imaginary body fat. Anorexia is a psychological problem but it can also become a medical emergency."

"So you're saying," Charlie began, "Sondra convinced Wendy..."

"Oh, no—no—no," Mrs. McKenzie interrupted. "I don't know why Wendy decided she is no longer happy as a girl. And since we don't have that information, we don't want to jump to conclusions. I'm just trying to illustrate how, especially for teens, social contagion or peer pressure can cause a girl to adopt a false body image. And it's somewhat the same with gender dysphoria. A sudden confusion about gender is often contagious within girl groups through social pressure of one kind or another."

"But—who would have pressured Wendy?" Tracy objected.

"No one had to pressure Wendy directly," her mom answered. "If she was distraught over something that happened at the party and she felt ashamed or fearful, she may have sublimated her distress over that incident. But then her simmering unhappiness coupled with the sudden transgender claims of other girls in your school could have convinced her that her problem was actually that she was *not a girl.*"

"Or maybe she felt like whatever happened at the party was her *fault* because she was a girl and if she was *not* a girl anymore it wouldn't happen again," Charlie suggested. "Could that make her so scared she just didn't *want* to be a girl anymore?"

Tracy was impressed by Charlie's reasoning. Her old chum was definitely smarter than she usually let on.

231

"That's possible," Mrs. McKenzie nodded. "Sometimes if a girl is sexually traumatized—either as a young child or by a single incident—she may come to dislike her body, as if her female body rather than some male's abhorrent behavior was responsible for whatever happened to her. Or she may become very fearful and feel that if she was no longer a female, she would be safe from further unwanted attentions."

"But with the gender dysphoria," she continued, "it can be something as simple as a young girl is confused and uncomfortable with the changes in her body as she starts maturing biologically. If her friends are feeling the same physical awkwardness, you can get this strange social feedback that says, *We don't want to be girls. In fact, we are actually boys.*"

"Well, Wendy was way past starting to mature biologically," Charlie persisted, "so do you think something really bad happened to Wendy at the party?"

"These are possible causes for gender dysphoria in general," Mrs. McKenzie stressed. "I'm not talking specifically about Wendy here. We don't know the details of Wendy's situation, and maybe it isn't any of our business. The best thing you can do for her when you see her is just to be kind, be friendly." Mrs. McKenzie paused. "It won't be easy. It might be awkward. But remember she must be very confused and distressed right now."

"But you said maybe more girls might get this ROGD," Tracy reminded her mom. "Why?"

"Rapid Onset Gender Dysphoria is sometimes almost like a fad. You know how suddenly every kid at school has to have a certain style—the same style—of pants or shoes? Well, some psychologists—even quite a few among those who support transitioning—say that for many teens gender identity is just an idea to experiment with, like a new hairstyle. One teenager told a psychologist, *'Going trans is the new black.'* The new popular thing to do, to try out."

"That's bizarre," Charlie commented.

"I agree," Tracy snorted. "That's dumb."

"Remember," Mrs. McKenzie chided gently, "although some teenagers may simply be playing games, others are seriously

232

confused and distraught. Just think how distressing it would be to actually think you—the inner real you—did not fit the body you were stuck in. No matter how unreasonable we may think those thoughts, they can cause these individuals deep pain."

The girls were quiet for a moment. Then Zoe, who had been unusually quiet, spoke up.

"Another sad thing is," she sighed, "if they go to see the school nurse, I know for sure that Ms. Kruger will reinforce their confusion, telling the girls that they are boys. After all, that's what she did with me!"

53

"That's called gender affirming," Mrs. McKenzie said, "and unfortunately many doctors, school administrators and others are jumping on the bandwagon and accepting whatever gender identity a child tells them they *feel*. It's not only a complete negation of common sense and biological science, but it doesn't help suffering kids discover the root of their discomfort so they can be helped to accept themselves as God made them."

The girls fell silent. Tracy felt a stirring of compassion for Wendy, even though she had never liked the girl. She had always thought she was shallow and her humor was a little coarse. Plus of course she was always attached to the ever-popular Sharon like a shadow.

Maybe Wendy had always fawned over Sharon because she felt insecure in her own personality—or identity. Even her identity as a girl. Which seemed odd, since she certainly had the figure of a girl. But, Tracy mulled, maybe there was a lot more going on underneath psychologically that— Hey, maybe that would be an interesting field to go into, she thought, interrupting her own soliloquy. Psychology. That might impress Josh—not that she cared whether Josh was impressed or not, of course.

But at that very moment the front door slammed open and the sound of boys' voices filled the entry hall.

"Because it's level!"

Tracy recognized her brother's voice. It sounded like he was half-laughing and shoving as he said it. The sounds of heavy footsteps and shoulders clunking against the wall reinforced her mental picture of the boys' boisterous progress down the hall.

"So—what does that matter?" came the response.

Mrs. McKenzie and the girls in the kitchen looked at each other and giggled.

"Boys!" Mrs. McKenzie smiled. "They're always so quiet, aren't they?"

"Yeah," Zoe spoke up. "That's Brett—the second one."

"And Nate was the first," Tracy added.

"Because there aren't any gullies or wadis!" came the third voice.

"That's Josh," Charlie whispered. "Those guys are like the three musketeers these days."

"So what are we?" Zoe giggled. "The three stooges?"

"You girls are too smart to be the three stooges," Mrs. McKenzie laughed. "I wonder what those boys are arguing about this time?" she added in a bemused voice.

The quartet of females sat quietly listening, trying to figure out what the topic of discussion was. But as the boys turned into the den across the hall, their voices dropped to a muffled roar.

The girls looked at each other in consternation. After a few seconds Charlie blurted, "Okay, I'm dying of curiosity. Let's find out what they're talking about!"

The girls were on their feet and dashing out of the kitchen in an instant, while Mrs. McKenzie waved them on, laughing.

The girls tiptoed to the arch opening into the den. The sofa faced away from the door about four feet into the room. The boys were sitting on the floor in front of the sofa, their backs against it. They were all three hunched over a laptop on the coffee table in front of them.

Tracy put her finger to her lips, warning the others not to make any noise. The girls inched forward silently and hung over the back of the sofa behind the boys, trying to see what they were looking at.

"See, right there it says," Josh was saying, "that if there had been millions of years between the layers, erosion would have created craters and gullies on the top of the bottom layer."

"Wait—wait—wait," Brett objected loudly. "What layer? Where?"

"Okay, look," Nate took over. "This example is in Grand Canyon. Look at the Hermit Shale layer. It's perfectly flat on top—no erosion evidence at all, which would certainly have occurred if there was a significant amount of time before the layer on top of it was laid down."

"Yeah, see the flat seam between the Coconino Sandstone on top and the Hermit Shale layer below?" Josh added. "That shows that the Coconino was laid down a short time after the Hermit Shale. There's no evidence of erosion from millions of years between these layers, or even thousands of years."

"Okay, you're saying these two layers were laid down rapidly," Brett nodded. "Which means?"

"Which means that the evolution narrative about taking millions of years to create the geology of Grand Canyon doesn't make sense," Nate responded.

"You're claiming you can lay down thick layers of different types of rock like you find in Grand Canyon in a short time, like what—less than a couple of hundred years?" Brett scoffed. "That doesn't happen."

Nate and Josh exchanged a glance and grinned.

"Oh-oh, I know that look." Brett rolled his eyes. "Okay, hit me with it."

"Mount Saint Helens," the two boys said in unison.

"Mount Saint Helens?" Brett wrinkled his forehead. "Wasn't that a volcano that blew up in Oregon about thirty or forty years ago?"

"Yep," Nate said. "But it was Washington State. In 1980."

"May, 1980," Josh filled in. "And when that mountain—which had been inactive since 1857—blew it's top, it released the energy of twenty million tons of TNT."

That's Josh, Tracy thought wryly, metaphorically rolling her eyes. He's always the one with the facts and figures on the tip of his tongue.

Brett whistled in appreciation. "Twenty million tons! Talk about a blast!"

Nate almost knocked over the two pals on either side of him as he suddenly threw his arms up, his action accompanied by sound effects imitating a blast.

Chuckling, Brett shoved back at Nate and pointed to the computer screen. "So what does this have to do with the Coconino?" he demanded with a grin.

"You doubted that different rock layers can be laid down in a short period of time," Nate reminded him.

"Okay, so how does a volcano erupting prove that they can?" Brett asked sceptically.

"On that day in 1980," Josh answered, "over three billion cubic yards of mud, dirt and rocks created a huge avalanche. It was a total mess of humongous mud and debris flows."

Brett snorted. "Yeah, so?"

"So the scientists assumed the whole mess settled below the original mountain in just that—a scrambled mess," Nate responded.

"But just two years later, in 1982," Josh explained, "there was another eruption—not as big as the first one, but still with huge mud flows. And that second mud flood cut channels through the earlier mud flows from 1980."

"That's when the scientists saw something surprising," Nate picked it up. "The mud flows from 1980 had already solidified into solid rock. In two years' time! And the new channels cut in 1982 exposed distinct layers of sediment and finely laminated or wafer thin layers, the kind of thing that only happens with a large flow of water."

"So where did Mount Saint Helens get the water?" Brett objected.

"There was an early steam blast in the initial eruption of magma from deep in the earth, but most of the water for the mudflows came from melting snow and ice at the top of the volcano," Nate answered.

"So okay," Brett persisted. "This was a volcano, like a weird once-in-a-lifetime explosion, and it made a bunch of distinct layers of rock in a day. Big deal. This is small potatoes compared to something like Grand Canyon. How can you compare the two?"

"Just add more water and you get layers like at Mount Saint Helens on a larger scale—voilà, Grand Canyon!" Josh explained. "See, scientists figured out that the deposition of thin layers of materials like clay and carbonate mud like you have in Grand Canyon occurs when you have fast flowing water."

"Come again?" Brett scoffed.

"They did flume studies using clay and lime mud in water tanks and found the clays clumped together and sank in fast-flowing water, with lighter materials and fine particles layering on top," Nate explained.

"Wait—what's a flume?" Brett interrupted.

"Have you ever seen pictures of logging operations where a massive trough filled with rushing water propels logs down a mountain?" Josh asked. "That's one kind of flume."

"Or you can see another example at our local amusement park," Nate grinned. "You know, where your canoe shoots down the fake mountain in a long channel until you splash into the artificial lake at the bottom. In a laboratory, a flume is a long box-like construction with fast-flowing water, which can be used to test sedimentation characteristics."

"See, it took vast amounts of flowing water for the huge rock layers in Grand Canyon like the Coconino Sandstone to be spread on top of the Hermit Shale—or the Tapeats Sandstone which is found not only in Grand Canyon but also blankets much of the United States and part of Canada," Josh said.

"So huge amounts of water—" Brett began.

"Over a very short period of time at Mount Saint Helens," Nate interjected.

"—created layers," Brett said. "Your point?"

"If we can explain the deposition of layers across the United States and Canada in a short period of time, maybe even as little as a year, by the force of huge flows of water—"

"Not again!" Brett groaned. "I should have seen it coming! You guys are pulling the Noah card again, aren't you?" He gave Nate a playful punch on the shoulder.

"Yep," both Nate and Josh laughed.

The girls were still hunched over the back of the sofa, listening with fascination. Zoe and Charlie looked at each silently with raised eyebrows.

"But the thing is," Josh continued, "if the layers formed quickly and Grand Canyon could be cut in a short period of time in the final whoosh of drainage at the end of the global flood—like the emptying of a bathtub—then the evolutionary time table for Grand Canyon is garbage."

"So you're trying to collapse the evolutionary epochs into a few thousand years?" Brett objected sceptically

"Well, I don't have to try too hard. The rocks tell their own story," Josh responded. "And without those millions of years, there's not enough time for a *fish to turn into a fisherman.*"

"You got that line from Dr. Thomas, didn't you, Josh?" Nate interjected.

"Yep," Josh grinned.

"Who's Dr. Thomas?" Brett puzzled.

"Dr. Brian Thomas. He got his Ph.D. in paleobiochemistry at the University of Liverpool," Josh answered.

Brett pursed his lips and nodded slightly. "Okay, that's impressive. So you're saying this Ph.D. in paleo-whatever is one of your creation experts?"

"Yep," Josh answered.

"You guys are really bugging me with this creation stuff," Brett laughed. "You're bound and determined to make a believer out of me, aren't you? But come on—our school texts, scientists, the media—they all talk about the earth being millions of years old."

"Actually, many scientists disagree with that story," Nate began, but at that instant out of the corner of his eye he caught a glimpse of his sister leaning over the back of the sofa. "Trace, what are you—!"

The other boys turned at Nate's exclamation. In a flash Brett grabbed a sofa pillow and lobbed it at Zoe while Tracy ducked one tossed by Nate. A second later Charlie and Josh were jostling for control of a throw pillow. Josh tugged so hard on the pillow that he pulled Charlie forward over the back of the sofa. The two of them tumbled together onto the carpet between the sofa and coffee table. For a few merry moments pandemonium reigned, but after a brisk pillow fight the six teens collapsed on the floor, out of breath and laughing.

Tracy was the first to catch her breath. "Come on girls," she urged, "let's get away from these monsters."

"Good riddance," the older brothers called as the girls scrambled to their feet and dashed to safety in the hall.

But Tracy noticed that Josh didn't echo his pals' big brother sentiments. In fact, she thought he gave her an odd smile—some kind of special smile—as she turned to go. Did his smile mean something—or was he merely amused by the girls' intrusion?

54

The last weeks of school before summer vacation always seemed to drag. But not this year. This year the halls buzzed every day with some new revelation, some shocking announcement of who had gone trans.

One of the oddest was the M's—the quintessential Dixie Duo with their fake eyelashes and dangling earrings. Only now they wore no make-up at all. They exchanged their low necklines and ruffles for utilitarian boys outdoor wear. Meghan—who was now called Max—spent a lot of time hanging around Sondra (a.k.a. Dran) and Wendy (a.k.a. Frederick) in the lunchroom, while Marline demanded to be called Marlin. That did sound more masculine but after all, a marlin was a kind of fish!

The most surprising thing was that the previously well-endowed Dixie Duo suddenly looked flat-chested. The only explanation for that physical transformation was chest binding, which sounded terribly uncomfortable—not to say unhealthy—to Tracy. But her mom said that with female gender dysphoria, chest binding was common. And just as her mom had said, so-called Rapid Onset Gender Dysphoria or ROGD seemed to be spreading like chicken pox at her school.

Weirdly Marline—that is, *Marlin*—did not hang out with Max and Dran at lunch but with Alicia, now called Brighton. Tracy had long since given up scratching her head over the name switches, or the fact that the school administration and the teachers all fell in lock-step with whatever the girls said to call them, but she was still puzzled over Alicia.

Alicia was the girl who had seemed as if she came from a foreign country—maybe Argentina or somewhere else in South America. She had always had a sort of lady-like air, but in a professional business way—not with the fake femininity of the Dixie Duo. And now, as Brighton, she still gave an impression of business decorum, but in a masculine way, right down to her polished patent leather shoes. She was the one Tracy had caught cribbing notes for the quiz that day in AP math. Now Tracy thought she was cheating in another way, by pretending to be something she was not—namely, a male.

But Marline—oops, *Marlin*—who had never seemed to notice that Alicia even existed, suddenly stuck to her like glue. And then after school, you could see Sondra (Dran), Wendy (Freddy), Meghan (Max), Alicia (Brighton) and Marline (Marlin) hanging out together with two other girls Tracy didn't know but who, from their clothes and hair, she guessed were also infected with this Rapid Onset Gender Dysphoria.

Meanwhile there was Sharon. With Deke and Pete seemingly out of the picture, Sharon blithely sailed onward with a new coterie of girls and boys in her wake, ever popular and doggedly oblivious to the whole trans phenomenon. She acted as if nothing had changed, and yet oddly, her group now included the two boys who had sometimes been seen kissing in the hall. Tracy wondered if despite her broadcasted exclusion of her erstwhile friend Wendy, her drawing in of the kissing boys was an attempt to show that she was ultra-tolerant—that is, that she was *inclusive*.

But what seemed to Tracy the most inexplicable reaction came from Josh. Suddenly he was curt and withdrawn, avoiding Zoe, Charlie and Tracy. He came and went mysteriously at school and his car never seemed to be available for rides anymore. Nate started acting odd also and refused to answer Tracy when she asked him what was going on.

But it all came out at dinner one night.

"I got a call from the school today," Mr. McKenzie said to Nate. "The secretary said you've been skipping physical education for the last six days."

"Yep," Nate answered laconically.

"That's not like you, son. What do you have to say for yourself?" his father asked patiently.

241

"I tried wearing gym-type clothes to class—I mean, my regular classes," Nate replied, "so I wouldn't have to go to the locker room to change. And I skipped the showers—just too bad if I was stinky after gym class. But that didn't work."

Tracy and Toby were all ears. Nate, the model big brother, was in trouble?

"What do you mean?" Mr. McKenzie prodded.

"I'm not going back," Nate answered stubbornly.

"You're refusing to return to gym class?" his dad questioned, puzzled.

"Yep. I won't go."

"Because..."

"Because they've got Sondra in there changing clothes and parading in the shower," Nate spit out in disgust. "Half the guys are mortified and won't look, and the other half are leering so hard you'd think their eyeballs were going to pop right out of their skulls."

"You mean—let me get this straight—you mean there's a *girl* changing clothes and showering in your locker room?" Mr. McKenzie sputtered.

"Yep," Nate muttered. "But it's not just me. About thirty of us guys are cutting gym class."

"I see," Mr. McKenzie answered in a voice that said he did not see at all.

Tracy hadn't had a clue what was going on with her brother. There hadn't been a single whisper in the halls. Normally you'd think a thing like that would be hot gossip fodder. But then again, everyone was afraid now. Afraid to get in trouble with the teachers and the administration if you said the wrong thing—anything that sounded as if you were critical of the gender switching. You could get in real hot water at school for that. Like she had today.

"Actually, I got in trouble today, too," Tracy said hesitantly.

Her parents looked at her in surprise. "What did you do?" they said in unison.

"I didn't *do* anything," Tracy sighed. "It was just like with Toby. I forgot and called Megan—*Megan.* I'm supposed to call her Max now. But Toby was brave enough not to. I mean, Toby wouldn't call Jason *Jessica,* so I decided I wouldn't call Megan *Max* either."

Her parents nodded. "And?"

"Well, it gets complicated. I needed to get a book back to Megan, so I gave it to Liliana, the girl who sits between us, and asked her to give it to—well, *Megan*. I couldn't even tell Liliana to give it to *her*, because that would get me in trouble, too," Tracy sighed. "I'm supposed to call her *him* now, but..."

Little Toby reached over and patted his big sister on the shoulder. "It's all right, Trace. I understand," he said softly.

Mrs. McKenzie had a look of sadness and incredulity on her face while her husband looked as though he was having difficulty controlling his anger—or to put it more accurately, he looked like he might explode.

"This is unacceptable," he erupted between clenched teeth. "Absolutely unacceptable. What does the school administration think they are doing?"

He turned to Nate. "Listen, can you give me the names of the thirty boys you say are skipping gym class?"

"Yes, most of them, I think," Nate answered.

"And phone numbers?"

"Well, I have numbers for some of the guys but not all of them. They're in different grade levels," Nate responded. "Josh might have numbers for more of the freshmen and sophomores, and Brett for the seniors."

"Brett's been skipping gym class?" Tracy gasped. "I thought he was a total jock. And what about his sports' scholarship?"

"There's a lot more to Brett than you think, sis," Nate shot back. "He and I were the first ones to join Josh in the boycott."

Tracy was stunned into silence. Was Nate saying that *Josh* had started the boycott? She had pegged him as a quiet nerd, not a leader—a bold instigator of revolt.

"Is that what this is—a boycott?" asked Mrs. McKenzie.

"Yes," came the determined answer. "We all agreed we're not going back to the locker room until they get the girls out of there."

"Good show," his dad muttered thoughtfully. "And I think we can take it further. Come on, I want you to write down as many names and numbers as you can."

243

When Mr. McKenzie and Nate had left the room, Mrs. McKenzie turned to Tracy. "How many weeks are left in the school year?"

"Five," Tracy said, then puzzled, "Why is the administration letting the girls go in the boys' locker room?"

"They're afraid of being sued, I suppose," her mom said. "I've been reading about other school districts where that's happened. I just didn't think it would happen here. After all, this is a fairly conservative suburb, not the big city."

"Well, it's happening," Tracy sighed. "But what I can't figure out is why such a strange assortment of girls is going trans. I mean, the Dixie Duo and Alicia and Sondra in a new clique? Before this weird gender stuff, they seemed to have nothing in common."

"Hmm, think about it," Mrs. McKenzie said. "There must have been some common element."

"Actually," Tracy mulled quietly, "maybe there was. They were all sort of outsiders and pretenders in a way—Megan and Marline from the Midwest masquerading as southern belles, Sondra putting on an act like a street savvy toughie, and Alicia a loner—never quite fitting in with her up-scale airs and foreign demeanor. They were always on the edge of things at school. They were the girls the other kids ignored or laughed at behind their backs."

"That doesn't sound kind," her mom said in mild rebuke. "But what about now?"

"Now they're the center of attention," Tracy answered. "It's like they have a kind of power with this gender business. They're demanding that teachers and students call them new names and new pronouns—Sondra even calls herself *they*, not *her* or *him.*"

"And the teachers and students are going along with this?" her mom asked.

"Yes," Tracy nodded slowly. "We're all afraid. We *pretend* to go along with it all or we'll get in trouble with the principal—who's afraid not to go along with it or the school will get sued?"

"That makes sense," Mrs. McKenzie nodded. "And I think you're right that some of it is for attention. The reason why such different girls are making this bizarre claim of being in the wrong body, that is. For girls who might feel they have been denied respect

244

or friendliness, it must feel good to be in the spotlight and to have this manipulative power. For a while, at least. But there's a lot of evidence of trans regret."

"What's that?" Tracy asked.

"Kids or adults who *transition* and embrace the *gender identity* and *gender expression* of the opposite sex, often even with medical interventions (like hormonal treatments or surgery) think that will make them happy. But months or years or even decades later, they regret having done that and return to their biological sex as their self-recognized gender. The problem is that time has been lost, the psychological wounds can be deep, and if they have used medical processes like hormones or surgery, some effects are irreversible."

"And that's called transgender regret?" Tracy repeated.

"Yes. It's becoming more common also, as more kids and adults jump on this popular bandwagon only to discover that their original gender—their biological sex—was not the source of their problems," Mrs. McKenzie said sadly. "They still have all the problems that caused their angst in the first place."

"Is that why the suicide rate is so high for transgenders?" Tracy asked.

"That seems the most reasonable answer," her mom replied. "LGBT supporters push the meme that it's because of bullying, but the research does not show good evidence of that."

Tracy was quiet for a moment, mulling over this new angle, *trans regret*. Then suddenly she burst out, "But going into the boys' locker room! That I don't get. I should think they'd be so embarrassed."

"If they were just playing a game—then yes, I would agree with you," her mom replied. "But if they are so confused and hurting that they have truly convinced themselves they are boys..."

Mrs. McKenzie fell silent. Toby and Tracy looked at her in bewilderment.

"What's going to happen to Nate—and Josh and Brett?" Tracy asked. "Do you think they'll be kicked out of school?"

The worried look on Mrs. McKenzie's face dissolved into a sly smile. "I think," she said, "that your father has a plan."

245

55

Tracy was impressed. She hadn't thought about it that much before. She knew her dad was smart and had a responsible job in business management. She just hadn't paid that much attention before. But now she was truly impressed.

By the next evening Mr. McKenzie—*her dad*—had organized a meeting of all the boys in the gym strike and their parents. And in three days' time, the school backed down.

At the first meeting Mr. McKenzie convinced each family to contribute to the expense of hiring a lawyer. The lawyer then forcefully explained to the school that he would instigate a lawsuit against the school district if they did not modify their policy of accommodating students who professed to be transgender in all of their demands. He pointed out that the school was acting at the expense of the rights and privacy of the majority of the students, and despite the claims of LGBT activists and the media, the voters in their community were overwhelmingly conservative. While no one wanted to discriminate against LGBTQ kids, neither was it fair to ignore the rights and liberties of the straight kids. Modest sensibilities were something to be celebrated, not condemned, he said. The flaunting of cross-gender nudity was not a community value.

A compromise of sorts was reached. The girls who claimed to be boys could participate in the boys' gym class and join school sports teams. But they would be given no handicap, no advantage in the trials for team positions. If they didn't make the cut, they simply wouldn't make the team.

Secondly, the new *trans boys* (biological girls) would have to change their clothes and shower in the small side room that had previously been reserved for the boys' coaches. The coaches agreed to hike across campus to the faculty lounge to use the men's room there if they needed to shower or change clothes.

This compromise applied to the last five weeks of the current school year, giving time over the summer for extended negotiations.

Tracy was proud. Proud of her brother and his friends for taking a stand. And proud of her dad for galvanizing community pressure, organizing the families of the boys into a group with a united purpose, and working with the lawyer to push the school to accept a compromise that was tolerable for everyone for the duration of the school year.

What it would mean for the next school year no one knew. But it gave the boys a respite for the closing weeks of the year.

Nate went back to gym class and stopped acting disgruntled and withdrawn at home.

Zoe said Brett also acted more like he always had, except that his focus had changed from sports to academics. He decided to attend the local community college for two years. He figured if he studied diligently, he'd have the grades for an academic scholarship at the university. He was interested in biochemistry.

Josh came to see Nate and Toby the week after the boycott, but he barely acknowledged Tracy's existence before quickly ducking into Nate's bedroom. And then the boys were quiet. There were no more sounds of good-natured arguments or mysterious building projects. Zoe said it was the same at her house.

Finally, with only two weeks of school left in the year, Zoe called. "The boys are over here," she said. "In the den. With three brothers plus Nate and Josh here, I'm outnumbered. Can you come over, Trace? I texted Charlie."

"Charlie is at band practice," Tracy told her. "But I can come. It'll take me ten minutes on my bike."

When Zoe opened her front door, she was laughing.

"What's up?" Tracy asked.

"Do you hear that?" Zoe responded, cocking her head to the side.

Tracy stepped inside, listened for an instant and began to grin. "I'm glad to hear those boys arguing again. They were way too quiet during the boycott and even after it ended."

"Yes, it's nice to have things back to normal," Zoe sighed. "Come on. Let's find out what the big discussion is about today."

The two girls tiptoed to the arch into the den. They stopped just out of sight with their fingers on their lips.

"The article was on WebMD. That's a respectable source," Brett insisted.

"It's a respectable source but the writer is still wrong," Nate countered.

"Specifics," Brett challenged.

"The writer just repeats the popular memes that we're having more violent weather patterns now," Nate countered, "and she says the fault lies with our use of carbon fuels."

"Or you can blame gassy cows," Josh added, laughing. "She says an increase in CO^2 emissions has caused droughts and food shortages."

"Global warming *is* causing crop failures," Brett objected.

"Not true," Josh came back. "There is no global warming, unless you are alarmed about a half degree rise in temperature over what—half a century? And even that is just a projection from computer models."

Nate added, "The U.S. National Oceanic and Atmospheric Administration (NOAA) records prove that neither the frequency nor the severity of droughts, floods, thunderstorms or tornadoes has increased for decades. Not in the U.S., and not globally either."

"Even the IPCC—which is the most radical U.N. Intergovernmental Panel on Climate Change—admits that," Josh emphasized.

"That's sure not what the media says," Brett responded doubtfully.

"Of course not," Nate chuckled. "Who's going to watch a report where the weather gal says, 'More boring normal weather is expected this month.'"

Brett winked and said slyly, "That depends on the weather girl."

Eavesdropping in the hallway, Zoe and Tracy rolled their eyes, then covered their mouths and giggled.

"But there *are* reports of an increase in droughts—and famine caused by drought," Brett insisted. "And it *is* because of increased human-caused carbon dioxide emissions."

"*Au contraire,*" Josh came back. "Global cereal production has been breaking records, and crop harvests are increasing even in areas of the world that have often had scarcer food supplies. For example, yields for rice and coarse cereals set records in India in 2017 and 2018. Similar positive records have been seen recently in Honduras for rice, wheat, maize, coffee."

"And our American corn yield is over the top," Nate cut in.

"But isn't an increase in CO^2 in the atmosphere bad for agriculture?" Brett objected.

"Listen to this," Josh said, scanning an article on his cell, "from a journal called *Nature Climate Change.* International researchers from *24 institutions in eight countries* state that up to half of the globe's vegetated areas have shown what they call *significant greening* over the last 35 years. And they say the reason for this beneficial increase is a slight rise in atmospheric CO^2."

"You're kidding!" Brett exclaimed.

"Nope. It says here that more atmospheric CO^2 increases plant photosynthesis," Nate read. "It also reduces water loss through transpiration and helps plants resist pests."

"I can't believe you guys," Brett groaned. "You're saying that fossil fuel consumption—like SUVs spewing out carbon dioxide into the atmosphere—is good for crop yield?"

"Yep."

"And I suppose this has something to do with Noah?" Brett sighed sarcastically.

Nate and Josh looked at each other in bewilderment for an instant, then tried to hold poker faces. "Absolutely," they chorused.

But in another instant they could no longer hold in their laughter. Brett gave them each a good-natured punch on the shoulder, which Nate and Josh returned. The three boys play-scuffled for a minute or two and collapsed on the floor of the den.

"Hey, you two bozos," Brett said when he had regained his breath. "So who's your expert here? Another creation guy?"

"I don't think so," Josh answered. "I didn't see anything like that in his bio. His name is Larry Bell. He's an expert in industrial design.

He's the head of the space architecture program at the University of Houston."

"Space architecture? What's that?" Brett scowled.

"It involves all the details of planning for a space mission or a space habitat," Josh said. "It's a multi-disciplinary field—math, physics, engineering and so on."

"Huh, never heard of it. Fascinating," Brett muttered.

"Or in Toby's words—" Nate began.

"Rad!" Nate and Josh yelled together.

Zoe motioned to Tracy and they tiptoed away from the den and crossed the hall to the kitchen. Zoe headed for the teapot while Tracy walked over to the back window, watching Zoe's younger brothers kick around a soccer ball on the grass in the back yard.

"At least the guys seem to be back to their old selves," Zoe chuckled. "Don't you think, Trace?"

"Yeah, it seems like it. I wonder why they were so weird for a while."

"I think they just didn't like to think of us—*the sisters*—as *girls* after the shower deal with Sondra and some of the other trans girls. Or I guess they are *trans boys*, aren't they? Because they are biological girls so when they go *trans* they are trans boys?" Zoe puzzled.

"You're right, Zoe," Tracy nodded. "When a bio girl transitions, she's called a trans boy."

"It's so crazy—" Zoe began, but she was interrupted by the three older boys surging into the room.

"Scoot, sis," Brett teased, shooing Zoe out of the way. "There's a hungry army here."

The boys crowded around the refrigerator, faces inside choosing soft drinks, joking and jostling each other. Zoe put several cookies, a couple of tea bags, and two mugs on a tray. As she reached for the teapot, Josh noticed the tray and turned to look around the room. His face blanched with surprise when he saw Tracy over by the window.

"Oh, hi Trace," he said gruffly. "I—uh, I didn't see you there."

"Uh, hi," Tracy answered.

Then he just stood there as if the cat got his tongue while Nate and Brett scrounged for cookies in the cupboard. Tracy couldn't think of anything to say either so she just stood there looking back at him and feeling stupid. Then Brett spotted the package Zoe had left on the counter.

"Here it is," he exclaimed as he pounced on the package. Turning, he saw Tracy by the window. "Aha," he grinned, "you girls were stealing all the cookies, eh? Don't you know us guys are famished?"

Tromping noisily, Brett and Nate swept from the room. Josh followed silently in their wake.

"Well, they may say there's been no increase in violent weather in decades," Zoe chuckled, "but those boys are a cyclone all by themselves!"

It was only when she felt her shoulders drop that Tracy realized how tense she had become during the face-off with Josh. Now she let a lopsided smile creep across her face.

"Yeah, they bring stormy weather all right," she muttered.

Zoe looked at her questioningly but let that pass. "How is Toby doing?" she asked with genuine concern.

"Fine," Tracy shrugged. "After he finished that lymphatic massage, he seemed completely back to normal. A pesky little brother," she finished with a grin.

"I'm glad," Zoe responded. "And speaking of little brothers..."

Zoe's two younger siblings burst into the kitchen from the back yard, inadvertently kicking their soccer ball into Tracy's shins.

"Oops, sorry!" they yelled. "Hey Zoe, you promised us a game of Monopoly this afternoon, remember?"

Zoe rolled her eyes but Tracy winked at the boys and whispered in a scary voice, "I'm an ace Monopoly player. Do you dare to take me on?"

Whooping, the boys disappeared down the hall, reappearing a minute later with the game board. Two hours later Tracy said good-bye to Zoe and her younger brothers and retrieved her bike from the side of the house.

She had pedaled only a half block toward home when a speeding car almost sideswiped her, forcing her to the right. Her front wheel caught in a storm grate, abruptly stopping the bike. It tipped over, dumping her unceremoniously on the curb. Tracy lay on her side struggling to extricate her right leg from under her bike.

"Here, let me help you," came a voice in her ear.

"Josh! Where did you come from?" Tracy asked in astonishment.

"My house," he answered simply. He made a butler face and continued in a silly super-dignified tone, "I feel it incumbent upon me to rescue all damsels in distress who plop themselves down on my curb."

"Yeah, sorry about that," Tracy said ruefully. "That crazy driver almost hit me. I had to swerve."

"I saw," Josh nodded, picking up her bike and laying it on the sidewalk. "There was plenty of room for him to drive in his own lane. He was really speeding, too. Are you okay?"

"Yeah, I'm fine," Tracy shrugged.

Josh took her arm and helped her to stand. "Well, you look okay except for that bloody scrape from the bike chain on your right ankle. Is your ankle twisted?"

"Naw—no, just a little stiff," Tracy said.

"Then you're doing better than your bike," Josh responded. He pointed to her front wheel, which looked more like an oval than a circle. "Come inside and we'll clean up your ankle."

"Oh, I don't want to be any bother," Tracy protested, suddenly shy. "I'm fine."

"Hey, you can't ride home with a bent wheel, and I don't mind sticking your bike in my trunk, but no way I'm letting you bleed all over the fine leather interior of my vehicle," Josh insisted with mock indignation.

Despite herself, Tracy began to giggle. "Fine leather interior, my eye!" she came back. "You mean the faded torn vinyl in your jalopy."

Josh grinned and put an arm behind her back, propelling Tracy across the lawn toward his front door. "All right, that remark earns you the iodine treatment," he growled.

"Not the iodine!" Tracy wailed in fake terror.

Propping her foot up on the bathroom counter, Josh used paper towels to wash off the blood, then smeared a disinfectant salve (no iodine!) on the scrape. He dried her ankle with more paper towels and liberally applied Band-Aids. Very liberally. About fifteen of them, overlapping and sticking six inches out all around the bloody spot.

"Enough!" Tracy yelped, holding her sides with laughter. "It's not a brain tumor."

"Just making sure to cover it," Josh grinned. Suddenly serious, he continued, "I had just stepped out to set the hose on the front lawn when I saw you coming. Then I saw that speeding car turn the corner and bear down on you. There wasn't even time for me to yell. You must have sensed it because you swerved suddenly to the right. Quick thinking! You probably saved yourself from serious injury—or worse."

He paused, then took both her hands in his. "My heart was in my mouth, Trace."

Tracy was taken aback as his eyes locked on hers. It was a little awkward, balancing on one leg with the other leg still propped up on the bathroom counter, twisted so the inside of her ankle faced up.

"Hey, I survived," she shrugged as nonchalantly as she could, pulling her foot to the edge of the counter until it abruptly crashed to the floor. "Did you know I was crowned Miss Graceful last year?" she added sarcastically.

"Come on, you!" Josh came back, laughing. "Let me get your bicycle and take you home."

In the car Josh asked, "Have you been to the new hike-and-bike trail out at Mesa Park?"

"No," Tracy shook her head. "Have you?"

"No, but I want to go this summer. When it cools down in the evenings."

"Sounds nice," Tracy said politely.

"I'm going to be working at the lumber yard this summer," Josh said.

"Josh the Lumberjack?"

"More like Josh-Restock-the-Hardware-Shelves," he grinned ruefully. "But still, summer evenings are long, and I'll have Sundays and Mondays off."

"So lots of time for biking," Tracy grinned.

Josh grinned back but kept his eyes on the road and said, "Actually, I thought maybe you'd like to go with me some time."

Caught off guard, Tracy froze, stretching her silence an awkward twenty seconds.

"It's really pretty up there," Josh continued hesitantly. "Are you okay with some hills?"

Exhaling, Tracy found her voice. "Yeah, sure. I can do hills." She paused, then added quietly, "That sounds like fun."

"Great!" Josh replied with vigor. "Yeah, yeah. It will be fun. When school's out..."

Parking in front of her house, Josh took her bike out of his trunk and wheeled it to the garage.

"Thanks for rescuing me, Josh," Tracy said.

"Anytime, my lady, anytime," he grinned. With a wave he turned, hopped into his jalopy, and pulled away.

Tracy watched his car traveling down the street, getting smaller in the distance. Then she limped to her front door. As she reached for the handle, it struck her.

Josh had asked her for a date.

Josh—the guy she alternately admired and derided as too logical—the fascinating, irritating, terrifying Josh—had asked her for a date!

Sort of. Nothing definite. But an invitation. Or a suggestion.

56

Tracy didn't say anything to Charlie or Zoe about what Josh had said. In fact, she didn't mention Josh at all. She just said her wheel got caught in a grate and was bent out of shape. Nate kidded her about watching where she was going. Of course, she had taken the mound of Band-Aids off her ankle and no one was particularly impressed by her bloody scrape, so the whole incident was quickly forgotten.

That was exactly what Tracy wanted. She wanted to privately savor Josh's invitation to ride bikes together in Mesa Park after school was out.

If they ever did. That is, if he ever followed through on his indefinite invitation. A lot of times folks said, "Oh, we must have you over to dinner." And then you never heard from them again. They really meant it at the time. It was just that people got busy. They had schedules, duties, distractions.

In Josh's case, a new job. Or a more interesting girl.

But he had asked her! Even if nothing ever came of it, she would treasure that.

Tracy felt a kind of happy glow as she sailed on automatic through the last two weeks of school, finishing projects, studying for finals.

At school most of the kids seemed to have settled into the new normal as if Dran, Max, Freddy, Brighton and Marlin had always been Dran, Max, Freddy *et cetera*. Sometimes Tracy felt as if she had moved to Mars, but like most of the kids, she just tried to ignore the whole business. With the school year drawing to a close, they were all absorbed in their own nightmares. Kids retreated into their individual distracted bubbles, studying frantically.

Charlie seemed more mellow even amidst these last frenzied days of school. But Tracy didn't see much of her these days—just a minute or two at the locker or between classes. At lunch Charlie swallowed a few bites and dashed off to the library. Even during finals, for *Charlie* that was odd. What was up with that?

Nate was spending more time over at Brett's house. But when Zoe mentioned that Nate had helped her finish her history project, Tracy realized her brother was no longer going over there just to see Brett. When she asked him about it, he said Brett was busy. He was helping Charlie study for some test.

"Brett is tutoring you?" Tracy asked in astonishment when Charlie poked her head around the corner of her locker.

"Yeah, I need to get up to speed quickly on the basics," Charlie answered before taking another bite of her energy bar.

"Why are you always eating those?" Tracy sniffed, giving her a playful jab.

"Breakfast!" Charlie grinned, waving the half-eaten bar like a flag.

Tracy scrunched up her face in mock horror. Then as Charlie slammed her locker shut, she spurted quickly, "Wait—basics of what?"

"Warning bell—gotta go!" With that Charlie turned and scooted down the hall.

"Vintage Charlie," Tracy laughed to herself. "Leave me hanging."

"So what is Charlie studying?" she asked her brother at dinner that day.

"Biology," he answered in an *of-course-didn't-you-know-that tone.* "Hey, Dad," he continued without a breath, "did you find that gear part we were talking about?"

Tracy tuned out the exchange between Nate and her dad. She was busy mulling over her brother's answer.

Biology? Why would Charlie be studying biology now? Biology was a sophomore class. Charlie would take biology next year along with Tracy, Meg—uh, Max, Marlin, Freddy, and Brighton. (Sondra—uh, Dran—had taken it this year since she—or *they,* as she preferred to be called—would be a junior next year.)

Tracy texted Charlie: *y bio?*

Charlie texted back: *told u. basics*

That was Charlie. She was as bad as Toby, Tracy thought, for enigmatic explanations.

But Tracy pinned Charlie between the open locker doors the next morning. Laughing, she demanded, "Explain, or I won't let you go to class!"

"I can't get in unless I pass the test, so I have to study," Charlie shrugged, with the same bored *everyone-knows-that* tone that her brother often used.

"Get in where? What test?" Tracy sputtered.

"Biology," Charlie yawned. "Bell—bye!"

With that she tickled Tracy in the ribs. When Tracy ducked away laughing, Charlie slipped by her down the hall.

But in the lunchroom Tracy would not be put off so easily.

"It's simple, Trace," Charlie sighed. "I have to pass a test on the basics in order to get into AP Biology in summer school. It will count—if I do well—for city college credit."

"But you're only a freshman—well, a sophomore after our finals this week. Why do you want to get AP credit for biology this summer? What's the rush?"

"No rush," she countered, suddenly coy. "It's just that—well, biology is really fascinating, you know? Brett was telling me some things about the ways plants can actually sense when a neighboring plant is being attacked by bugs or drought and—well, you know, it's just fascinating. I got interested, is all," she finished with a shrug.

Ah, Brett was telling her, Tracy thought with amused enlightenment. But Charlie sounded sincerely enthralled with the science. In fact, Charlie seemed to have grown up overnight in the last few weeks. She was still Charlie—effervescent and enigmatic—but the gossipy part seemed to have disappeared. She seemed calmer somehow, more grounded. Kinder. Definitely happier.

Tracy was glad. She felt almost a motherly satisfaction in seeing this new more mature side of Charlie.

And Zoe. Tracy couldn't think of another girl she would be more excited to see Nate be interested in. She was fun and sweet and smart and compassionate. From the start—as soon as her *trans* misdirection got settled—she had seemed more mature than either Charlie or herself, Tracy thought. She deserved a really nice friend and hey—her brother was really a nice guy, after all.

257

Tracy was a little shocked by how her own emotions had morphed in the last few weeks. A lot of her own insecurities and petty jealousies seemed just that—petty. Silly. Not worth giving a minute's attention to.

She felt a growing appreciation for her family and friends. Her mom and dad were amazing, Nate was really an okay big brother, and Toby was a sweet little guy.

Charlie was still fun but she was displaying a new depth of character. And the more she got to know Zoe, the more she appreciated her compassion, intelligence, and humor. And then there was Brett—even for Brett she had developed a new admiration. He wasn't just a jock. He was serious about biochemistry. He was serious about a lot of things. In fact, Nate said he was even investigating Christianity now. Nate loaned him a book called *The Case for Christ* by a guy who was an investigative reporter—and an atheist when he started his research.

So wow—she had a great family and some neat friends. Even if the world was getting a little wonky.

And then there was Josh.

A good friend. A great guy to take bike rides with this summer. And—and—

Tracy left that thought unfinished. After all, she was only fourteen—almost fifteen.

For now, *friends* was enough.

258

APPRECIATION

My first reader, Marianna Mancini, responded from the perspective of a young teenage girl with positive enthusiasm, and she was a great proofreader!

John David Miller, another teenage previewer, answered my question about its appeal to boys. John simply said, "I like it—and I'm a guy!" Many thanks to both of these young people.

Renate Sims, the mother of four teens, was the first mom who read the text to check it for appropriateness and interest to tweens and teens, and even adults. I appreciate her thoughtful support.

Through articles and videos by Dr. Michelle A. Cretella I learned a great deal about gender dysphoria, and it was her impassioned expression of the need for a teen novel dealing with gender confusion that inspired me to write *CHOOSING*. When I eventually told her what I was attempting, she was a continual source of support and encouragement.

Dr. Andre Van Mol carefully edited the sections dealing with biological science and transgender issues, but his suggestions were not limited to factual corrections. His expertise in the area of teen sexuality was invaluable to improve the text.

Dr. Tim Clarey and also Dr. Brian Thomas checked sections relating to their areas of scientific expertise and offered useful corrections. I am indebted to them for taking the time to insure the accuracy of the text.

And to my dear husband, Philip—the one who rescues me when my computer goes wonky, who puts up with my being glued to the screen for hours on end, and who is my faithful cheering squad—I cannot express the depths of my gratitude.

NOTES AND
FURTHER READING

The following articles, videos, and books are not an exhaustive list of resources. But why put any references at the end of a work of fiction? Because some of you are probably saying, "Oh, really? Is that true? *Or is this author talking through her hat?*"

The list within each chapter is not in alphabetical order. Rather, references more or less correlate to the order that information pops up in a chapter. Some references are repeated in more than one chapter.

5

"Kohlberg's Cognitive Developmental Theory of Gender."
Science Aid. Jamie, et al, Ed.
https://scienceaid.net/psychology/gender/cognitive.html

9

Here is a screen shot from the Planned Parenthood website (viewed July 26, 2019) titled "How do I talk with my preschooler about their body? See the box labeled, "Who has what? A note about Gender."

> While the most simple answer is that girls have vulvas and boys have penises/testicles, that answer isn't true for every girl and boy. Boy, girl, man and woman are words that describe gender identity, and some people with the gender identities "boy" or "man" have vulvas, and some with the gender identity "girl" or "woman" have penises/testicles. Your genitals don't make you a boy or a girl.

https://www.plannedparenthood.org/learn/parents/preschool/how-do-i-talk-my-preschooler-about-their-body

"Gender Identity Issues in Children and Adolescents."
American College of Pediatricians. Articles and videos. Various dates.
https://www.acpeds.org/the-college-speaks/position-statements/sexuality-issues/gender-identity-issues-in-children-and-adolescents

Cretella, Michelle A. (Primary Author). "Gender Dysphoria in Children."
American College of Pediatricians. November, 2018.
https://www.acpeds.org/the-college-speaks/position-statements/gender-dysphoria-in-children

Cretella, Michelle A., Quentin Van Meter, and Paul McHugh.
"Gender Ideology Harms Children."
American College of Pediatricians. September, 2017.
https://www.acpeds.org/the-college-speaks/position-statements/gender-ideology-harms-children

Higgins, Laurie. "Formerly 'Trans' Young Women Speak Out."
Illinois Family Institute. March 4, 2019.
https://illinoisfamily.org/homosexuality/formerly-trans-young-women-speak-out/

"Gender Dysphoria in Children: Understanding the Science and Medicine."
The Heritage Foundation. Video, October 11, 2017.
https://www.heritage.org/gender/event/gender-dysphoria-children-understanding-the-science-and-medicine

10

Gosselin, P. "Fears of Global Cooling Very Real In 1970s ...Scientists Devised Ways To WARM The Planet!" *No Trick Zone.* May 10, 2016.
http://notrickszone.com/2016/05/10/fears-of-global-cooling-very-real-in-1970s-scientists-devised-ways-to-warm-the-planet/

Morano, Marc. "Climate Depot's Factsheet on 1970s Coming 'Ice Age.'"
Climate Depot. October 6, 2009.
http://www.climatedepot.com/2009/10/06/dont-miss-it-climate-depots-factsheet-on-1970s-coming-ice-age-claims-2/

Seymour, Julia. "That's the Way It Was: In 1972, Cronkite Warned of
'New Ice Age.'" *mrcNewsBusters.* March 5, 2015.
https://www.newsbusters.org/blogs/julia-seymour/2015/03/05/and-thats-way-it-was-1972-cronkite-warned-new-ice-age

Whitestone, Gregory. *INCONVENIENT FACTS, The science that Al Gore doesn't want you to know.* Silver Crown Publishers, 2017. Print.

14

Hilt, Robert. "Cannabis and the Adolescent Brain."
Healio Pediatric Journals. March 1, 2014.
https://www.healio.com/pediatrics/journals/pedann/2014-3-43-3/%7Bce5d451b-9559-4c9d-980e-c849f00ba261%7D/cannabis-and-the-adolescent-brain#divReadThis

See the American College of Pediatricians web page with multiple articles
on marijuana and its effects on adolescents:
https://www.acpeds.org/?s=marijuana&Submit.x=0&Submit.y=0

Veritas, "What Parents Should Know about Marijuana."
American Academy of Pediatricians, Blog. February 25, 2019.
https://www.acpeds.org/what-parents-should-know-about-marijuana?highlight=patient%20hand%20out%20on%20marijuana

Micozzi, Marc. "Is marijuana as safe as they claim?"
INSIDERS' CURES. February 24, 2014.
http://drmicozzi.com/is-marijuana-as-safe-as-they-claim

Nicholson, Lucy. "ER Visits for Kids Rise Significantly After Pot
Legalized in Colorado." *NBC News.* May 4, 2017.
https://www.nbcnews.com/health/health-news/er-visits-kids-rise-significantly-after-pot-legalized-colorado-n754781

University of Otago Press Release. "Illicit Drug Use Starts With Cannabis."
SCOOP Health News. March 14, 2006.
http://www.scoop.co.nz/stories/GE0603/S00045.htm

Forrester, Mathias and Ruth D. Merz. "Risk of Selected Birth Defects with Prenatal Illicit Drug Use, Hawaii, 1986-2002." *Journal of Toxicology and Environmental Health*, Hawaii Birth Defects Program. January, 2007. https://www.dalgarnoinstitute.org.au/images/resources/pdf/researchmaterial/2019/Selected_Birth_Defects_w_Prenatal_Drug_Use_-_Cannabis_Hawaii_Forrester_2007.pdf

Goldman, Russell. "Here's a List of 58 Gender Options for Facebook Users." *ABC News*. February 13, 2014. https://abcnews.go.com/blogs/headlines/2014/02/heres-a-list-of-58-gender-options-for-facebook-users/

Williams, Rhiannon. "Facebook's 71 gender options come to UK users." *The Telegraph*. June 20, 2019. https://www.telegraph.co.uk/technology/facebook/10930654/Facebooks-71-gender-options-come-to-UK-users.html

Min, Jessica. "Common App to Increase Gender-Identity Options." *The Harvard Crimsom*. April 27, 2016. https://www.thecrimson.com/article/2016/4/27/common-app-gender-identity/

For how counselors separate sex assigned at birth, legal sex, and gender identity, see the blog:
"Gender Identity Options." *commonapp*. September 28, 2016. https://www.commonapp.org/whats-appening/college-counseling/gender-identity-options

Sax, Leonard. "How common is intersex?" Journal of Sex Research, *Scholarly Publications*. August 1. 2002. http://www.leonardsax.com/how-common-is-intersex-a-response-to-anne-fausto-sterling/

Van Mol, Andre. "Intersex: What It Is And Is Not." *CMDA's The Point*. May 2, 2019. https://cmda.org/intersex-what-it-is-and-is-not/

18

For a book about a young mother making do in primitive conditions in Big Bend, Texas in the middle of the last century:
Koch, Etta. *LIZARDS on the MANTEL, BURROS at the DOOR, A Big Bend Memoir.* University of Texas Press, Austin. 1999. Print.

19

White, C. Michael. "The difference between real and synthetic cannabis." *Newshub.* February 9, 2018.
https://www.newshub.co.nz/home/lifestyle/2018/09/the-difference-between-real-and-synthetic-cannabis.html

"Seventeen percent of teens who start using pot become addicted." *National Institute on Drug Abuse , NIH.* June, 2018. https://www.drugabuse.gov/publications/research-reports/marijuana/marijuana-addictive

A list of articles on NIDA (National Institute on Drug Addiction) about marijuana addition:
https://www.drugabuse.gov/search/seventeen

24

"Researchers Identify 6,500 Genes That Are Expressed Differently in Men and Women." *Weizmann Wonder Wander, News, Features and Discoveries from the Weizmann Institute of Science.* May 3, 2017.
https://wis-wander.weizmann.ac.il/life-sciences/researchers-identify-6500-genes-are-expressed-differently-men-and-women

Cretella, Michelle A. "I'm a pediatrician. Here's what I did when a little boy told me he was a girl." *LIFE SITE NEWS.* December 11, 2017.
https://www.lifesitenews.com/opinion/im-a-pediatrician.-heres-what-i-did-when-a-little-boy-told-me-he-was-a-girl?utm_source=LifeSiteNews.com&utm_campaign=21233b4472-Daily%2520Headlines%2520-

Cretella, Michelle A. "College President Speaks on Transgender Ideology." *American College of Pediatricians.* July 10, 2017.
https://www.acpeds.org/college-president-speaks-on-transgender-ideology?highlight=cretella%20transgender

Van Mol, Andre. "Transing California Foster Children & Why Doctors Like Us Opposed It." *PUBLIC DISCOURSE, The Journal of the Witherspoon Institute*. October 28, 2018.
https://www.thepublicdiscourse.com/2018/10/42612/

"Mastoid part of the temporal bone." *Wikipedia*. June 1, 2019.
https://en.wikipedia.org/wiki/Mastoid_part_of_the_temporal_bone

Sameen. "25 Biological Differences Between Men And Women That Aren't Commonly Known." *List 25*. Updated August 29, 2016.
https://list25.com/25-biological-differences-between-men-and-women/
Johnston, Elizabeth. "Study Finds a Stunning 1500 Differences Between Boys and

Girls, Undermines Leftist Gender Theory." *Activist Mommy*. May 15, 2018.
https://activistmommy.com/study-finds-stunning-1500-differences-boys-girls-undermines-leftist-gender-theory/

Cretella, Michelle A. "I'm a pediatrician. Here's what I did when a little boy told me he was a girl." *LIFE SITE NEWS*. December 11, 2017.
https://www.lifesitenews.com/opinion/im-a-pediatrician.-heres-what-i-did-when-a-little-boy-told-me-he-was-a- girl?utm_source=LifeSiteNews.com

Van Mol, Andre. "Scapegoating the Church for LGBT Suicide and Stigma." *CMDA'a The Point*. June 27, 2019.
https://cmda.org/scapegoating-the-church-for-lgbt-suicide-and-stigma/

Dhejne, Cecilia et al. "Long-Term Follow-Up of Transsexual Persons Undergoing Sex Reassignment Surgery: Cohort Study in Sweden." *PLOS ONE*. February 22, 2011.
https://journals.plos.org/plosone/article?id=10.1371/journal.pone.0016885

26

Quote from Wiki: "A chromosome is a deoxyribonucleic acid molecule (DNA) with part or all of the genetic material (genome) of an organism." "Chromosome." *Wikipedia*. July 22, 2019.
https://en.wikipedia.org/wiki/Chromosome

"What is a chromosome?" *YG Topics*. Genome Campus, Publisher. n.d.
www.yourgenome.org/facts/what-is-a-chromosome

27

Hrala, Josh. "Mount Everest Isn't Really The Tallest Mountain on Earth."
Science Alert. May 2, 2018.
https://www.sciencealert.com/mount-everest-isn-t-really-the-tallest-mountain-earth-science

Puru, Tibi. "What's the tallest mountain in the world? Hint: it's not Mt. Everest."
ZME Science. February 1, 2019.
https://www.zmescience.com/other/feature-post/tallest-mountain-world/

Unke, Beata. "Height of the Tallest Mountain on Earth."
The Physics Factbook. n.d.
https://hypertextbook.com/facts/2001/BeataUnke.shtml

31

Kelly, Mike. "Before NJ legalizes weed, why not consider its impact on health?"
North Jersey Record. February 22, 2019.
https://www.northjersey.com/story/news/columnists/mike-kelly/2019/02/22/nj-legal-weed-why-not-consider-its-impact-health/2940948002/

Quote: "The prefrontal cortex of my teenage son's brain isn't fully developed."
"TEENS AND THE REAL DANGER OF MARIJUANA EDIBLES, What Parents
Need to Know." *GROWN AND FLOWN*. 2019.
https://grownandflown.com/teens-danger-marijuana-edibles/

Quote: "One of the brain areas still maturing during adolescence is the
prefrontal cortex—the part of the brain that allows people to assess
situations, make sound decisions, and keep emotions and desires under
control."
National Institute on Drug Addiction. "Drugs, Brains, and Behavior."
NIH. July, 2018.
https://www.drugabuse.gov/publications/drugs-brains-behavior-science-addiction/drug-misuse-addiction

Marcu, Matthews, and Lee. "IS CBD REALLY NON-PSYCHOACTIVE?"
Project CBD. May 17, 2016.
https://www.projectcbd.org/science/cbd-really-non-psychoactive

Logan, Jennifer. "CBD Oil: Health Benefits and Risks."
News-Medical. December 19, 2018.
https://www.news-medical.net/health/CBD-Oil-Health-Benefits-and-Risks.aspx

34

Micozzi, Marc. "Is marijuana as safe as they claim?"
INSIDERS' CURES. February 24, 2014.
https://drmicozzi.com/is-marijuana-as-safe-as-they-claim

"TEENS AND THE REAL DANGER OF MARIJUANA EDIBLES, What Parents
Need to Know." *GROWN AND FLOWN*. 2019.
https://grownandflown.com/teens-danger-marijuana-edibles/

Schollenbarger, Price, Wieser, and Lisdahl. "Impact of cannabis use on
prefrontal and parietal cortex gyrification and surface area in adolescents
and emerging adults."
Developmental Cognitive Neuroscience - Science Direct. December, 2015.
https://www.sciencedirect.com/science/article/pii/S1878929315000699

Jacobus and Tapert. "Effects of Cannabis on the Adolescent Brain."
National Insitute of Health. January 1, 2015.
https://www.ncbi.nlm.nih.gov/pmc/articles/PMC3930618/

Crean, Crane, and Mason. "An evidence-based review of acute
and long-term effects of cannabis use on executive cognitive functions."
National Institute of Health. March 1, 2011.
https://www.ncbi.nlm.nih.gov/pmc/articles/PMC3037578/

University of Otago. "Illicit Drug Use Starts With Cannabis."
SCOOP Health News. March 14, 2006.
http://www.scoop.co.nz/stories/GE0603/S00045.htm

McIlhaney, Joe. "Happy New Year – Updated Hooked Book."
Medical Institute for Sexual Health. December 12, 2018
https://www.medinstitute.org/2018/12/founders-corner-happy-new-year-
updated-hooked-book/

35

Williams, David B. "Rock or Stone: Is there a difference?"
Geology Writer. November 2, 2011.
http://geologywriter.com/blog/stories-in-stone-blog/rock-or-stone-is-there-a-difference/

Osgood, John. "The Date of Noah's Flood."
Creation Minstries International. March, 1981.
https://creation.com/the-date-of-noahs-flood

"The Bible Timeline." *Bible History.* 2013.
http://timeline.biblehistory.com/period/noah-and-the-flood

36

For more reading on deep space background radiation, glacial ice cores,
biological adaptation mechanisms and other issues relating to the age
of the earth, check out and search the ICR (Institute for Creation Research)
website. From "Publications" choose "ACTS & FACTS" and use the search
box at the top of the page.
https://www.icr.org/homepage/

Ham, Ken. "Dinosaurs and the Bible." *Answers in Genesis.* January 5, 2015.
https://answersingenesis.org/dinosaurs/dinosaurs-and-the-bible/

Thomas, Brian. "Jungle-Covered Ruins May Hold Surprising Hints."
ACTS & FACTS, Institute for Creation Research. June 24, 2013
https://www.icr.org/article/jungle-covered-ruins-may-hold-surprising

Sachatello-Sawyer, Bonnie and Charlesworth, Liza.
"When Was the First Dinosaur Discovered?" *Scholastic.* n.d.
https://www.scholastic.com/teachers/articles/teaching-content/when-was-first-dinosaur-discovered/

Main, Douglas. "Javan Rhino Officially Extinct In Vietnam."
Planet Earth. January 3, 2013.
https://www.livescience.com/25967-vietnam-rhino-extinct.html

39

"gender." Oxford English Dictionary. c. 2019.
http://www.oed.com/viewdictionaryentry/Entry/77468

Heyer, Walt. *Paper Genders*. Make Waves Publishing. 2011. Print.

Reisman, Judith. *Kinsey: Crimes & Consequences.*
Institute for Media Education. 4th Ed. 2012. Print.

Sax, Leonard. "How common is intersex?"
Journal of Sex Research, Scholarly Publications. August 1, 2002.
http://www.leonardsax.com/how-common-is-intersex-a-response-to-anne-fausto-sterling/

40

Park, Jonathan. "Dinosaurs and the Bible—Shocking Evidence."
Jonathan Park Journal. March 9, 2018.
https://www.jonathanpark.com/blogs/journal/dinosaurs-and-the-bible-shocking-evidence

Jackson, Wayne. "The Hava Supai Dinosaur Carving." *Christian Courier*. 2019.
https://www.christiancourier.com/articles/871-hava-supai-dinosaur-carving-the

Butt, Kyle. "Evidence That Humans Lived With Dinosaurs."
Apologetics Press. 2004.
http://www.apologeticspress.org/apPubPage.aspx?pub=2&issue=823&article=1576

Anderson, Pastor Chuck. "Native Americans Made Clay Figurines of Dinosaurs 2,000 Years Ago!" *Discovery World*. 2017.
https://www.discoveryworld.us/dinosaur-world/dino-figurines/

Natasha, P. "Archeologist Discovered the Ancient Dinosaur Figurines of Acambaro in Mexico." *History & Tech News*. October 26, 2018.
https://www.histecho.com/archaeologist-discovered-ancient-dinosaur-figurines-acambaro

48

Clarey, Tim. "Marine Fossils Mixed with Hell Creek Dinosaurs."
ACTS & FACTS, Vol. 48, No. 4, Pg. 10. Institute for Creation Research.
April 2019. Print.
https://www.icr.org/article/11249/

Thomas, Brian. "Mongolia, Montana, and My Bible."
ACTS & FACTS, Vol. 48, No. 5, Pg. 13. Institute for Creation Research.
May 2019. Print.
https://www.icr.org/article/11269

Thomas, Brian. "Does the Toast Model Explain Fossil Protein Persistence?"
ACTS & FACTS, Vol. 3, Pg. 12. Institute for Creation Research. March 2019. Print.
https://www.icr.org/article/11133

Disregarding the dates cited in this article, it has some interesting
information about T. rex Sue:
Solomon, Alan. "The Secrets of Sue the TRex." *Trvl Channel*. n.d.
https://www.travelchannel.com/interests/arts-and-culture/articles/the-secrets-
of-sue-the-trex

52

Anderson, Ryan T. *When Harry Became Sally, Responding to the Transgender
Moment.* New York: Encounter Books, 2018. Print.

Robbins, Jane. "The Cracks in the Edifice of Transgender Totalitarianism."
Public Discourse. July 13, 2019.
https://www.thepublicdiscourse.com/2019/07/54272/

53

Clarey, Tim. "Four Geological Evidences for a Young Earth."
ACTS & FACTS, Vol 48, No. 6, Pg. 10-11. Institute for Creation Research.
June 2019. Print.
https://www.icr.org/article/11291

Thomas, Brian. "How Mount Saint Helens Refutes Evolution."
ACTS & FACTS, Vol. 48, No. 6, Pg. 14. Institute for Creation Research.
June 2019. Print.
https://www.icr.org/article/11291

55

Bell, Larry. "Debunked: CO2 will not cause a food shortage."
CFACT. June 5, 2019.
https://www.cfact.org/2019/06/05/debunked-co2-will-not-cause-a-food-shortage/?mc_cid=9a77db4ccd&mc_eid=18507eb0f4

Grayson, Audrey. "Shooting for the Stars: UH's Larry Bell Discusses Space
Architecture." *University of Houston, Cullen College of Engineering.*
September 11, 2013.
https://www.egr.uh.edu/news/201309/shooting-stars-uhs-larry-bell-discusses-space-architecture

Herzog, Katy. "The Detransitioners: They Were Transgender, Until They
Weren't." *the Stranger*. June 28, 2017.
https://www.thestranger.com/features/2017/06/28/25252342/the-detransitioners-they-were-transgender-until-they-werent

Heyer, Walt. *Trans Life Survivors*. Amazon. 2018. Print.
https://www.amazon.com/s?k=Heyer%2C+Walt.+Trans+Life+Survivors&ref=nb_sb_noss_2

Higgins, Laurie. "Formerly "Trans" Young Women Speak Out."
Illinois Family Institute. March 4, 2019.
https://illinoisfamily.org/homosexuality/formerly-trans-young-women-speak-out/

ENDORSEMENTS

I am often asked by parents how they can arm their middle and high school children against the lies of transgenderism. My answer: CHOOSING, a novel by Ellie Klipp. Targeted for tweens and teens, it masterfully weaves science and logic throughout an engaging tale about Tracy McKenzie, her family and her closest friends. The unfolding story also helps adults understand this issue and how young people are swept under transgenderism's spell. Buy a copy for yourself, and for the tweens and teens in your life today!

> Dr. Michelle Cretella
> Executive Director of the American College
> of Pediatricians

With her brave and insightful novel CHOOSING, Ellie Klipp entertainingly equips teens, tweens, and parents against the assault of gender and transgender ideologies—what many call the "trans craze." Kids are being targeted by highly organized and lavishly financed activist, philanthropic and corporate organizations standing to benefit from promoting ("affirming") and medicalizing sexual ("gender") confusion that otherwise overwhelmingly goes away by adulthood. Get copies of CHOOSING for yourself and the children you care about today. It's a fun read and a potent tool.

> Andre Van Mol, MD
> Co-Chair of Adolescent Sexuality Committee,
> American College of Pediatricians

Tracy's mother, a nursing student, provides empathic and scientific information for Tracy and her high school friends that guides them through the dangerous and deceptive transgender maze. Dad models action steps for parents. Mystery, friendship, adventures in science and faith—served with cookies and hot chocolate! I didn't want the book to end—a real page turner!

> Dr. Laura Haynes, Retired Psychologist
> Chair of Research and Legislative Policy,
> National Task Force for Therapy Equality

In her new book *CHOOSING*, Ellie Klipp tackles a rather controversial topic in a unique and positive way. Along the way, she introduces the reader to some real and surprising scientific discoveries. I commend her for another great effort that is both eye-opening and accurate.

> Dr. Tim Clarey,
> author of *Dinosaurs: Marvels of God's Design*

CHOOSING is an informative, educational and entertaining novel. Most parents are unaware of what goes on at school, where our kids face daily indoctrination in LGBTQ lies. The extensive research done by Ellie Klipp can be used to educate our kids about the strange and confusing idea called transgenderism. *CHOOSING* shows the truth of our identity according to God's work. *To counter the un-Biblical and unscientific lies of LGBTQ activists*, I recommend this novel. Your teens will enjoy it, I guarantee. I also encourage pastors to read this book, take the truth and preach it. You will have your congregation on the edge of their seats, as I was while reading it.

> Jorge Tovar,
> Senior Pastor – Jordan River Church, Laredo, Texas

Ellie Klipp is a retired teacher. She received her B.A. from Biola, her Teacher's Credential from California State College at Los Angeles (now CSULA), and her M.A. from Masters International University of Divinity.

Visit her online at ellieklipp.com

Made in the USA
Monee, IL
30 October 2023